Also by Richard Poirier

The Comic Sense of Henry James
In Defense of Reading
A World Elsewhere
The Performing Self
Norman Mailer
Robert Frost: The Work of Knowing
The Renewal of Literature
Poetry and Pragmatism

Trying It Out in America

RICHARD POIRIER

TRYING IT OUT
IN AMERICA

Literary and Other
Performances

for Richard,
love,
Dick

06/16/99

FARRAR, STRAUS AND GIROUX / NEW YORK

Farrar, Straus and Giroux
19 Union Square West, New York 10003

Library of Congress Cataloging-in-Publication Data
Poirier, Richard.
    Trying it out in America : literary and other performances / by
Richard Poirier. — 1st ed.
        p.   cm.
    Includes index.
    ISBN 0-374-27941-1 (alk. paper)
    1. American literature—History and criticism.   2. United States—
Civilization.   I. Title.
PS121.P58   1999
810.9—dc21   99-22467

Grateful acknowledgment is made to the following publications in which most
of these essays first appeared, in somewhat different form: *The London Review
of Books; The New Republic; The New York Review of Books;* and *The Times
Literary Supplement.*

To Frederick Seidel

CONTENTS

PROLOGUE

Without going on at any great length, I want by way of introduction to accomplish two things: first, to describe in a sketchy way the essays that make up this book; second, to characterize my own critical stance or deportment and why it seems to me appropriate to the American works, writings, and performances that I focus on.

Only two of these are works of literary criticism: about an important recent book on the late writings of Henry James, and about a study of what are imagined by its author, erroneously in my view, to be some distinctly American ideas of manhood. Two other essays were prompted by the publication of large-scale biographies: the first biography of a leading poet of the so-called New York School, Frank O'Hara; and a very ambitious "cultural biography" of Walt Whitman.

Five are essays occasioned by the appearance of collected editions of works, some of them never previously published, of especially important American writers. These include the first substantial collection of the letters of Marianne Moore; a massively annotated, first edition of some of the earliest (and most personally revealing) of T. S. Eliot's poems, many of which he hadn't meant to make public; an edition of what may have been the first version, as reconstructed by a renowned Melville scholar, of Melville's provocative, extremely troubled novel *Pierre*; the final volume of the nine-volume day-by-day, sometimes hour-by-hour chronicle of the last years of Whitman's life by his devoted younger friend, confidant, and attendant, Horace Traubel. I have also included a summary essay on the career and literary accomplishments of Gertrude Stein, prompted by two large volumes in the Library of America, the most comprehensive edition of her writings now available; and, as a sort of addendum to the Stein essay, a brief, very intensive analysis of a passage in Emerson's "Self-Reliance" which discloses a surprising degree of kinship between his skepticisms about language and hers.

Another essay focuses on the often bizarre, always fascinating diary of the brilliant, reclusive, hypochondriacal Arthur Inman, with his uniquely detailed reports on the daily lives, habits, economies, and sexual adventures of working-class Americans in the 1930s and 1940s, those he employed and the many others who were brought in to talk with him in his darkened rooms in Boston. Along the way are three animadversions on books about the United States, one written by the French sociologist-philosopher Jean Baudrillard, the others by two British observers. Two celebratory essays strike a far more appreciative note: on the concert performances of Bette Midler, and on that greatest of all choreographers, the Shakespeare of dance, who found in America a home and an inspiration for his work, George Balanchine.

Finally, I have included essays on three American novelists, though they write in a number of other forms, who, since World War II, have also made themselves conspicuous as public personalities: Norman Mailer, Gore Vidal, and Truman Capote. Vidal and Mailer will continue to deserve the most serious kinds of attention; Capote will be remembered for one book only, I think, *In Cold Blood*.

Most of the American works I discuss are by now regarded as canonical and others as likely candidates to become so. As if to mark this claim to canonicity, it seems that no matter how long ago some of these works were written, no matter how often read, reread, quoted, and exhaustingly analyzed since then, many of them have maintained, even augmented, that aura of mystery, of some irreducible integrity of difficulty that fascinates even while it frustrates one generation of readers after another. While Emerson, as a prime instance, is among the most frequently quoted of writers, with page after page devoted to him in collections of familiar quotations, it remains the case that each time we return to his essays, any familiarity we may be supposed to have acquired gives way to unfamiliarity and strangeness. "Oh you man without a handle!" exclaimed his old friend and often exasperated admirer Henry James, Sr., "Shall one never be able to help himself out of you, according to his needs, and be dependent only upon your fateful tippings up?"

Like Emerson, though in a manner peculiar to each of them, nearly all the writers featured here manage to resist translation into formulaic meanings, to reward but still evade interpretive curiosity, which only continues to stimulate still greater interest over generations. Robert Frost could have been speaking for many of them when, in a letter in 1917, he observed: "You get more credit for thinking if you restate formulas or cite cases that fall easily under formulae." But, he goes on, "all the fun is outside, saying things that suggest formulae but won't formulate—that almost but don't quite formulate. I should like to be so subtle at this game as to seem to the casual person altogether obvious." I intend to be popular and saleable, he is saying, but in a way that can be understood as an evidence of my genius and not of my having in any way compromised it.

Nearly all the American writers I'm most concerned with here have ambitions for themselves that are similarly in an always precarious, quite often faltering equilibrium. They hope to appeal to a large contemporary audience who buys, reads, and spreads the good word about books. At the same time they write in a fashion meant to be taken as original and likely to be thought difficult, though by about 1925 "difficulty" had itself acquired a kind of fashionability. They like to imagine that they write for future generations as much or even more, if Whitman is to be believed, than for their own. They want, one might say, to be always and forever ahead of the time.

The most compelling example of such a writer in the history of literature is, unquestionably, Shakespeare. This may account, in part at least, for the particular kind of esteem expressed for his work late in their lives by three American writers who are especially favored in this book, writers who by now are nearly assured, as they so much wanted to be, of some measure of literary immortality: Ralph Waldo Emerson, Henry James, and T. S. Eliot, covering the span of two centuries. Thus Emerson, in a *Journal* entry in 1866, at age sixty-three, quite directly links the difficulty felt by the best readers of Shakespeare, when trying to account for his genius, with the related difficulty of restraining their sense of wonder at his achievement. "It is, I own, difficult not to be intemperate in speaking of Shakespeare; and most difficult, I should say, to the best readers. Few, I think none, arrive at any intelligence of his methods."

A century later, Eliot, four years before his death in 1965, and at a time when he was complaining in *The Frontiers of Criticism* that given developments in academic criticism over the previous three decades literary analysis "may even come to seem too brilliant," observes in "To Criticise the Critic" that "so great is Shakespeare that a lifetime is hardly enough for growing up to appreciate him." Shakespeare's language, like Dante's, has become for him a "comfort and amazement of my age."

Finally, more fully (and out of chronological order), I turn to Henry James and to his magnificent yet scarcely ever mentioned introduction in 1907 to the last play fully written by Shakespeare, *The Tempest* (which I discuss more fully in chapter 15,

"In Praise of Vagueness: Henry and William James"). Like Emerson and Eliot, James is nearing the end of his career and contemplating his own chances for literary immortality. His appreciation is phrased with an eloquence and passion uncommon even for him. It is a remarkably self-enhancing kind of eloquence. Here, all as much as in the late novels that precede it—*The Ambassadors, The Wings of the Dove, The Golden Bowl,* where James so unabashedly exhibits a determination to absorb into himself his principal characters, seldom allowing any one of them a distinctive style of speech marked off from his own— James's celebratory description of Shakespeare's career and particularly of his style, sounds, increasingly as they go along, like a description and celebration of his own stylistic accomplishments, especially in the late phases of his work.

It is as if he, too, needs to be defended from "interpretative zeal" or "interpretative heat," from efforts, that is, to erase the complexities of his style, so as to reduce him to the kind of clarity that his critics, including his brother William, often demanded of him. Having described his own response to *The Tempest* as full of "a strange, an aching wonder," he then writes:

> It may seem no very philosophic state of mind, the merely baffled and exasperated view of one of the supreme works of all literature; though I feel, for myself, that to confess to it now and then, by way of relief, is no unworthy tribute to the work. It is not, certainly, the tribute most frequently paid, for the large body of comment and criticism of which this play alone has been the theme abounds much rather in affirmed conclusions, complacencies of conviction, full apprehensions of the meaning and triumphant pointings of the moral.

The phrasing at the end of this passage, when he is characterizing the critically primitive and yet triumphantly all-knowing responses of most commentators on *The Tempest*, becomes measurably more agitated. Very likely, his contempt for Shakespeare's interpreters was substantially increased by insensitive disparagements of his own later works very close to home. In the very year when he wrote this passage, 1907, he received a letter from his older brother William reminding him,

> you know how opposed your whole 'third manner' of execution is to the literary ideals which animate my crude and Orson-like breast, mine being to say a thing in one sentence as straight and explicit as it can be made, and then to drop it forever; yours being to avoid naming it straight, but by dint of sighing and breathing all round and round it, to arouse in the reader who may have had a similar perception already (Heaven help him if he hasn't!) the illusion of a solid object, made (like the 'ghost' at the Polytechnic) wholly out of impalpable materials, air, and the prismatic interferences of light, but ingeniously focused by mirrors upon empty space.

Though William goes on to concede that "you do it, that's the queerness!" it is only to discover in this concession the grounds for renewing the attack:

> You can't skip a word if you are to get the effect, and 19 out of 20 readers grow intolerant. The method seems perverse: 'Say it *out* for God's sake,' they cry, 'and have done with it.' And so I say now, give us *one* thing in your older directer manner, just to show that, in spite of your paradoxical success in this unheard-of method, you *can* still write according to accepted canons.

Such advice, phrased in so supercilious or kidding a fashion, would be galling to any poet or novelist, even one of modest ambition. It would be especially offensive to a writer like Henry James who felt that his was a sacred calling to which the canon would be obliged to adapt itself. Which of the American poets who have renewed and reinvigorated our language, and thereby our perception of the world around us, would have ever chosen to "say it out" or even to concede that the phrase could mean much of anything to any greatly aspiring writer? Not Whitman or Dickinson surely, not Eliot or Stevens or Frost, not Hart

Crane or Elizabeth Bishop. And even while they take evident delight in the detailing of objects or the techniques of work and of physical accomplishment, American novelists like Melville or Mailer can be said to "create" each of these things by very particular, unfamiliar shapings of words, and these words are intended to function meanwhile in specifically contributory ways within the works' larger imaginative design.

Henry James seems to be defending his own practices, as much as Shakespeare's, and repudiating his brother William's dogmatizing, when he writes exaltingly of Shakespeare's plays: "It is by the expression of it exactly as the expression stands that the particular thing is created, created as interesting, as beautiful, as strange." It should be noted, however, that James very deftly corrects the flight path of this sentence, so that the initial and too simple assertion, that things are created by style, is modified to say, rather, that style creates a particular *mode* for the existence of things.

Nonetheless, James's overall claim for what at one point in his introduction he calls "the absolute value of style" requires, in my view, some further adjustment. Greater accommodation should be made for the fact that words used in a poem or a novel are not the invention of any writer; they carry with them, wherever they are put, an immensely long history of their own, not only from the literature of the past, but from their political, religious, economic, institutional uses, and from other languages. And always, to some degree, words call up for the reader images and sounds from everyday experience outside the immediate experience of reading. While an author's style may, during our exposure to it, become powerful enough to blur or diminish the vividness of such reminders and correspondences, this can be accomplished only by great effort, by a writer's conspicuous acts of contention with the already inherent power of words. These efforts can be discerned in syntactical and structural strains, in usages that are and seem to be eccentric or peculiar, even ingenious, to a point where the strains become an essential part of the reader's felt experience of the work.

American writers exhibit a fondness for highlighting the effortfulness of their literary endeavors. They like to compare it metaphorically to work done in a bean field or an apple orchard or on a whaling vessel, to warfare, as in Stein and Stevens; to athletic competition, prowess, and the disciplines of the body, all much favored metaphors in Frost and Hemingway, Marianne Moore and Mailer; to exploration and to pathfinding, in William James and Parkman. "Every poem," says Frost, "is an epitome of the great predicament; a figure of the will braving alien entanglements." I try in these essays to attend very closely to this figure of the will, to celebrate its still active and activating authorial presence, as it continually moves through sentences and paragraphs, reanimating words that might otherwise stagnate in their acquired inertias.

Trying It Out in America

MARIANNE MOORE:
ACCURATE GUSTO

Writing poetry, criticism, or, several times each day, letters of advice, sympathy, and chastisement to her numerous and celebrated friends, matching wits with the formidable mother she adored—the only person with whom she ever lived—editing *The Dial* during its great years in the 1920s, rewriting poems submitted by Hart Crane, or rejecting a section from Joyce's work-in-progress, *Finnegans Wake*, working as a librarian, attending literary parties night after night in Manhattan, traveling, lecturing, picking up nearly every prestigious award available in her time to an American poet: whatever Marianne Moore chose to do in her long life, from 1887 to 1972, she did with élan and determined care. In all her actions—writing and reading were, she maintained, forms of action—she unerringly achieved a balance between what she called "gusto" and, another favorite word, "discipline," between an abundance of energy and the self-fashioned rigors of form, between freedom and reticence. In a talk in 1949 entitled "Humility, Concentration, and Gusto," she remarks that "gusto thrives on freedom, and freedom in art, as in life, is the result of a discipline imposed by ourselves."

Gusto and discipline are everywhere on display in her letters. Especially in the first two sections of *The Selected Letters of*

Marianne Moore ("The Early Years: 1907–1919," which includes her student years at Bryn Mawr, and "The Dial Years, 1921–1929"), the letters are extraordinarily long, even after the editors wisely chose, in a few cases, to abridge them from their original thirty, forty, even fifty pages. She consumed space with dizzyingly minute descriptions of apartments and buildings down to addresses and how best to get there, of city and country landscapes, rare plants, animals, and fish, the personal attire of people she meets or the articles on a cluttered table, or plays and operas and dinner menus, and the back-and-forth of smart conversations.

Very little of this is meant to be comic, though it reads at times like those moments in Jane Austen when, to show the boredom of country life, she satirizes conversations on the weather or on the proper consistency of really good gruel, or like Eudora Welty's superbly sad and funny story "Why I Live at the P.O.," given over to the ruminations of a paranoid woman who prefers to be alone rather than endure family conversations, amplified in her mind as insidiously against herself. Though justly famous for her wit, Moore isn't given to comedy at her own expense. Readers who patiently plow through such descriptive thickets will better understand why the editors seem occasionally to nod off when an explanatory note comes due. The notes, glossaries of names, and introductions to the four sections of *Selected Letters* are helpful and lucidly written, but a good encyclopedia should be kept handy by those who want to track down the names of certain exotic plants or animals, baseball players, politicians, writers, literary characters, and the like.

The close pileup of detail in some of Moore's writing can work to the advantage of certain of the poems, if not to some of the letters, and it was a feature of the poetry admired by Elizabeth Bishop. Bishop was sent to meet Moore in 1934 by the librarian at Vassar, where she was then a student. The two struck it off immediately when the young woman invited the now-famous older one to go with her to the circus. Soon Bishop was sending drafts of her early poems to Moore and her mother for comment and, sometimes, correction and revision. It was a practice she gradually discontinued, especially after the Moores objected in 1940 to Bishop's use in her poem "Rooster" of the expression "water closets" and to other "sordidities," as Bishop superciliously called them.

In a 1966 interview Bishop speaks positively of Moore's descriptive zeal as an aspect of an instinctive democratic feeling, and compared her in this respect to John Dewey, whose daughter was by then a close friend of Bishop and whose pragmatist writings Moore had read as far back as 1917, copying out passages she admired. Both Dewey and Moore, despite the complexities of their writings, had a rare capacity among literary intellectuals to "talk to everyone, on all social levels, without the slightest change in their manner of speaking," with a kind of instinctive respect. And both, Bishop adds, "loved little things, small plants and weeds and animals."

Bishop could have had in mind Dewey's belief, evidenced no less by Moore in some of her forty poems about animals, that "to grasp the sources of aesthetic experience it is necessary to have recourse to animal life below the human scale," to "the activities of the fox, the dog, and the thrush," and his appreciative comments on "the tense grace of the ball-player." In her poem "Baseball and Writing," she, too, makes watching a ball game little different from the experience of writing or reading a poem. In sports, in the instinctive grace and measure of animal movements, no less than in the choreographed movements she admired in a dancer like Arthur Mitchell of the New York City Ballet—a dancer who can at once, as she puts it in a poem about him, "reveal/ and veil/ a peacock tail"—Moore found confirmation of her commitment to restraint not as a limit so much as an incentive to exemplary forms of extravagance.

Moore's fascination with baseball emerges early, in the baseball lingo in letters from Bryn Mawr to her brother, and intensifies with the years. Her enthusiastic review in 1961 of *Out of My*

League by George Plimpton, with whom she became friends and attended ball games and prizefights, was followed by a 1968 piece on the local library, where she expresses her admiration for the great New York Giants pitcher Christy Mathewson. In the early 1920s, on visits to the Hudson Park Children's Room, she liked to recommend his book, *Pitching in a Pinch,* to the boys. The 1961 poem "Baseball and Writing" has resemblances to Frost's earlier poem "Two Tramps in Mud Time," where the wood-chopping poet, under the envious gaze of tramps who covet the job for wages, tells himself that it is his duty as a poet, even during the Depression, to "play/ With what was another man's work for gain." He reasons that the physical sensation of woodcutting is akin to the sensation that goes into the activity of poetic creation, and that he is thereby able to "unite/ My avocation and my vocation."

When Moore refers to Frost in her letters she sounds more distantly admiring than she does of other comparable poets, Stevens, Eliot, Auden, and Williams, with whom she more frequently corresponded. But she is undeviatingly reverential about him and immensely appreciative of whatever attentions he paid her. Writing to Elizabeth Bishop in 1956, she is delighted to report that, in James Merrill's introduction of her at Amherst College, "I was compared with Robert Frost," the poet who wrote that "the work is play for mortal stakes." Though she nowhere compares, as he does, the bodily movements of sexual intercourse to "the figure a poem makes," she is as determined as he is to find analogies for the work of poetic creation in all kinds of other movements, human, animal, or botanical. In her poem "Nevertheless," she praises the sap struggling to fulfill itself as it works its way through a final "little thread," not just to make a cherry, but "to make the cherry red." Like Frost (or Dewey), she is less interested in production as a form of perpetuation than as a form of enhancement, of excess, of aesthetic excitation, spirit, and tenacity.

Moore's writing, whether in poetry or in her letters and essays, is a celebration of those who have the discipline required to shape this excess of energy into any form of play, including poetry. The virtue of formal play, like baseball, poetry, or dance, is that it is publicly available to others, perhaps inducing in them some comparable degree of discipline and caring. Thus, in a poem entitled "Hometown Piece for Messrs. Alston and Reese," the latter better known as Pee Wee Reese, she says of the manager and captain of the Dodgers: "Zest./ They've zest. 'Hope springs eternal in the Brooklyn breast.'" After remarking in a 1966 essay that "writing is a fascinating business," she goes on to quote Faulkner: "'And what should it do?' William Faulkner asked. 'It should help a man endure by lifting up his heart.' (Admitting that his might not always have done that.) *It should.*"

It is evident from the difficulties posed by Moore's own poetry that the way in which art or writing or other shaped activities might "lift up the heart" is not by exhortation or inspirational anecdote. It is by the artist's or athlete's performance, the aesthetic excitements called forth by intricate displays of human creative prowess. Thus, in a 1933 review of the letters of Emily Dickinson, Moore could easily be talking about herself when she writes:

> Against near rhyme or no rhyme where rhyme is required, complaint seems general. But Emily Dickinson was a person of power and could have overcome had she wished to, any less than satisfactory feature of her lines. . . . To some her Japanesely fantastic reverence for tree, insect, and toadstool is not interesting; many who are "helped" by a brave note, do not admire the plucked string; by some the note of rapture is not caught; and by the self-sufficient, Emily Dickinson has been accused of vanity. A certain buoyancy that creates an effect of inconsequent bravado—a sense of drama with which we might not be quite at home—was for her a part of that expansion of breath necessary to existence, and unless it is conceited for the hummingbird or the osprey to not behave like a chicken, one does not find her conceited.

A bit further on, she praises Dickinson for her capacity to "attain splendor of implication without prefatory statement, for her conciseness was an extreme of her largesse." Thirty years later "conciseness" is a virtue she ascribes (on the dust jacket of his *I Am the Greatest*) to Cassius Clay, as Ali then called himself: "He is a master of concision. Asked, 'Have you ever been in love,' he says 'Not with anyone else.'" Matching his own high spirits she remarks, "He is literary—in the tradition of Sir Philip Sidney, defender of Poesie. . . . He fights as he writes. Is there something I have missed? He is a smiling pugilist."

Moore's mention of Sidney is one acknowledgment that for centuries some of the most artistically venturesome writers have claimed that their work with language required something like the prowess, skill, discipline, and fortitude of athletes and warriors. In 1815 Wordsworth remarks that the poet of genius "will be called upon to clear and often to shape his own road: he will be in the condition of Hannibal among the Alps." The reader must therefore be correspondingly inspirited, and cannot expect "to be carried like a dead weight." Frost, who pitched softball in high school and well into his seventies, was invited to write in 1956 on an All-Star Game by *Sports Illustrated,* and in a piece called "Perfect Day—A Day of Prowess," he wrote, "Prowess of course comes first, the ability to perform with success in games, in the arts and, come right down to it, in battle. The nearest kin to the artists in college . . . are their fellow performers in baseball, football and tennis." And he says of his dear friend the Welsh poet Edward Thomas, killed in the last moments of World War I, that he had "come to look on a poem as a performance one had to win." Hemingway and Mailer are obvious additions to any little anthology of writers as would-be athletes, on the page and off. In a letter of February 5, 1965, Moore reports that she sat next to Mailer at Toots Shor's, where she had been taken by George Plimpton after the Floyd Patterson–Chuvalo fight at Madison Square Garden. "I liked Norman Mailer immensely," she writes to her brother, "and on getting home read his article in the Jan 31 *Times*; 'Cities Higher than Mountains'—in which he says 'Man is always engaging the heavens. Now the jungle is replaced by a prison.' Really ingenious article. He lives at 128 Willow. George P. is always alluding to him. I now see a reason."

Wallace Stevens, who seldom revealed any interest in sports beyond sailing, and made the mistake once in Key West of drunkenly picking a fistfight with Hemingway in which he broke a hand and was knocked down, was nonetheless intent, as in the epilogue to "Notes Toward a Supreme Fiction," on comparing the poet with the soldier fighting in World War II: "Soldier, there is a war between the mind/ And sky. . . ." This war is the endless war fought by the poet against already determined forms of reality. It is a war, he concedes to the soldier, that "depends on yours." For the Stevens of the lecture "The Noble Rider and the Sound of Words," delivered the year after the United States entered World War II, poetry represents "a violence from within that protects us from a violence from without. It is the imagination pressing back against the pressure of reality." Moore had a devoted if complex regard for Stevens, reviewing brilliantly and at length all but one of his volumes. He in turn wrote two lengthy essays on her and trusted her to make the selection, for publication in England, of some of his poems. Writing to Winifred Bryher in 1935, she speaks of "all my efforts in writing criticism and in writing verse having been for years, a chameleon attempt to bring my product into some sort of compatibility with Wallace Stevens."

Moore's reticence is so instinctive, her endorsements so tentative, that even in the relatively free form of her letters, no less than in her poems and critical writings, there is apt to intrude a word or phrase of quiet curtailment just as she seems to be surrendering to an enthusiasm. Thus, after her praise of Mailer in the letter to her brother, she says she now sees "a" reason (only one?) why George Plimpton so frequently alludes to him; Emily Dickinson is described as a "person" of power, raising a good question of why she isn't, by another woman poet, called a woman of power. And her apparently ever varying or ever modified ("chameleon") attempts at achieving some similarity to the work of Stevens are at most aimed, in her words, only toward "some sort" of similarity. The elegantly scrupulous inflections of her language—which makes her longest poem "Marriage" into a wonderful riddle on the subject—nearly always point to something important that can be discovered only by a reader's close inquisitiveness.

Moore's carefully measured sense of her compatibility with Stevens turns out to be of considerable importance to our understanding of both of them. Her restraint has little to do, for example, with the fact that she sometimes felt mystified by him, as any friend sometimes can be by another. To William Carlos Williams in November 1944, she writes: "Wallace Stevens is beyond fathoming he is so strange; it is as if he had a morbid secret he would rather perish than disclose and just as he tells it out in his sleep, he changes to an uncontradictable judiciary with a gown and a gavel and you are embarrassed to have heard anything." In a correspondence that lasted some thirty-five years, she continued calling him Mr. Stevens in her salutations even after he, in March 1953, momentarily relented and addressed her as Marianne.

Stevens always remained the contemporary poet she most admired—for what, in her first review of him, of *Harmonium* in 1924, she called his "accurate gusto" and because, as she said in 1937 of later poems, "they embody hope that in being frustrated becomes fortitude." And yet her poetry is distinctly and tellingly different from his, and she knew it. The persistent celebratory thrust of her poetry is not importantly conditioned by intervals of any perceived threat to it, as his quite often is, aside from the incontestable fact that life is inherently dangerous, as suggested in her poem of 1932 "The Steeple-Jack," one of her best. It is a poem in which she seems to endorse a town's complacently idyllic view of itself. And yet, as in the last stanza, she gently qualifies her endorsements, so gently as to suggest that the town could not bear any less delicate reminders that no place is immune to the perils of human existence. The ending seems to affirm the presence of dangers even as it denies them. Why else must the church steeple carry so visible a reminder of the need for hope?

> It could not be dangerous to be living
>   in a town like this of simple people,
> who have a steeple-jack placing danger-signs by the church
> while he is gilding the solid-
>   pointed star, which on a steeple
>   stands for hope.

Moore was acutely responsive to historical tragedies, like World War II, the depression of the 1930s, economic dislocations, racial injustice at home, and the horrors of anti-Semitism in Europe. But she exhibits nothing like Stevens's persistent sense of the threat, to poetic creativity, of imaginative desolation, of creative (and sexual) impotence. There are in her poetry no Frostean desert places or Stevens's mind of winter. The affirmative, optative mood of nearly all her writings presumes the facts of mortality and that "life," as William James puts it, *"feels like a real fight"* ("Is Life Worth Living"), a fight in which it is well to accept that there will be real winners and real losers. These inevitabilities are for her welcome incentives to scrappiness, discipline, and creativity, to "song" itself, as she suggests in her poem "What Are Years?":

>   The very bird,
> grown taller as he sings, steels
> his form straight up. Though he is captive,
> his mighty singing
> says, satisfaction is a lowly
> thing, how pure a thing is joy.
>   This is mortality,
>   This is eternity.

In thousands of letters written over sixty-four years, from 1905, when she entered Bryn Mawr, to 1969, after an incapacitating stroke which led to her death two years later, there will inevitably be a few confessions on her part to private, personal depression—amazingly few and far between, though, at least in this ample selection, for a woman who worked exceptionally hard, cultivated a number of difficult and troubled friends, and was never known to have had a single romantic or sexual or even very exclusive relationship with anyone other than her mother. Her mother was her closest friend and confidant, a brilliantly cultivated, loquacious, vigorously moral woman, the daughter of a Presbyterian pastor, in whose house Marianne was born. Her mother, when pregnant with Marianne and already with an infant son, had separated from her husband—for the rest of her life, as it turned out. He had lost what fortune he had in speculation and, with it, at least temporarily, his mental stability. Marianne was never to meet her father. The mother, who shared in many of Moore's literary and personal friendships, was, like her daughter, pointed and original of speech, and her aphoristic phrasings can be heard in some of her daughter's poems. She died in 1947 at the age of eighty-five, after a succession of illnesses during which she was cared for mostly by Marianne, who often fell ill herself from exhaustion. It was the greatest loss in Moore's life, not alleviated by the succession of honors lavished upon her in the years close to it: the Shelley Award, the Harriet Monroe Poetry Award, a Guggenheim Fellowship, election in the year of her mother's death to the National Institute of Arts and Letters, and, in one year, 1951, the Pulitzer Prize, the National Book Award, and the Bollingen Prize.

In this period of exceptional private loss and public acclaim, she wrote an uncharacteristically distressed letter to Ezra Pound, to whom she was always trustingly direct in her dealings, especially in her criticisms of his politics, though she was herself a Hoover Republican all her life. At the time of her writing,

Pound was confined to St. Elizabeths Hospital, exposed to the kinds of trouble she herself was experiencing. In July 1946, she writes:

> I sound dull because I *am* dull. You know our propensity for illness; the gloom of which you helped dissipate by visiting our infirmary. This time it is hard. My mother is having a battle to eat; or rather swallow (because of an injury to the nerve controlling the palate). I have been telling people I cannot write letters or even receive them; but we think of you, Ezra, and wish you could be comfortable. Don't be embittered. Embitterment is a sin—a subject on which I am an authority.

If, somehow, she had in fact become an authority on the sin of embitterment, it was not for reasons deducible from any but three or four of these letters or from her published writings or the reports of her friends or the fine account of her life given by Charles Molesworth in his biography of her. She scarcely ever complains about financial problems, beyond those of other people during the Depression, though they are inferable from her letters of thanks to her brother and to Winifred Bryher, H.D.'s very wealthy and generous companion, for gifts of money. Far from feeling aggrieved about her literary standing, the letters reveal a reluctance to allow the first book publication of poems already printed in periodicals. They didn't by then seem to her to represent the best she would do. The publication was arranged, nonetheless, by H.D. and Bryher. There's no evidence either that she felt any so-called anxiety of influence with respect to poets past or contemporary. She was cheerfully candid about the exceptions she took to poets she knew, and she knew nearly all the best known, especially so when it came to Williams, and to the critic Kenneth Burke, her fellow editor of *The Dial* (who reportedly called her one of the sexiest women he ever met), to Stevens, Crane, Cummings, and her dear friend Elizabeth Bishop. These criticisms focused mostly on the use in their work of language she or her mother considered tasteless or obscene.

It was on that score, it would seem, that Williams once said, "I am in perfect terror of Marianne," whose association with him and his family was all the while particularly affectionate on both sides. Just how formidable she could become on the subject of the off-color is apparent in her brilliantly rendered account, in a letter of 1923 to her brother, of a conversation with the American poet-critic Matthew Josephson. It is the kind of letter that makes one hope to see at least part of the novel she worked on for years but for which she could never find a publisher. In her salutation she addresses her brother as "Badger" and calls her mother (to whom she also occasionally referred as "he") "Mole," and herself, signing off, "Rat," these being among the pet names they used with one another, some of them drawn from their mutual appreciation of characters in Kenneth Grahame's 1908 classic *The Wind in the Willows*:

Dear Badger,

. . . Mole described somewhat our conversation with M[atthew] Josephson and it was an ordeal. He said at one point of the salvos, "well, I hope we can still be friends." "Surely; one's interest in human beings" I said "transcends a difference in tastes." Previous to this, he had said that abroad nobody "studied over" obscenity: that grossness and sensuality were part of life, one didn't make a point of it or avoid it, it was just there like the trees on the street and he thought if I had lived abroad I would have a different feeling about it. I said, "I'm afraid not and what makes me sure I wouldn't is that none of the writers who write the fiction & poems you speak of ever discuss face to face with me any of the questionable matters that they write about. Mr. Burke when I am talking with him never borders upon a discussion of any of the details I object to in his writing because he would be embarrassed." He said, "that is a point I have raised myself in my own mind, but" etc. I said, "Shakespeare exhilarates me; These writers don't. When a piece of work focuses attention so strongly upon his grossness or its funniness that you can think of nothing else then all question of the writer's potential greatness disappears; he's not an artist, & signifies only as [a] moral problem." More of this and at length he said "Then I wonder what you think of my book—if you've troubled to read it." I said of course I had read it & and there was much I didn't like—much that I felt was unconscious & instinctive, not meant aggressively but that I deplored & felt was reflected from the society that perhaps he had happened to be in. He looked downcast & somewhat slyly defiant and then I said I liked 2 of his poems in which I felt that he escaped from impinging influences when I hadn't the feeling that he was writing with a view of the thing's being read by Gorham Munson & Slater Brown & James Joyce & Scofield Thayer. We laughed outright but he was displeased & we had a real carnage of skin & fur for 2 hours or more. Words couldn't do justice to the revolting inanity of it & as I said to Mole, the man's limitations which should enlist one's pity merely alienate me. However he will be here again & on that occasion I shall ignore the existence of offal & smelly fishheads and treat him as if he were a little mister in society & thus eventually fly away from him.

With love,
Rat

Absent from Moore's own writing are any of those "questionable matters" she objects to. Absent, too, especially from the published correspondence, where if anywhere it might be expected, are evidences of any sexual feelings she might have harbored. Even the highlighting of human physical attributes that might offer some clue to such feelings isn't to be found and isn't inferable from her metaphors. Perhaps her descriptive voraciousness about every other subject is related to her diligent neglect of sexuality or of the human body in her writing. This extraordinary avoidance of the sexual, even in the long poem "Marriage," ought to call particular attention to two letters written from Bryn Mawr when she was twenty, letters which the editors have commendably made available, but without comment. The letters are remarkable because they reveal her intense, close to self-shattering sexual feelings for young women, a crisis in her life which her interpreters, except Cristanne Miller, have not noted or discussed, so far as I can discover. Still more, the two letters show that her recognition of these feelings caused in her an intensity of depression not to be found again in her letters until close to forty years later, with the final illness of her mother.

The letters are addressed to Marcet Haldeman, a classmate at Bryn Mawr who was off campus for the semester. In one of these, at the end of January 1908, when Moore was twenty, she confesses, "I have lost my heart to Frances Stewart and call her my lady-love." Two weeks later, in another letter to Marcet, she describes a most marvelous sunset witnessed alone with Frances from the roof of a college building. In her account of this moment of shared enthusiasm, Moore confesses, "I could have kissed her." She also refers here to another college friend, Peggy James, daughter of the philosopher William: "I get nervous as a horse though when [I] get to touching certain parts of her," she writes, adding:

> I don't believe she has "understanding" or the shadow of it. Alas some deficiencies do not, however, keep one from being a Circe, if the instinct to please, and a gentle feeling aspect and a mind over which passions show color as they run, are present. I hate to make Peggy an *objet d'art* and it is her fault that I do—but if she *can*not acknowledge me as a man without giving me a black, she *can*not.

Earlier in this same letter, she makes one of her very rare admissions of depression:

> I am sorry you have to think upon my Sunday's broken growl of anguish. I don't mind your knowing that I slip into a black frenzy occasionally but I insult your understanding by *retailing* you the mess of it, and not taking for granted that I have your sympathy unconsciously whether or not I say I need it and why.

Here, much as in the letter to Pound forty years later during her mother's final illness, Moore's famous reticence comes into play. Here, too, she hastens to assure her correspondent, who is apparently already familiar with the problems Moore is experiencing, that she won't burden her with details. And she goes on, as she will when warning Pound and herself against the sin of embitterment, to declare her resolve to master her depressions:

> Silvia—where is Silvia? in all this. At the bottom of it I fear. She will not do. She cannot reach. I feel like molten lead inside once and a while. It's terrible to the place where you feel. Sampson! wake up. You stand trying to conjure up for yourself a phantom Delilah. Dig your poor sensitive mortal's foot into the earth and *run* with yourself till you are a *man.*

This is troubled prose, and it is likely that Moore wasn't in control of its implications. It's clear enough, however, that Silvia is not a reference to yet another student, a third along with a Frances and Peggy, with whom Moore, at least in her own mind, is involved in an intense and unrewarding romantic relationship. Throughout her correspondence she refers, with no attendant explanations, to literary and mythological figures as casually as she might to close acquaintances. In this instance, she can count on someone she's taken classes with to recognize Silvia as the much courted young heroine in Shakespeare's *The Two Gentlemen of Verona*: "Who is Silvia? what is she,/ That all our swains commend her?" But Moore was likely referring to some less famous lines in the play: "Except I be by Silvia in the night,/ There is no music in the nightingale." Moore had already published some of her poems in the Bryn Mawr magazine *Tipyn O'Bob,* and in her very next letter to Marcet, in the midst of much talk of the need for "courage" and to be "master of your fate," she announces, and not for the first time, "I have come to the conclusion that I want to write." That she meant to become not just any writer but a great one is suggested in a letter close by to her mother and brother: "Writing is all I care for, and for what I care most, and writing is such a puling profession, if it is not a great one, that I occasionally give up."

So even as her allusion to Silvia momentarily evokes the nightingale, a traditional poetic figure for poetic song, and with it the notion that perhaps one needs a Silvia in one's arms to be inspired to song, she immediately banishes this same idea: such a romantic hope for an idealized Peggy or Frances "will not do. She cannot reach." Instead, Moore will go it alone, *"run* with yourself till you are a *man."* Indeed, to become a "man" in the form implied here requires that she *not* ask someone like Peggy "to acknowledge me as a man," that is, as the substitute for a male lover. She seems to have held to this decision even as, all through her life thereafter, she found close friendships and comfort with women like Elizabeth Bishop, Hilda Doolittle, and Katherine Jones, whose various lady-loves also became good friends and who made her comfortable in their homes, even babied her, on some of the few vacations she took.

What, then, or who is this "man" she is determined to become by henceforth running "alone"? It is the same man, I would argue, called into being by two great women writers of whom Moore wrote most appreciatively, Emily Dickinson and Gertrude Stein. Stein goes so far as to propose, through the puns and play of her language, that her own genitalia are the full equivalent of a male phallus, and in the little poem "Essential Oils are Wrung" Dickinson makes clear her intention to be the equal of any illustrious male poet with a pun on "sun": "The attar of the Rose/ Be not expressed by Suns—alone." In light of this, one can better appreciate why Moore refers to Dickinson not as a "woman" but as "a person of power." She means to suggest that Dickinson is a full equal, not a tolerated exception, in the nearly exclusively male line of great poets. She is a full inheritor, and if she will not join in the line of sexual reproduction of the race, she will hold a leading place, as Stein intends to do, in the exalted line of cultural reproduction, destined to be inherited by future generations. It is a thrilling moment in Moore's letters, like Stephen Dedalus's walk on the beach, written at the very beginning of her career, and the implications call for the kind of attention that the publication of these letters ought to excite. Meantime, Moore can be believed when she alludes, in a letter to William Carlos Williams in 1952, to "my case," and immediately adds, "disregarding gender—something I have always done."

2

ELUSIVE WHITMAN

In August 1890, Walt Whitman, by then a revered, monumentally grand, and infirm old man, received another importunate letter from John Addington Symonds, one of the earliest of his many English admirers. Best known for his writings on Greece and Italy, Symonds was once again asking in a guarded way the same question he had asked in a letter of 1872, still unanswered eighteen years later: Did Whitman's recurrent stress on the beauty of male comradeship mean that the poet was a lover of men—the term "homosexual" wasn't welcomed into the language until 1892, the year of Whitman's death. And wasn't this factor essential to the meaning of the Calamus series of poems, which, with the publication of the third edition in 1860, had become part of the ever evolving *Leaves of Grass*? Symonds hinted that his discretion could be counted on, as might be expected of someone reputed to be homosexual himself, married, and the father of four. While "burning for a revelation of your more developed meaning," he hoped besides for "some story of athletic friendship from which to learn the truth."

It wasn't until 1888 that Whitman showed the unanswered letter of 1872 to his confidant and future biographer of his last years, Horace Traubel, remarking, as Traubel recalls, that, while

Symonds is "a royal good fellow," he is "always driving me about that: is that what Calamus means?" When he finally does respond to Symonds's "urgent persistence" two years later, it is to reject the intimations about the Calamus poems as "morbid inferences which are disavowed by me and seem damnable." He meets the inferences about himself with a glaring lie: "Tho' unmarried I have had six children—two are dead—One living southern grandchild, fine boy, who writes to me occasionally. Circumstances connected with their benefit and fortune have separated me from intimate relations." He here uses an elaborate falsification of "intimate relations" to excuse or deny the true absence of such relations in his life. He does no less everywhere in his poetry.

The lie about fathering six children is important to an understanding of Whitman as a man and especially as a poet, and so is the maneuver by which he concludes the letter: "I see I have written with haste & too great effusion—but let it stand." In other words, what I say can be believed since I admit to saying it without calculation, hastily and effusively. This claim, too, is made repeatedly in *Leaves of Grass*, where fictions about his life are meant to be verified by further fictions about the nature of his writing. If this is to be judged immoral, so then is a lot of great poetry.

The letter reveals a truth about the gregarious-seeming and yet truly isolate Whitman of the poetry, the Whitman who wants continually to insist on a fiction of "intimate relations" with the reader. The reader is the "you" referred to in his poems, when "you" doesn't refer to the poetry itself or to the poet's "soul." Even as this Whitman amorously cozies up to you, he is already preparing to withdraw, to disclaim the intimacy he initiates. Time and again in his greatest poems, mostly published between 1855 and 1860, he tells us that Walt Whitman *is Leaves of Grass*, and that you hold him in your hand—though only for a moment. "Camerado, this is no book,/ Who touches this touches a man, (Is it night? are we together alone?)/ It is I you hold and who holds you,/ I spring from the pages into your arms—decease calls me forth." The sexuality of Whitman's poems—which need not mean the sexuality of Whitman—is in a long tradition of erotic mysticism, wherein "insubstantial death," as Romeo calls it in the tomb, "is amorous." To come is to go; to leap into a beloved—the reader in this and many other instances—is at the same time to be called away: "So Long!" is the poem's title. "Is it night? are we together alone?—" You bet; see you later. "Missing me one place search another," he concludes "Song of Myself," "I stop somewhere waiting for you."

Whitman was ever fearful of getting detained in a personal, particularly a sexual, relationship, or of being locked into one identity, to the point where he creates a cartography of himself including "my self," "my soul," and "Me myself," or the "real Me." Soul in his poetry has less of the conventional religious connotations usually assigned it and is more closely identified with the ancient poetic figure of Inspiration, the descendental muse. Indeed, in section 5 of "Song of Myself" the soul as muse quite graphically descends on Whitman by apparently going down on him: "I mind how we lay in June, such a transparent summer morning:/ You settled your head athwart my hips and gently turned over upon me,/ And parted the shirt from my bosom-bone, and plunged your tongue to my barestript heart,/ And reached till you felt my beard, and reached till you held my feet." By contrast, the "real Me" or "Me myself" is a figure of awesome severity who would never put itself in the positions here imagined for "my self" and "my soul." In the great, and greatly despairing, poem written five years later, in 1860, "As I Ebb'd with the Ocean of Life," Whitman describes himself walking along the shoreline at Paumanok thinking of "the pride of which I utter poems" and feeling

> O baffled, balk'd, bent to the very earth,
> Oppress'd with myself that I have dared to open my mouth,

Aware now that amid all that blab whose echoes recoil upon me I have
    not once had the least idea who or what I am,
But that before all my arrogant poems the real Me stands untouch'd,
    untold, altogether unreach'd.

Even after David Reynolds's *Walt Whitman's America: A Cultural Biography* (1995) and the twenty or so biographies that have
preceded it, Whitman's "real Me" remains "altogether unreach'd,"
remains a mystery. I don't mean to be ungrateful for Reynolds's
industrious labors as a cultural historian, but I regret to say that he
is trying to do something that cannot work when the writer in
question is a poet of Whitman's genius. He intends to demonstrate that a proper understanding of Whitman's poetry, which is
after all what any critical labor is finally about, depends on its
being read in a reciprocal relation with other cultural and political
materials assembled from roughly the last half of the American
nineteenth century. This sort of procedure can sometimes pay off
when the writer in question is less dauntingly original. But in the
case of Whitman the results could have been predicted, which is
that his poetry more or less escapes untouched.

Even while Whitman in his poetry often invites culturalist, historicist, and political explanations, the poetry all the while resists
them almost as much as does that of his near-contemporary
Emily Dickinson, who in her lifetime published only a handful
of her over seventeen hundred poems. Reynolds attempts to
demonstrate, for example, that Whitman's extensive journalistic
writings and cultural-political involvements before 1855 inform
and even predict the sudden, otherwise baffling, and little
noticed appearance that year of the first edition of *Leaves of
Grass.* No one is likely to be persuaded who knows how to read
the poetry or who has read such essential interpreters of it as
Harold Bloom and Kerry Larson, to name two, neither of whom
is mentioned in this book of nearly seven hundred pages, or
Michael Moon, who is mentioned only once.

Reynolds's cultural and chronological efforts at dovetailing are oblivious to an evident and stubborn fact: the poetry in the 1855 volume, particularly the as yet untitled "Song of Myself," is one of the inexplicable wonders of human literary creation, as strange as great poetry has ever been or is ever likely to become. Unexplained, too, is why, if the poetry is indeed as expressive of prevalent cultural assumptions as Reynolds assumes, it was resistant to clarification back then and it still is. He had some admiring readers from the beginning, notably Emerson, but they were few in number for a poet who claimed to belong to everyone and who said he wanted to absorb America and to be absorbed by it. It wasn't that Americans ignored American poets. Reynolds records the fact that, while the first edition of *Leaves of Grass* met with mixed reviews and sold less than a hundred copies, Longfellow's *Hiawatha,* published the same year, sold ten thousand in its first month, a figure that rose to thirty thousand in the next six. One reason for this disparity is that at their best Whitman's poems, in what they have to impart, were not easily available to a culture for which he imagined he was writing, then or now, and out of which he developed, if one is to believe culturalist readers like Reynolds. Eventually he became a legendary national figure, helped along, as Frost was later to be, by English admirers. How to explain the phenomenon that so great and difficult a writer ever became legendary in America? It doesn't mean in the least that the writings themselves were or are now widely read, much less understood, outside the literary minority. Gertrude Stein, a grateful and shrewd admirer of Whitman, remarked during her triumphant American tour in 1936 that enthusiastic audiences turned out to see her and listen to her readings, not because of any work of hers the audiences *did* understand, but because of the famous work of hers that they didn't understand; they were interested in her because they couldn't forget and yet couldn't figure out something as simple-sounding as "a rose is a rose is a rose is a rose."

The discipline of cultural-literary criticism, even when practiced as skillfully as it is by Reynolds, is the discipline of the collector: it requires the collection of writings meant to explain the significance of the literature that provides the essential incentive to the inquiry, like *Leaves of Grass.* It's taken for granted that all the writings thus assembled, canonical and journalistic, are on the same negotiating track, that they share in "discourses," vocabularies, and assumptions, allowing for differences in style and formulation. That such evidence is available goes without saying, since a literary work, no matter how recondite, must always use some version of the language already understood by its readers. It isn't surprising, therefore, that Emerson, a most difficult American writer while also proposing to be a popular one, should offer as lucid a rationale for cultural-literary or new historicist criticism as it is likely to get. In the essay "Art," he remarks, "No man can quite exclude the element of necessity from his labor. No man can quite emancipate himself from his age and country, or produce a model in which the education, the religion, the politics, usages, and arts, of his times shall have no share. Though he were never so original, never so willful and fantastic, he cannot wipe out of his work every trace of the thoughts amidst which it grew. The very avoidance betrays the usage he avoids."

In one of her many Emersonian moments, even the outrageous Miss Stein concedes that no writer can invent new languages: "So every one must stay with the language their language that has come to be spoken and written and which has in it all of intellectual recreation." You are necessarily stuck, she is saying, with the inheritance of language. You can, however, recreate it and look for evidences within it of its having been recreated or troped many times before by still other writers. So that while any poet must perforce use a language others have used, including the language of one's own earlier writings, this immediately ceases to be a burden, since there is also to be discovered in language an inherent power to re-create and transform it, to make it do new things.

Nothing, according to Whitman in the 1855 preface, exists only in its own moment; "no result exists now without its being from its long antecedent result and that from its antecedent, and so backward without the farthest mentionable spot coming a bit nearer the beginning than any other spot." Readers of Whitman are always surprised to discover how conservative he can sound, and when he speaks of that antecedent result which is the English language itself, it is without any of the nationalistic or insular bluster popularly associated with him. "The English language befriends the grand American expression," he says, and he calls it "the powerful language of resistance . . . it is the dialect of common sense. It is the speech of the proud and melancholy races and of all who aspire."

For Whitman, occasional venerations of the past aren't to be understood as venerations of objects or texts created in the past. Their value has far less to do with any abstractable meanings than with the discoverable traces of the actual work of writing that went into their creation. What is to be admired is the inferable compositional enterprise more than the finished composition itself, an enterprise that continues in the form of later critical revisions and interpretations made by countless others. Emerson in 1844 was already speaking for the Whitman of 1855 and thereafter when he said, "Our poetry, our language itself are not satisfactions but suggestions," and earlier, in 1841, "The real value of the Iliad, or the Transfiguration, is as signs of power . . . tokens"—a favorite word of Whitman's for his own poems—"of the everlasting effort to produce, which even in its worst estate the soul betrays."

This Emersonian and, later in the century, pragmatist imagination of poetry is one wherein Whitman, with the first *Leaves of Grass*, immediately takes a predominant place. From that moment to the present, this huge gathering of poems has proved immensely difficult, for the reason that he places at its core the veritable drama of its making, the problems that attend the coming into being of a work which in this instance is without any apparent origin or license other than his own voice, a voice now exuberant, now embattled, sometimes defeated. "My voice," he says, "goes after what my eyes cannot reach." This incessant "going after," this will to figuration, as some would call it, moves many of his best poems off any position of rest they even temporarily offer themselves or the reader. *Leaves of Grass* is incessantly revising, amputating, adding to what it has done, disowning its metaphors even as these begin to shape themselves into a design, while the figure of Whitman in it will characteristically embrace his lovers only when he is leaving them.

Whitman is a poet much given to abandonment, however frequently he wishes to be thought of as the poet of absorption. Each of these activities gives way to the other, often so precipitously that the speaker is caught off guard, seems no longer in control of the process, but filled suddenly with surprise or interrogation or consternation: "Is this then a touch? quivering me to a new identity" or "O Christ! My fit is mastering me!" or "I discover myself on the verge of the usual mistake" or "My lovers suffocate me!"

In a good many of his poems the interplay between intense involvement and abrupt disengagement will suggest to some, as it did to Symonds, that his poetry is at times an encoding of actual preferences and conflicts in a sexual life that dares not more directly speak its name. Obviously he cherished the spectacle of Manhattan streets, and just as obviously, to me at least, he entered those streets partly on the sexual prowl, which occupied him no less on the Brooklyn ferry, in Pfaff's underground restaurant and saloon at Broadway just north of Bleecker Street, and in the streetcars. It was there that he met a conductor named Peter Doyle, whose intimacy with Whitman lasted longest of the many in the poet's roster of relations with semi-literate, working-class young men, most of whom, though not Doyle, went on to be married.

As I read the letters and notebooks, they indicate that he cruised in search of new "camerados" with vigorous regularity, and the notebooks for the 1850s, 1870s, and 1880s list dozens of young men not otherwise identified. Paul Zwieg, in the biography that most closely preceded Reynolds's, asks incredulously, "Were these men Whitman's lovers? Possibly, but so many?" Why not hope that most or all of them *were* his lovers, since in that case he'd be less likely to find himself immobilized with any one of them. Like most of Whitman's biographers, Zwieg prefers to believe that if Whitman ever did go to bed with men, it was only on a very few occasions and that these "were not happy experiences." Really? How can we know? Or is it simply to be assumed that such experiences can't (shouldn't) be happy ones? As represented by his biographers, Whitman's sex life is already a Woody Allen film script.

Even while Reynolds is prepared to believe—for good enough reasons, it seems to me—that in 1841, while teaching school in Southport, Long Island, Whitman may have been tarred, feathered, and ridden out of town on a rail for sodomizing one of his male students, he nevertheless leans toward the view that he was more homoerotic than homosexual. This quibble is, I suspect, another instance of how the culturalist biographical method dictates rather than validates its findings. Like many academics these days, Reynolds is overawed by the idea that it is of enormous importance that "homosexuality" and, indeed, "heterosexuality" are terms of relatively recent invention. This leads to the assumption, as fallacious as it is widespread, that prejudice against "homosexuals" was markedly less in evidence before they were classified as such late in the nineteenth century. And yet it's preposterous to maintain that a phenomenon such as homosexuality or the prejudice against it has ever waited upon a particular classification. The convenience of believing otherwise promotes a further belief, which is that homoeroticism met with far more tolerance in earlier times, like

1855, than it does now, presumably because folks were blissfully ignorant of the unspeakable acts to which it might lead. Meanwhile, back on planet earth, any observer of advertisements for male underwear that nowadays adorn billboards and buses, or of the televised goings-on at breaks in football games or at the end of other sporting events, knows that homoeroticism in public is having a good run, at least as good as it ever has had, while this in no way means that the public is ever likely to condone homosexual acts in changing or locker rooms. Sodomy, or "the great sin against nature," was punishable by death well into the eighteenth century, while homoeroticism was supposedly in full sway (as Foucault, who is partly responsible for some of these historicist perpetrations, acknowledges).

But this is a digression from my primary concern, which is Whitman's poetry, a digression made necessary by large-scale ones on the same subject, running to chapters of books and books in their entirety, that have vitiated many a discussion of this, the greatest poet America has ever produced. It's not possible to argue on the basis of his poetry that he was or was not a homosexual, though it is evident to me on the basis of his notebooks, letters, and the patterns of his personal relationships that he clearly was one. Poetry is metaphor, and it can offer none of what Iago derisively calls "ocular proof" of anyone's sexual conduct; poetry is sound, and it's utterly vain to listen to it for audible proof of anyone's sexual conduct. And yet the issue of Whitman's sexuality has been made so central to considerations of him that even some distinguished critics who would otherwise scorn and deride interpretations of poetry which treat it as a species of sexually specific self-revelation repeatedly turn to *Leaves of Grass* as if something close to revelation might be found there.

So what if the poem likens itself to "his seminal muscle," or, as in "Spontaneous Me," he refers to "this poem drooping shy and unseen that I always carry and that all men carry." The penis as

poem is a conceit found in a number of poems; poetic inspiration, on bad days, can be imagined as a shriveled penis in the
work of Whitman, but it appears also in the works of Wallace
Stevens. Which brings to mind, too, that Stevens's dedication of
"Notes Toward a Supreme Fiction," "To Henry Church," is
immediately followed by a stanza beginning "And for what,
except for you, do I feel love?" Stevens was in no degree homosexual and the feelings he was expressing were directed toward
what, in another poem, he called his "interior paramour," the
muse of his poetry, embodied for him, as it often was, in a book
that he said he could "press . . . Close to me, hidden in me day
and night." "Who touches this touches a man."

What can be gleaned from Whitman's letters and notebooks
about his wariness of any too committed an attachment to young
men like Peter Doyle or Harry Stafford does indeed lend an
autobiographical dimension to the repeated abruptions that
occur in the poetry. And yet the same maneuvers are a crucial
feature of Emerson's essays; they are his way of abandoning
positions and formulations on which he has for a paragraph or
two become overly dependent. "The way of life is wonderful,"
he says in "Circles," "it is by abandonment." Thus it is that a
poetic figure or a stylistic movement which in Whitman's poetry
can be adduced in support of a contention as to his homosexuality can also be shown to have no such connotation whatever
when it occurs in the work of writers closely allied to him
who were not homosexual. Emerson was no more homosexual
than Stevens. He gives little evidence even of homoeroticism,
although when he was a seventeen-year-old at Harvard, he confesses in his journals, he was infatuated with another student in
the all-male freshman class. There was an exchange of stares
over many months, an exchange of a few words, but beyond that
he speaks of their being "entirely unacquainted," and while in
the final entry on the subject he admits to "being agreeably
excited by the features of [this] individual," he then adds that the

young man was "personally unknown to me." This is hardly
enough to justify Reynolds's decision to include this touching little episode in a list of what he calls "intense male pairings" confessed to by notable American men in the early nineteenth
century. Maybe the freshman's name, Martin Gay, proved an
irresistible inducement. It is fair to point out that this is only one
incidental reference to Emerson among many more extensive
ones in Reynolds's book, but it's nonetheless indicative of how
little of importance he finds to say about the connections
between the two writers.

I hadn't supposed that the centrality of Emerson to any study
of the cultural contexts for *Leaves of Grass* should still need to
be insisted upon, much less the centrality to our literature of the
affinities between Emerson and Whitman. Indeed, Whitman
himself insists upon them, despite occasional disclaimers. His
preface to the 1856 edition takes the form of a letter to Emerson; his advertisements for this and other printings eagerly
exploit (without the author's permission) Emerson's famous letter to him in 1855, which begins: "Dear Sir—I am not blind to
the worth of the wonderful gift of 'Leaves of Grass.' I find it the
most extraordinary piece of wit and wisdom that America has yet
contributed. I am very happy in reading it, as great power makes
us happy." Coming from a writer of by then immense international stature and addressed to a writer with none at all, someone Emerson had never met or heard of before, this is among
the most magnificently generous and clairvoyant endorsements
of one writer by another in the history of literature.

In failing to recognize the deep links between Emerson and
Whitman, Reynolds, along with all the other biographers of
Whitman and of Emerson, cannot go on to see how *Leaves of
Grass,* from the very outset, in 1855, contextualizes itself within
a tradition that extends not only to Thoreau, close at hand, but
also to William James, who frequently expressed admiration
for Whitman, and, still later, to three great twentieth-century

American writers, all of whom were at one time or another students at Harvard while James was a dominant figure in its philosophy department—Frost, Stein, and Stevens. These, along with
Emerson, Thoreau, and Whitman, are all on the same road
together, though frequently out of step, while the too easily
acclaimed if sometimes appealing runts of the litter, like Allen
Ginsberg and Jack Kerouac, trail behind. "I greet you at the
beginning of a great career," wrote Emerson from the pinnacle
to which his own had taken him, "which yet must have had a long
foreground somewhere, for such a start." These are the accents
of one great man's self-exaltation, merited in this instance, as
he accommodates another great man who has unexpectedly
appeared on the scene. And yet, in the last half of the sentence,
there is also, to my ears, a hint of inquisition in the tone, as if to
ask if the "somewhere" of that "long foreground" isn't possibly
discoverable in Emerson's own writing.

I've already alluded to some of the evidence that such discovery is there to be made; an important example is Emerson's
mythologizing of the poet in relation to America, both to the
idea that is America and to the continental stretch, "To the land
vaguely realizing westward," as Frost memorably phrases it
in "The Gift Outright." "America," Emerson says in 1844, "is a
poem in our eyes." As in Whitman, it is a visionary possibility, a
poem not yet finished. As for the figure of the poet, it is for
Emerson what it will later be for Whitman: the man "without
impediment," Emerson calls him in "The Poet," "who sees and
handles that which others dream of, traverses the whole scale of
experience, and is representative of man, in virtue of being the
largest power to receive and to impart." Emerson would have
heard the voice of this poet in the first line of the volume Whitman was to send him in 1855. "I celebrate myself,/ And what I
assume you shall assume,/ For every atom belonging to me as
good belongs to you."

As imagined by Whitman in his prefaces and especially in his
poems written before the Civil War, the poet is as mythological a

figure, and therefore as undependable a source of autobiographical confession, as he is in Emerson's essays or in the writings of
Wordsworth or Shelley or Sir Philip Sidney's 1598 *Apologie for
Poetrie.* For all these, the poet is a "maker" in the archaic sense
of the term; he is himself a god, capable of creating a new or second nature.

Whitman inherits nothing that he does not change, however,
and his poet is conjoined, very early in "Song of Myself," with
Whitman's unique invention of himself in tripartite form: "my
self," "my soul," and the "real Me." The poet in Whitman thus
can become uncommonly beset by doubts as to his mission and
his capacity to fulfill it. The very existence of the "real Me," in its
disdainful aloofness, casts doubt upon the poet's poetic achievements and, like some terrifying, retributive in-law, is capable at
any time of disrupting the creative intercourse between "my
self" and "my soul." It is, of course, Whitman's choice to create
this conflict to begin with, and the impetus for some of his most
intricately conceived and emotionally wrenching poems, including, among many, "Song of Myself" (not at all the uninterrupted
"celebration" it's usually made out to be), "Crossing Brooklyn
Ferry," "The Sleepers," "As I Ebb'd with the Ocean of Life,"
"Out of the Cradle Endlessly Rocking," and (less often included
in such lists) some of the poems in Calamus, especially "Scented
Herbage of My Breast," "Whoever You Are Holding Me Now in
Hand," which in every respect anticipates Stevens's "The Rock,"
and the infinitely gentle purposefulness of "The Last Invocation," first printed in 1868.

Whitman's misleading, often mendacious self-promotions
as America's public poet, intelligently enough recounted by
Reynolds, his posturings as a celebrant of the nation, even when,
as in the poem "Respondez!," he could write of it with unmodu-
lated bitterness, and his celebration of himself as one of the
indefatigably gregarious "roughs"—all this succeeds so well that
many still assume his poetry is rather stridently simple. In fact,
he exhibits a density of feeling and language not exceeded in the

poetry of Emily Dickinson, in the novels of Henry James, or by modernist "difficulty," as Eliot defines it. Perhaps he had it coming to him when a scholar as intelligent as Symonds could be led to ask if the Whitman of Calamus and the Whitman living in Camden, New Jersey, weren't really one and the same, making out with the boys in the one place as he seemed admittedly to have done in the other.

Even posing as the poet of democracy, he is among the most elusive and easily the foxiest and most manipulative of American writers, which is saying a good deal. The recurrent reminders in his poetry, and in his promotional writings about it, that you get what you see—Walt Whitman, American—has always stimulated in readers their natural tendency to reduce any hard-going poetry to something more manageable. He knew that, and knew also that the posturing was essential to the success of his entire poetic project, requiring great audacity of calculation. First of all, he induces in the reader the belief that the poem is in important respects a true representation of a representative life, of the flesh-and-blood Walt. He then willingly tolerates the consequent misunderstandings, to the extent that in the case of Symonds he doesn't even try to clear them up for more than eighteen years and, when he does get round to it, first dismisses these "morbid inferences," goes on to tell a real whopper of a lie, and then ingeniously tries to verify it on the spot by pretending to have written without premeditation.

Whitman's answers to any of the questions about himself occasioned by his poetry are always and everywhere evasive, if not utterly false. So that while he prompts such queries as those made by Symonds and by generations of readers since then, his response consists only in raising more questions. Questions are finally all we're left with, which is of course all we're left with by most great poetry. What regularly appear to be literalizations and identifications ("I was there") eventually drive the reader to recognize the metaphoric status of his words; he forces the reader back into his metaphors, back into the poetry-as-poetry, and away from it as historical representation. And once we get there, into the poetry, cultural biography or cultural study of the kind now being practiced turns out to be less than helpful. Whitman contrives that his poetry will at last hold each of us, all alone, in its grasp.

Speaking of which, I note that one of Whitman's tart and most telling comments on Symonds is missing from Reynolds's commendably researched book. In 1890, when he received a copy of Symonds's essay "Democratic Art, with Special Reference to Walt Whitman," the old poet is reported by Horace Traubel to have remarked, "I doubt whether he has gripped 'democratic art' by the nuts, or L of G. either." Women readers, who in the nineteenth century were the staunchest defenders of L of G against charges of indecency, need not feel left out. After all, it's only a figure of speech.

3

REACHING FRANK O'HARA

In 1966, on the shore of Fire Island Pines, Frank O'Hara, forty, was struck down and mortally injured by a beach buggy. It was two o'clock on an August morning, and he had been cruising and carousing with some friends. Five years later there appeared the now long-out-of-print *Collected Poems.* Covering five hundred large and closely packed pages, the poetry is at times brilliantly accomplished and challenging. But very little of it has received the kind of close reading that it deserves. This is a pity, because the poems tell us something essential about what O'Hara was like, beyond the vast store of gossip and anecdote that abounds in the only full biography of the poet, Brad Gooch's 1993 *City Poet: The Life and Times of Frank O'Hara.*

O'Hara's work also includes a number of still-important essays on contemporary American painting, which are no less slighted by Gooch, and some efforts at filmmaking and playwriting. In these writings, as in his poetry and letters, O'Hara emerges as someone almost evangelically convinced by the Manhattan of the 1950s and early 1960s that America has become the most culturally exciting place in the world. His enthusiasms for European styles, of which a great deal has been made, seem to me to have been more decorative than real, as when, in a letter to his friend Kenneth Koch in

1956, he admitted, "I'd rather be dead than not have France around me like a rhinestone dog collar." Things French were rapidly assimilated into the New York blend of popular culture and high culture, but they were to be further mixed, without O'Hara or his associates being altogether aware of it, with American traditions that go back to Emerson. Those native traditions anticipated the need for, if not the doctrine of, surrealism, and foreshadowed other avant-garde developments like "action painting," whose practitioners assumed, along with O'Hara, that the exemplary characteristics of a work of art are the traces of performative energy coursing through it, not its thematic significances.

O'Hara's intellectual audacity, his volubility, his immense social vigor were all in the service of a conviction, expressed in a poem of 1951, that "New York is everywhere like Paris!" The Cedar, a tavern for painters where O'Hara was a mascot to the likes of the de Koonings, Pollock, and Michael Goldberg; the more ecumenical San Remo, mostly a haunt for writers, along with a contingent of gays who were not much welcomed at the Cedar; the all-night or all-weekend parties in Greenwich Village and in the Hamptons; the endless panel discussions and readings (at one of which Kerouac shouted at O'Hara, "You're ruining American poetry, O'Hara," to which the quick-witted poet immediately replied, "That's more than you ever did for it"): all these places and occasions were as essential to artistic and intellectual bonding in New York as were such uptown institutions as Balanchine's New York City Ballet, which O'Hara frequented with his good friend Edwin Denby, that most supple of dance critics and essayists, or the Museum of Modern Art, where in 1951 O'Hara found work selling postcards at the front desk and before long became a curator who helped to select contemporary American paintings for exhibition in Europe.

O'Hara thrived on coteries. He was the Demosthenes of the telephone. He liked to triangulate one-to-one relationships so as to involve some of his many close women friends with his even more numerous male cohorts, thereby leaving him free to move on to someone entirely new. Over the years he found his way into bed, often drunkenly, with some of the women to whom he felt especially close, such as Patsy Southgate, a writer who was then married to Michael Goldberg. But these encounters never got past affectionate petting, and according to Joseph LeSueur, his roommate of nine years, "the impotence had nothing to do with heterosexuality. It was pervasive. It also had to do with homosexuality. He had a difficult time with an erection." Like many of his long poems, O'Hara's sexual infatuations with men, often heterosexual men, seldom found a satisfying way to conclude themselves.

Gooch is best about O'Hara's life before New York—about his childhood, his high school, his service in the Navy during World War II, which eventually took him to the Pacific, his years at Harvard on the G.I. Bill, where he was part of that unprecedented concentration of talent that filled American colleges and universities between 1946 and 1950. O'Hara was the first of three children born to a prosperous and cultivated Irish family long settled in farming businesses in western Massachusetts. He became a good swimmer and a good rider; later in life he reported to Larry Rivers that he had his first sexual experience, when he was sixteen, with a boy who took care of the family horses. (This is probably "the stable boy who gave me the diamonds" in the poem "Commercial Variations" of 1952.) But the young O'Hara seems to have especially enjoyed sitting on the porch discussing books and musical scores with his doting aunts.

O'Hara's first aspiration was to be a pianist and a composer, and his playing became accomplished enough to please Robert Fizdale (who was, for a brief spell, also O'Hara's lover). In high school he spread his enthusiasms for Toscanini, for Lily Pons, and for almost any movie, especially if it featured Marlene Dietrich. Though he seemed aloof, as he later did in the service and at Harvard (where he met his lifelong friends John Ashbery and Kenneth Koch), he was simply on the lookout for kindred spirits, one of whom, Elsa Ekblau, the daughter of a professor at nearby Clark University, dressed only in black and lined her lips with purple lipstick. Along with his redoubtable aunts, Elsa was among the first of a succession of women in O'Hara's life who displayed great independence of spirit and assertive style. Others of this kind included Bunny Lang, a colorful figure at the Poets' Theater that O'Hara helped to establish in Cambridge, whose early death plagued his memory for years, as well as the painters Jane Freilicher and Grace Hartigan, both of whom, along with Southgate, figure importantly in his poetry.

O'Hara in New York is the story of an emotionally reckless man, wasteful of affection as well as anger. He was endlessly generous in his support of friends but had a habit, especially when drunk late in the evening, of brutally taking them apart, only to try to put them back together again still later on the telephone. In his short life he created a large body of work, some part of which will always matter, and he managed, up to his death (and thereafter), to keep the love of any number of discriminating, lively, and talented people. It was a good life, on the whole, and Gooch is to be commended for getting it onto the page without presumption—he never calls his subject "Frank"—and with a minimum of constraining moral or psychological intrusion.

Yet Gooch seems unwilling or unable to discover much about the sadder side of O'Hara's effervescence. A man of O'Hara's conflicted erotic disposition could never reach the kind of fulfillment that Gooch novelistically celebrates in a late chapter called "Love," devoted to O'Hara's affair of some eighteen months (not the two years Gooch gives to it elsewhere in his book) with a nineteen-year-old ballet dancer named Vincent Warren. And Gooch does no justice to O'Hara's work. He is not disposed to read the poems as inquisitively as he should. In O'Hara's case, this amounts to a failure of criticism that is at the same time a failure of biography. For in the best of his poems O'Hara's

complications of feeling are much the same as the complications
that frustrated his chances of finding more than fleeting satisfac-
tion in his love affairs. In his poems, as in his romantic attach-
ments, there is a fateful contradiction between the eager
reachings-out, the intense solicitation of passing sights, sounds,
and people, and the hints of a despairing pensiveness about
where his life might be heading. O'Hara had a very affecting
need to feel enchanted, to believe that there must be something
magical or mysterious lurking within the immediate offerings of
daily experience, even though he could not get to it.

Being of the same generation as O'Hara and from much the
same Irish Catholic background, having been in the service at
roughly the same time as he, and then at Harvard just after he
left, I was not surprised to discover that he, too, experienced an
early and peculiar shock of recognition when reading Joyce's *A
Portrait of the Artist as a Young Man.* The appeal of the book to
someone like O'Hara cannot only have been, as Gooch would
have it, that it told the story of a young Irish Catholic renegade
who turned against his Jesuit training in pursuit of the religion of
High Art. Much more powerfully for any gay Irish Catholic
teenager, Joyce's novel, which was first published in America in
1916, is a story of how the Church can produce in late adoles-
cence a tortuous guilt about sexual desires and fantasies. Reading the book again in the Navy in 1944, O'Hara wrote to his
parents that "in some places Joyce's character is uncannily like
me." By then Catholic boys were no longer feeling anything like
Stephen Dedalus's guilt about wanting girls, but a Catholic boy
secretly wanting sex with other boys could powerfully identify
with the hero's plight, as O'Hara did. To escape the guilt, and to
retaliate for its imposition, the fledgling Catholic artist in Joyce's
novel finds himself turning the trappings and the devices of the
Church into artistic properties, so that, as I read them, Stephen's
pretentiously worded theories of art become a grotesque mixture of the theology of Aquinas and the aestheticism of Walter

Pater. "To burn always with this hard, gemlike flame," as Pater recommended, is to make hellfire itself into a stage device.

"A sexual bliss inscribe upon the page of whatever energy I burn for art": that is O'Hara's Dedalean–Paterean request, in his 1958 "Ode on Causality." He was able to put his Catholicism behind him more decisively than Stephen Dedalus ever did, but his lifelong admiration for the figure in the novel points to the interplay within his own work between an aesthete's ideal of continuous responsiveness and an intellectual's suspicion that the products of art cannot adequately represent this responsiveness. That suspicion was a part not only of his Catholic inheritance but also of his American inheritance. And it broaches the kind of literary inquiry that Gooch avoids, and that might have opened the way toward important biographical speculations.

The poems tell us a great deal about O'Hara's day-to-day experience but in a manner contrived not to tell us much about who he really is. In their local details, the poems are everywhere autobiographical. And yet, like Whitman—referred to in the opening line of "Ode: Salute to the French Negro Poets" as "my great predecessor"—O'Hara made verse catalogues of the things, persons, and places that impressed themselves upon his attention and these were not intended to be confessional. In "Meditations in an Emergency," O'Hara is Whitman become a little soigné: "It's not that I'm curious. On the contrary, I'm bored but it's my duty to be attentive. I am needed by things as the sky must be above the earth. And lately, so great has *their* anxiety become, I can spare myself little sleep." Along with the occasional Russian poet such as Pasternak, or the occasional French poet such as Rimbaud, the announced heroes of O'Hara's poetry were Whitman, Crane, and Williams. These three are the only ones "of the American poets," as he opines in his mock-manifesto "Personism," who "are better than the movies."

But finally his citations of "things" are different from theirs, far less publicly recognizable, more private, more obscure even

than "things" are for Crane. In "Mayakovsky"—a poem whose
four parts were quite haphazardly put together from a pile of
manuscripts on O'Hara's desk during a visit from James
Schuyler, who then gave the poem its title because he saw on the
same desk a well-thumbed copy of Mayakovsky's poems—we
come abruptly on the lines

> That's funny! There's blood on my chest
> oh yes, I've been carrying bricks
> what a funny place to rupture!
> and now it is raining on the ailanthus.

In a note to the poem in *Collected Poems,* Donald Allen quotes a
letter from Schuyler saying that "the bricks he was carrying were
the supports of a John Ashbery bookcase, which O'Hara and
Fairfield [Porter] helped John with." O'Hara loves to be casually
arcane in this fashion, as if talking not to a reader but to some
close intimate ("oh yes") of the unidentified people involved.

I suppose the editor's note does assist us with a minor puzzle;
and yet this little passage is testimony to the peculiar nature of
O'Hara's writing, in that finally the annotation does *not* really
help us understand the poem, only some isolated words in it.
The reader of this poem comes to notice that his attention is
being drawn, not to this or that particular thing, but to O'Hara's
rapid movement away from it and his swift transit to something
to which it bears no discernible relation at all: "and now it is rain-
ing on the ailanthus." Things like "bricks" are not allowed to
initiate, or to become a part of, any narrative or metaphoric
development. Coherence among these things derives only from
the variable ranges and inflections of the voice, which is always
moving past one of them and on to another.

Thus, in one of O'Hara's most splendid achievements, the
poem dated 1956 called "In Memory of My Feelings," it is probably worth knowing that in the lines "One of me is standing in
the waves, an ocean bather,/ or I am naked with a plate of devils

at my hip," O'Hara is referring first to Matisse's *Bathers by a River* and then to a painting by his friend Grace Hartigan called *Frank O'Hara and the Demons.* Still, of greater importance to any grasp of O'Hara's presence in the poem is his repeated use, here and elsewhere, of the phrase "one of me," meaning that another is on the way, and his use of that little word "or," with its suggestion that neither of the two allusions matters more than the other. What keeps the poem going, what keeps O'Hara going as a poet (and as an aspiring lover), is the need to extricate himself from any figure with whom he has just been involved. He does not extend one image into another, he substitutes one for another; and he is especially apt to do this when both images are derived from existing works of art.

Biographers of poets are seldom any help with their poetry, but Gooch can be altogether a hindrance, as in such summary observations as this: "If the poets of the New York School could be grouped together because they wrote in language that was illogical and often meaningless, O'Hara's particular tone was surrealist, Ashbery's was philosophical, and Koch's was comic." No poet or reader of poetry has ever been served by this kind of boilerplate. A sure way to diminish O'Hara as a poet is to call him, as many of his interpreters like to do, a surrealist or a poet of the New York School. (The latter label was concocted in 1961 by John Bernard Myers, a friend to the poets in question and an art dealer at the Tibor de Nagy Gallery.)

O'Hara's poetry and his theories of art are obsessively shaped, rather, by a concern found everywhere in the work of the great American predecessors whom he read and admired, Emerson and Whitman, and in their successors Crane, Stevens, and Gertrude Stein, who was of particular interest to O'Hara. These writers have much in common, including a high degree of communicated suspicion that they are being betrayed even by the language they use, and they share, too, another suspicion: that variations they try to bring about experimentally in the language are themselves arbitrary and impositional. To enjoy such writing is to cope with its difficulty, without simply translating it into clarity. The difficulty is a sign of the poet's fascination with the medium.

These poets are saying, in effect, that while the language available to you has to some degree already shaped and determined your experiences all day long, your use of that language in writing or reading, no matter how innovative or how much a challenge to the existing order of things, becomes still another instance of the possibility that composition flattens, deadens, or makes into a monument the very things it is meant to represent. And yet, in supposing this to be true, the writer finds a good excuse to keep on writing, to begin again, as Stein recommends.

From the opening of a short poem called "Poetry" in 1951— "The only way to be quiet/ is to be quick, so I scare/ you clumsily, or surprise/ you with a stab"—to the lengthy "In Memory of My Feelings" five years later, whose first lines are "My quietness has a man in it, he is transparent/ and he carries me quietly, like a gondola, through the streets"—O'Hara, like his American forebears, proposes to save the idea of a free-floating self from entrapment in the artifact of language and from other historical and cultural inheritances. He talks of transparency, indulges in spontaneous lurches away from the direction just laid down by his own phrases, and writes favorably about his own "quickness" or mobility: "my force is in mobility it's said," according to "Poem (Now it is the 27th)."

When he occasionally seems to pause in the middle of a poem to let us settle on a line he has just written, it is usually when he has just made a joke, at times in the manner of S. J. Perelman ("the sound/ is that of a bulldozer in heat stuck in the mud where a lilac still scrawnily blooms and cries out 'Walt!'"), or Milton Berle ("you were made in the image of God/ I was not. I was made in the image of a sissy truck driver"), or a latter-day Oscar Wilde ("I have discovered that beneath the albatross there is a goose smiling"), or Noel Coward imagining himself as a 1940s

American teenager ("from hours of dusk in bushes playing tag, being called in, walking on the porch and crying bitterly because it wasn't a veranda"). The brilliance of O'Hara's wit, even as it is meant to suspend us for a moment in admiration, is itself a reminder of his outrageousness, of his impatience with convention; and it is meant as evidence that he has not become trapped within himself. He is no Hamlet, as we are assured by his joking echo of the play in "For the Chinese New Year & for Bill Berkson": "oh oh god how I'd love to dream let alone sleep."

In the same poem, O'Hara says that "the strange career of a personality begins at five and ends/ forty minutes later in a fog . . ." In an interview with Edward Lucie-Smith in 1965, he speaks derisively of "the confessional manner of Robert Lowell," alleging that it lets Lowell "get away with things that are really just plain bad but you're supposed to be upset because he's supposed to be so upset." By contrast, O'Hara has already asked us to believe, in "Post the Lake Poets Ballad," that he "has no more self-pity than Gertrude Stein/ before Lucey [sic] Church," and that

> I think of myself
> as a cheerful type who pretends to
> be hurt to get a little depth into
> things that interest me.

Note that it is not because "things" already have "depth" that they interest him. Rather, when for whatever reasons they do interest him, he will con his audience into believing they are deep. Whenever a poet so openly admits that he is indulging in a hoax, he is usually positioning himself for another hoax—the claim that there are no sincerities whatever behind what he is doing, nothing to be looked for except immediacy. But what is immediacy, as O'Hara himself sometimes wonders, if not simply an idea, a pretense, a guise, a fiction out of which the poet manages to generate more poetry? In "My Heart," he says:

I'd have the immediacy of a bad movie,
not just a sleeper; but also the big,
overproduced first-run kind. I want to be
at least as alive as the vulgar. And if
some aficionado of my mess says "That's
not like Frank!," all to the good!

As O'Hara knows, his "immediacy" is not only a fabrication
but an "overproduced" one, and it is inferentially compared in
"For the Chinese New Year & for Bill Berkson" to the flowers in
the glass flower collection at Harvard: "It's a strange curse my
'generation' has we're all/ like the flowers in the Agassiz
Museum perpetually ardent." This is a resonant, Keatsian figure.
It suggests that the reason O'Hara so much wants a life of immediacy is that he feels so irrevocably cut off from it: he is like a
replica of what was once natural and alive—and is going about
the business of reproducing itself. In this light, O'Hara's infatuations throughout his life with straight painters such as Larry
Rivers or Michael Goldberg, or with straight poets such as Bill
Berkson and scores of others, can be understood as the expression, I think, of his desire to have been straight himself. And his
poetic fascination with immediacy is part of a corresponding
wish to live absolutely in the present, since only death hovers in
the past, with dead family and dead friends, and since at his own
death he will leave no biological heir.

O'Hara's frequent references to death in his poetry—"I histor-
ically/ belong to the enormous bliss of American death," is the
Whitmanian ending of his poem "Rhapsody"— are seldom so
complexly motivated as in his reference to being "like the flowers
in the Agassiz Museum." Still, that complexity should be kept in
mind when reading any of his poems, and when assessing his long
and recurrent mourning for friends who have died, especially
Bunny Lang. He has a painful but quickening awareness that his
poetic creativity is partly a compensation for what he knows he
cannot otherwise give to life. The immediacy of responsiveness
that he likes to register in his poetry is a reprieve from the deaths

in his life and the death that awaits him, a gift from the city, with its buzz of happenings and accidental sightings.

"Everything/ suddenly honks: it is 12:40 of/ a Thursday," he remarks in "A Step Away from Them." By the title he means that he is only one step away from loved ones now dead: "First/ Bunny died, then John Latouche,/ then Jackson Pollock. But is the/ earth as full as life was full, of them?" While the poem ends unfortunately with the assurance that his heart is all the while in his pocket, where he carries a volume of Pierre Reverdy's poems, the poem itself is determined to celebrate an alternative to death, not in any works of art, but in the sheer fact of the poet's being, at that moment, alive to random sights and sounds: "hum-colored cabs," "yellow helmets," "bargains in wrist watches," "neon in daylight," "several Puerto/ Ricans on the avenue today, which/ makes it beautiful and warm."

The splurge of the world's random creativity finds an expression in the poet and his poetry but does not depend on these. In recognition of this, Emerson, Whitman, and Stein generate yet a further recognition, more happily assented to by Stein than by the others: that the finished works of any artist are expendable and that their value lies chiefly in the performative, even barbaric energies that produced them. The particular poet and the particular textual evidences of poetic activity are themselves inclined toward death or, in an image O'Hara favors, toward "statuary." The acknowledgment of this by poets or artists can have the effect of releasing them into celebrations of performative power itself, into moment-by-moment exercises of production. But it can also understandably lead to moments of despair, as in Emerson's "Experience," or Whitman's "As I Ebb'd with the Ocean of Life," a poem especially predictive of O'Hara, where Whitman admits to being

> Oppress'd with myself that I have dared to open my mouth,
> Aware now that amid all that blab whose echoes recoil upon me I
>   have not once had the least idea who or what I am,

But that before all my arrogant poems the real Me stands yet
    untouch'd, untold, altogether unreach'd,
Withdrawn far, mocking me with mock-congratulatory signs and bows,
With peals of distant ironical laughter at every word I have written,
Pointing in silence to these songs, and then to the sand beneath.

Except for its "ironical laughter," Whitman's "real Me" is associated with silence, disdainful of "all that blab," which is Whitman's writing. O'Hara's equivalent figure is "my quietness,"
which we have already heard about in the opening of "In Memory of My Feelings": "My quietness has a man in it, he is trans-
parent/ and he carries me quietly, like a gondola, through the
streets." And just as Whitman's "real Me" is said to be "both in
and out of the game and watching and wondering at it," monitoring his other selves (his "I" or "my self" or "my Soul"), so O'Hara
imagines "a number of naked selves" who are responsible to his
"quietness":

My quietness has a number of naked selves,
so many pistols I have borrowed to protect myselves
from creatures who too readily recognize my weapons
and have murder in their heart!

In O'Hara as much as in Whitman, none of the gregarious,
loving, cruising selves who write and talk and befriend multitudes—"there are at least sixty people in New York who thought
Frank O'Hara was their best friend," said Larry Rivers at his best
friend's grave—ever expresses the "real Me." In fact, the "real
Me" feels endangered by these others, whom O'Hara calls
"creatures." Whitman similarly complains, "My lovers suffocate
me!/ Crowding my lips, and thick in the pores of my skin,/
Jostling me through the streets and public halls. . . . Calling my
name from flowerbeds or vines or tangled underbrush." Far
from being imagined as a revelation of a true self, poetry is taken
to be a projection of false selves. The paradox for both poets is

that the only way to protect the "real Me" is by continuing the volubility that hides it, since to fall silent would be to give finality to what has already been characterized as "blab" or, in O'Hara's variant, as a "ruse."

"In Memory of My Feelings" is self-consciously brought to an end with an expressed fear that the energies that have gone into this and other poems, like the energies that have gone into his love affairs, are deadened when any particular embodiment of them is treated as final. "I have forgotten my loves," he complains, because "against my will/ against my love" they have "become art." He imagines himself the dupe of his own compositional successes, which include the very poem he is in the process of giving us:

> and I have lost what is always and everywhere
> present, the scene of my selves, the occasion of these ruses,
> which I myself and singly must now kill
> and save the serpent in their midst.

The poem must abruptly be cut off so as not to trap the spirit coursing through it. This, I take it, is what he intends to mean by his recurrent use of the figure of "the serpent," which is also meant as a sign of O'Hara's allegiance to what Blake calls "the Devil's party." His poetic movements, in sum, are best seen as movements of insinuating resistance to any created order of things.

"In Memory of My Feelings" is the best of O'Hara's many long poems, touching upon perplexities in him that twist and turn his verse in extraordinarily productive directions. The poem draws him inexorably toward recognitions that he often tries to evade by means of an impenetrability that sometimes passes for surrealism when it is merely cute, by razzle-dazzle cleverness, and by prolixity. Critics have largely ignored another exceptional and beautiful short poem, "To the Harbormaster," written in 1954, two years before "In Memory," though it is

admired by fellow poets such as Richard Howard, who quotes
most of it in *Alone with America,* his brilliant study of American
poetry since 1950; and by John Ashbery, who broke down while
reading it at O'Hara's funeral. Like the longer "In Memory of
My Feelings," "To the Harbormaster" seems to be turned away
from the reader, as if intent on finding its way privately toward
significances the poet only intuits as he goes along.

Here, more powerfully than in any of his other poems,
O'Hara discovers that he yearns for something that all the while
he denies himself, something on the far side of his "ruses,"
which on this occasion he calls "the forms of my vanity":

> I wanted to be sure to reach you;
> though my ship was on the way it got caught
> in some moorings. I am always tying up
> and then deciding to depart. In storms and
> at sunset, with the metallic coils of the tide
> around my fathomless arms, I am unable
> to understand the forms of my vanity
> or I am hard alee with my Polish rudder
> in my hand and the sun sinking. To
> you I offer my hull and the tattered cordage
> of my will. The terrible channels where
> the wind drives me against the brown lips
> of the reeds are not all behind me. Yet
> I trust the sanity of my vessel; and
> if it sinks, it may well be in answer
> to the reasoning of the eternal voices,
> the waves which have kept me from reaching you.

Surely this asks to be read as a love poem, and a note by Donald Allen in the *Collected Poems* says that O'Hara told him in
1959 that the poem, which was written five years earlier, was
"about Larry Rivers." It is not clear to me just what O'Hara
could have meant by "about": his own love for Rivers? Rivers's
own aspirations in love? To be "about Rivers" is already to be
"about" the elusiveness evoked in the lovely Steinean ending of a

1953 poem called "Larry": "So we're great friends constant and true/ to not being sure of your being sure/ of my being sure of your being sure of you."

Be that as it may, "To the Harbormaster" is among a large number of poems that Gooch simply decides to forget when he alleges that Vincent Warren, whose affair with O'Hara began in 1959, was "the first muse to inspire O'Hara to openly gay love poems." I don't wish to deprive Gooch of his simple assumption that when O'Hara finally did link up for a while with an openly gay man, even though they never lived under the same roof, he must have been more in love than he could ever have been in his liaisons with men who were predominantly straight. But Gooch cannot be allowed the even simpler supposition that to be inspired to write "openly gay" love poems requires a recipient who is also gay.

As the dates indicate, long before O'Hara even met Warren he had written some beautiful love poems to Rivers, who, he charmingly complains in 1953 in "Round Robin," "is moved by my smile like a public accusation/ of homosexuality against the Great Wall of China"; and he wrote several more love poems to the emphatically heterosexual Bill Berkson during his affair with Warren. Along the way there are numerous and graphic allusions to homosexual sex in early poems such as "Homosexuality," which includes an informal gay men's guide to cruising in Manhattan in 1954, beginning with subway latrines: "14th street is drunken and credulous,/ 53rd tries to tremble but is too at rest. The good/ love a park and the inept a railway station . . ."

The ambiguity of what O'Hara might have meant by "about Larry Rivers" is lodged in the language of the poem itself and in brilliantly consequential ways. The word "you" introduced in the opening line, "I wanted to be sure to reach you," may well refer to Rivers, making him the harbormaster who is already securely at the place O'Hara is striving to reach. Yet it is evident that Rivers is also being referred to in the lines "or I am hard

alee with my Polish rudder/ in my hand and the sun sinking."
(Rivers was born of Russian-Polish-Jewish parents, and he used
to delight O'Hara by speaking in his parents' heavily accented
English, as can be heard in some lines of "Walking with Larry
Rivers.") It can be inferred, then, that Rivers represents, in one
sense, the goal of O'Hara's efforts, and in another sense he represents a detour; ". . . my Polish rudder" is a synecdoche for
Rivers, for his phallus, which steers O'Hara off course into a
merely temporary haven, thwarting his attempts to battle the
storm as he tries to reach the Rivers who is the harbormaster. A
roughly similar terminological complication of roles occurs in
the fifth section of "Song of Myself," where Whitman describes
intercourse between "my Soul" and "the other I am" in terms of
sexual intercourse between himself and another man:

> I mind how we lay in June, such a transparent summer morning;
> You settled your head athwart my hips and gently turned over
>   upon me,
> And parted the shirt from my bosom-bone, and plunged your tongue
>   to my bare-stript heart,
> And reached till you felt my beard, and reached till you held my feet.

The meditative nobility of O'Hara's poem, and its sadness, is a
result of his chosen syntactical confusions, which seem to com-
pel him to accept his fate even as he still contends with it. The
expression of O'Hara's desires cheats him, in life and in his
poetry, of anything commensurate with them. The "you" that he
cannot reach is finally himself.

    Much more could be said about this poem, especially of those
moments where its nuanced modulations of voice dispel any
hints of self-pity or resentment or complaint, where his admissions of personal deficiency become instead a heroic rejection of
the theatrical posturings to which he is all but invited by the
poem's highly conventional images of the stress and storms of
love. The poem's sincerity of feeling is never in doubt, but it is
everywhere a measured and performed sincerity within an

already stylized mode that goes back to a much earlier poet whom O'Hara admired, the sixteenth-century Sir Thomas Wyatt, specifically to "My Galley Charged with Forgetfulness," which is itself indebted to Petrarch and Horace. "To the Harbormaster" echoes the Wyatt poem in even more detail than does the earlier and weaker O'Hara poem of 1951 called "After Wyatt."

The literary allusiveness in O'Hara's poetry is no less pervasive than is the allusiveness to people and places in New York; and if the effect of the latter is to induce in the reader an outsider's yearning to be initiated into some exclusive circle, the effect of the former is to demonstrate that O'Hara is intent on making his way into the far more exalted and historically select company of great poets. Anyone who can refer to Whitman as "my great predecessor" has convinced himself that his poetic ambitions, even when it comes to representing himself in love, are not local or social but universal and cultural. With that other "city poet," the Whitman of "Crossing Brooklyn Ferry," O'Hara aspires to be alive "a hundred years hence, and ever so many hundred years hence," not only as a trace on the Manhattan scene, but also as a voice in American poetry. As a first step, however, he had to establish that his days alive in America were as glamorous as he believed them to be. This was the point of a letter he wrote in August 1950 to a younger writer who had sent him some of his work:

> I can see certain tendencies in you which we all have to get rid of. With me it was Ronald Firbank, with you it looks a bit like the divine Oscar (have you read that PRETTY poetry!). We Americans are all more lonely for glamour than for each other, and until we learn to find it in each other and around us, that is to lay in something we can comprehend, relax with and *use*, glamour is just an elder brother's cast off exoticism.

O'Hara's literary ambitions were considerable, and the assurance with which they were expressed, even at so early an age, was owed to the similar accents that he heard in the American writers from whom he had descended. We are not easily allowed by O'Hara's writings, any more than by the writings of his literary forefathers, to distinguish his ambitions for himself from his ambitions for America.

4

BALANCHINE IN AMERICA

✧

I am recalling a season at the New York City Ballet, spring of 1980, two years before Balanchine's final season in 1982, when he added to the repertory four essentially new works. *Ballade,* to the music of Fauré, featured Merrill Ashley, a dancer refined to a kind of beaming technical brilliance, and Ib Andersen, who, less than a year after he left the Royal Danish Ballet, became one of the best dancers in a company so strenuous for newcomers that it took even the superbly confident Peter Martins three years to find his proper place in it. There was *Walpurgisnacht Ballet,* an independent ballet of a work staged originally for the Paris Opera production of Gounod's *Faust* in 1975. Like Balanchine's earlier *Tchaikovsky Suite No. 3,* it is a romantic piece full of fast, open, loose-haired movement by the women, though with little of *Ballade's* complex elasticity, and it was led by the great Suzanne Farrell, with her sometimes dizzying, seemingly off-balance improvisations. There was also *Le Bourgeois Gentilhomme,* to music by Richard Strauss, which shows unabashedly Balanchine's taste for theatrical lavishness, for romps and high jinks, as against the minimalization of costume and decor in his *Agon* or *The Four Temperaments.* Peter Martins, its star, was a

dancer of such noble and exact bearing that it was always surprising to observe his capacity for comedy and dramatic characterization, though it shouldn't have been, given what he did in
Coppélia and in *Union Jack.*

But the great event of the season was *Robert Schumann's
"Davidsbündlertänze."* "If you can't pronounce it, don't come,"
Balanchine remarked in an interview with the critic Anna Kisselgoff, adding that Schumann was too great a composer to have a
ballet named after anything but his own music. Still, the title is
unprecedented in the emphasis it gives to the composer's full
name.

Balanchine meant the title as a signal homage and also, I
think, as an indication that the dance, like the music, has much
to do with Schumann's life, which ended in 1856 at the age of
forty-six, in a sanatorium he entered in 1854 after the most
severe of his nervous collapses. The title refers to a suite of eighteen piano pieces composed in 1837 and to a society, the League
of David, or Davidsbündler, which was entirely the creation of
Schumann's fantasy, "a conspiracy of himself alone," as Balanchine put it to Kisselgoff, to fight the philistines of his day. These
are represented onstage, during a nightmare solo danced by
the Schumann figure, by five figures in massive top hats and
cloaks, completely shrouded in black, and holding huge quill
pens. Not merely Schumann's critics but all his enemies, these
are "the other side," including his father-in-law; at one point,
before it proved technically unfeasible, the ballet was to end
with a huge flood: "I always like to get rid of those dark people who don't understand anything," Balanchine charmingly
admitted.

Schumann marked most of the eighteen pieces of the *Dance
of the League of David* with an E or an F, a few with both letters,
referring to the contrasting alter egos in the League: Florestan,
passionate and exultant; and Eusebius, lyrical and contempla-
tive. The music, played at a piano onstage—Gordon Boelzner,

performing brilliantly, at the premiere—with the pianist dressed in formal black attire of the period against a backdrop that might have been created by the nineteenth-century romantic painter of Gothic sublimity, Kaspar David Friedrich: white drapery closes off the sides of the stage at an angle, directing our attention to a background lit by some strange mixtures of sunset and dawn, in which a blurred visionary Gothic cathedral rises out of water. Within this space of the past, four couples dance in increasingly complicated sequences: Karin von Aroldingen and Adam Lüders, Ib Andersen and Kay Mazzo, Suzanne Farrell and Jacques d'Amboise, Peter Martins and Heather Watts. Lüders danced the part meant to be an aspect of Schumann, "stranger than the rest," as Balanchine put it; von Aroldingen the part that might be his wife, Clara; and the other couples represent alternative, happier possibilities for partnering that could have belonged at some point to Schumann's, and Clara's, imagination of their life together. But the qualities of Florestan and Eusebius belong, in varying proportions, to all four couples, and none wholly represents one side or the other.

Anyone who watches the ballet or listens to the music with these clues in mind will have about as much fun as anyone who reads *Ulysses* with Joyce's guidebook hints—that is, some but not much. Great artists need and use such schematizations or frames not to discipline the work but to release it to freer play than it would have if it had to stabilize itself as it went along. Such structures are like a trampoline or an exercise bar. The ballet is exceptionally meaningful, though really no more so than, say, Balanchine's ballets that are "about" Tchaikovsky, like *Divertimento from "Le Baiser de la Fée"* or *Suite No. 3* or the very early *Mozartiana,* set to Suite No. 4. But whatever the ballet "means," the meaning wasn't there before it was choreographed, preexistent in some story or biography to which the dance is responsible. The movements of the four couples are dictated primarily by the music and by the temperamental and physical characteristics of the dancers. Balanchine's conception of these materials precedes and in fact creates the occasion for any thematic meanings the ballet might be said to develop. These have ultimately to do, I think, with the whole idea, in life and in the dance, of what can be called "support." With an intensity at once very poignant and very beautiful, we are shown versions of the problem—or is it the delight? the opportunity?—of physically and psychologically holding up a partner or would-be partner, and of being held up or supported in return. Of course this is a kind of meaning inherent in any dance with couples, but once again, and after glorious renditions in the Stravinsky *Violin Concerto* and *Duo Concertant,* it is revealed as a central generative force in Balanchine's imagination of himself, of his art, and of a composer who infused classical forms with intense personal emotion. The psychological ambiguities and mysteries that for Balanchine were inherent in dancing, especially in partnering, had unusually direct and vivid analogies in Schumann's life and music. That is why the ballet seems so emotionally charged— even, to some viewers, overwrought.

And yet it is never possible to say of the work of a genius that it is unprecedented. The Joyce of *Portrait of the Artist as a Young Man* can be found in so fragile a story as "The Sisters"; the Eliot of *The Waste Land* in his early "Preludes"; and for this ballet there are preparations that may go as far back, if accounts can be depended on, as a strange piece in 1935 called *Transcendence,* which had something to do with the mesmeric appeal and technical prowess of Franz Liszt. The drama of sexual, psychological, and social support in *Davidsbündlertänze* gives a retrospective enhancement to gestures in *Orpheus, Prodigal Son, Serenade,* the ball scene in *Don Quixote,* to the mysterious coda to *Divertimento from "Le Baiser de la Fée"* and to the remarkable ballets, like *Coppélia* and *The Steadfast Tin Soldier,* which explore the difference between dancing with mechanical proficiency, as a doll might, or with a heart, as a man and a woman must.

At the center of *Davidsbündlertänze* is the balletic drama of
the Schumann figure and his wife, Clara. Neither Lüders nor
von Aroldingen ever danced so wonderfully. The very qualities
in each to which some fans of the company objected were shown
always to have been part of their value to Balanchine. Lüders, a
remarkably able dancer, was, nonetheless, with his large body
and small head, his unhappy and somewhat distraught expression onstage, like someone who got into dance for therapeutic
reasons only to discover that he had a career on his hands; no
matter what the role, he looked as if he might be remembering
some original and unhappy reason for being there. Of von
Aroldingen it was said that she had no transparency, that she was
too physical a presence, a sort of aristocratic German nurse,
happy in her dictatorial efficiency and just about as stimulating
to the imagination. But I always admired both of them, especially von Aroldingen, so it's pleasing that Balanchine found a
way, as he always did, to turn these very characteristics, if that is
what they were, to his work's advantage. They danced together
with the pathos of a couple who know that there can be no one
else for either one of them, and who know why. The arms and
hands of the Schumann figure move toward clumsy touches,
failed claspings, reachings-out to take a wrist or an elbow when
the hand of another is what he most wants and needs to find. He
can barely give Clara support, and she disguises this—what dar-
ing on Balanchine's part and what confidence on Lüders's!—
with that precise tenderness which can come from the pain of
habit. She wants to need the support he tries to offer, but we
know that, really, she doesn't need it; and the fact that no one
can give him the support he requires is made clear enough even
before his frighteningly real "mad" solo.

Intermittently, the other couples, first one and then another,
take over the stage. In the d'Amboise–Farrell sequences there
are indications on the man's part of romantic proficiency, going
ever so slightly to seed, as he reaches out for her while she

moves away from him and finds his arms and head resting pathetically, for a second, on her waistline. In his always decorous and controlled anxieties, he is barely able to keep pace with Farrell's gorgeous and speedy eccentricities of movement. By contrast, Martins with Watts and Andersen with Mazzo are like two younger couples matched in will and capacity, untouched, as yet, by distress. Support is mutual between the men and the women, and it is clear that there are resources for it not even being called upon. And yet at alarming and peculiar moments one or another of the couples freezes into a nearly paralytic attitude, a posture of holding in place that looks like immobility, the stasis of boredom or platitude.

Not to press the point, *Davidsbündlertänze* may have to do, finally, with the tribulations of genius as it tries to live within the circumstances of the ordinary or the given. It is a work that can move you to tears because ultimately what is being asked for by the couples onstage is supposed to be so simple, so natural, and yet it is shown to be precarious for everyone, and all but unavailable to a genius like Schumann.

Balanchine was probably as powerfully involved in this music, with these dancers, and in the significances he drew from them as he ever was in his long career, but it would be extremely misleading to take the ballet as a species of autobiographical revelation. Insofar as it is about Schumann, the ballet, within the larger Balanchine repertoire, suggests why Balanchine could reinvest Schumann's life, even his music, with value that Schumann himself could not recover from either. Balanchine could dramatize Schumann's alienation and collapse precisely because he was not subject to them.

Demonstrably, Balanchine made peace with the ordinary aspects of life, of American life. To the surprise and dismay of certain admirers, he had a taste for many of the things that might have been supposed to offend him, like Western dress, Western films, popular culture, *Charlie's Angels*, even motel accommodations. More important, since the beginning of his life in America, he exulted in what he took to be its special tempo, the athleticism of long-limbed American women, the oddly unemotional quality of American dancers, including popular dancers like Ray Bolger, the jazz beat, the sense of space, and the fast movements needed to accommodate oneself to it. Even while rehearsing one of his most rigorously tempered works, *Concerto Barocco,* to Bach's Concerto in D minor for Two Violins, he allowed the corps, especially in the first and third movements, syncopations that Edwin Denby long ago called "wonderfully American." Almost a "Charleston on pointe," said Suki Schorer, who performed the soloist role, so that "in many of my most brisk and classical movements Balanchine kept saying, 'Make it jazzy.' 'Lead with the hip.'"

Balanchine can be found, that is, only in some constellation of all his work, and especially of those movements where he appeared to be an artist at once classical by choice and popular by some gregarious extension of interest, an extension that was well sustained by the contemporary culture of his adopted country. His was a rich and complicated effort, without parallel in the history of dance. On the final evening of that spring 1980 season, the Schumann had on either side older masterworks that bore subtle but characteristic testimony to the fact that Balanchine felt none of Schumann's alienation with respect to the culture within which he did most of his work. On the one side was *Square Dance,* to the music of Corelli and Vivaldi, in which he discerned the perfect metric for classical dance along with an opportunity to adapt to it the forms and terms—even, in its first version, the "caller"—of the American square dance. On the other side was *Symphony in Three Movements,* with thirty-two dancers moving at astonishing speeds in sometimes dangerous physical proximity to one another, all to the music of Stravinsky wherein, again, Balanchine could hear an occasion for classical dance that frequently took shapes made familiar by the *Goldwyn Follies* and Broadway musical shows (both of which Balanchine had once choreographed).

Such a conjunction of works is by no means unusual at the New York City Ballet, and it is part of the evidence, it seems to me, that the genius of Balanchine looks for parallels to the careers of Shakespeare, Mozart, or Verdi. It is common enough to call Balanchine a genius, but to put him in such company makes doing so a matter of some gravity, because if this is praise for his accomplishments, it is also an imposition on him and on his audiences, a sort of encumbrance. It immediately makes the reception of his work a problem for those who don't expect, who resent even being asked, to give to ballet the kind of wondering, anticipatory, meticulous, even awed attention required and rewarded by any work of genius. No choreographer in history ever created works at once so theatrically available and yet structurally so complex, so pleasing each by itself and yet offering still greater pleasure if seen within a pattern created by his vast balletic repertoire, not counting his choreography for film and stage. Which is another way of saying that no other choreographer in history deserves to the same extent the title of genius. It's therefore no wonder that those who might want to deny him the title often know a lot about ballet but not much about him. To be educated by other companies, even very good ones like the Royal Ballet or American Ballet Theatre, or by other choreographers as remarkable as Sir Frederick Ashton or Paul Taylor or Jerome Robbins doesn't prepare one for what can be seen at the New York City Ballet in Balanchine's work, any more than in the age of Queen Elizabeth regular attendance at other theaters would prepare anyone for what was going on at the Globe in Shakespeare's work. In fact, it could be said that people had been prepared *not* to see or to hear what was going on in Shakespeare even though, clearly, they could love whatever they did see or hear.

It is characteristic of genius that in individual cases it produces a great abundance and variety of works and that these works, on reflection and in retrospect, appear to comment on each other and on their own procedures in astonishingly complex ways. Yet somehow this doesn't prevent the works from becoming popular. Peculiarly, genius traditionally exhibits not agony in production, regardless of the agony in the life, but speed and abundance. Think of Schumann's prolific accomplishments as pianist (before his hand injury), as composer, and as writer, until he died at forty-six, or Shakespeare's before he died at fifty-two. After a famously hard life, D. H. Lawrence produced enough before his death, at the ridiculous age of forty-five, to be recognized now as one of the indispensable literary critics of his time, one of the important poets of the century, a talented painter and dramatist, and a very great writer of fiction and travel. Such abundance is necessarily accompanied by complexities in the work somehow so natural and indigenous to it that they seldom obtrude in such a way as to offend popular taste.

Genius is seldom afraid of popularity or of popular culture, nor does it condescend to either. That is, men and women of genius are unique in their apparent ease of production coupled with a richness of invention that doesn't impede the immediate pleasure one may take in what they produce. Genius therefore raises the issue of specialness, of the *Übermensch,* even of the Muse, which can sometimes offend ordinary people. To men and women of genius the possibility that they are different from ordinary people may be offensive, too, and it's almost always frightening. No one fears the potentially alienating effects of genius more than the people who have it, as Wordsworth so often assures us. Balanchine said that "my personal life is not very interesting." Doubtless this was the case, and most surely it must have seemed the case to him. How, indeed, could anyone's perception of his own life have been interesting when he was at the same time capable of perceiving and creating such extraordinary abundance of life as can be found in the works I've been discussing?

The nature of Balanchine's genius is best accounted for by the kinds of detailed, nuanced, and historically informed writings done by Arlene Croce in *Afterimages* and a few others, like Robert Garis and Joan Acocella. Little ground is gained by exaggerated and general claims that his variations on classicism repudiate the very traditions he worked in. It is sometimes said, for example, that he rescued classical ballet from subservience to story and plot, from narrative conventions and motifs conspicuous in *Swan Lake* or *Giselle*. To begin with, it's inconceivable that cultured people ever watch the great classics of traditional ballet in expectation of some point-by-point correspondence of movement to story or meaning, as if, say, a deep *plié* on one leg and the other foot off the ground in the *passé* position is an encoding of "meaning" or narrative, instead of something beautifully or not so beautifully executed by a dancer. This sort of crudity about classical ballet, with the assumption that it minutely enacts stories which in fact are never more than a pretext, has been decisively challenged by, among others, the philosopher Marshall Cohen; but it nonetheless persists, as much among detractors of Balanchine as among defenders of his innovations. To quote a Soviet critic in *Leningradskaia Pravda* of September 30, 1972: "We were delighted by the ballet technique of the American dancers in *Violin Concerto* of Stravinsky, by their purity of movement, correct 'fifth position,' rapid gyrations . . . but it occasionally lacks that 'life of the human spirit' without which any technique grows dim." One person's "life of the human spirit" is another's soap opera, and to ask such critics to conceive that certain exercises of technical brilliance may in and of themselves be an expression of the "life of the human spirit" is to expect too much. The argument over whether Balanchine's work does or does not have "life," does or does not permit his dancers the expression of "life," is vitiated by critical and popular misconceptions not only about Balanchine's work but about the classical tradition of which he is both student and master.

Like any great artist, Balanchine first of all had to be a great reader, a critical reader of the tradition. It can be said confidently that he read the classical syllabus of dance and music more deeply and intelligently and with a keener sense of its possible mutations than anyone had before him. And having fully possessed it he then had the freedom to condense, accelerate, distort it in a way that immeasurably enriched the vocabulary and syntax of classical dance. Out of his incredibly varied repertoire could be fashioned a highly traditional corpus, if by that one means merely ballets that adhere to stories (*Orpheus, Prodigal Son*), or two- or three-act ballets (*Harlequinade, Don Quixote*), or ballets with plots central to the classical canon (*Pulcinella, The Nutcracker Suite, Coppélia*), or ballets that allow dancers a chance for individualized characterization and dramatic expression onstage, for evidence of which one need only have observed the marked differences over the years in the portrayal of Apollo by d'Amboise, Villella, Baryshnikov, Tomasson, and Peter Martins.

But none of this is to the point. It is an unnecessarily defensive response to detractors. An innovative genius must, again of necessity, be a critic if he is also to be the savior of the traditions out of which he emerges. Balanchine may be said to have erupted into the traditions of classical dance as Picasso did into Western painting, and by so doing he revealed the sharp and beautiful contours hidden under the slag that had accumulated on top of them. More than anyone, Balanchine allowed us to see that there really is a vital, mythic life in classical dance, and that it consists of more than stories, and more also than techniques and a grammar of movement—the "fifth position" or whatnot. The classical ballet without Balanchine would be like the novel without James or Joyce, Proust or Lawrence, novelists whose fictions are also criticisms and acts of devotion directed at the forms of literature they inherit and transcend.

Forms of art, techniques of expression, are also to any genius of this kind forms of life that excite similar intensities of emotion.

The duet, for Balanchine, is an image of the opportunities, perils, difficulties, and creative glories of partnering. It is Adam and Eve, and the dancing technique invented for the conduct of a duet represented to him some of the ways in which human beings have imagined partnering and the central human myths from which it issues. To receive and to transform a tradition in the arts, to nurture it with this primitive simplicity, with what Schiller would call the naïveté of genius, is nothing less than a matter of life and death. It involves not a solemn, not even a conscious, but rather an instinctive and joyous sense of art as a corporate human enterprise. The vital transmission and variation in the codes of dance or of poetry are as natural, and as mysterious, as the transmission of genetic codes. In the light of this, phrases like "the human spirit" are seen to be hopelessly banal. More appropriate than "spirit" would be "will," the human will compelled by its creative necessities.

Genius disdains snobbishness, which is one of the havens of the talented. It wants to be lavish, it wants to be popular, it wants always to move. Balanchine preserved in this century, as did Verdi in the last, a Shakespearean velocity, range, and theatrical inclusiveness. The sumptuousness of *Jewels*, with its assembled company for the concluding polonaise; the massed dancers, flags in hand, signaling the end of *Union Jack* with "God Save the Queen," in semaphore, are as joyously exuberant as is the line of sixteen women stretched diagonally across the stage at the beginning of *Symphony in Three Movements.* In glistening white leotards and their hair in ponytails, they move to Stravinsky's music with a jazzy, sweeping menace. The menace, which is clear in the shock tactics of the music, is meant to say something about the period in which it was written—one section was supposedly a response to newsreel footage of Nazi soldiers—but it also catches something of the frightening power that we recognize on the spot as a suppressed reaction that audiences, especially men, might always have had to the large, powerfully coordinated female chorus lines of the 1930s and 1940s. In each of these works the idioms of popular dance and popular music are also invoked: by the emulation of street-gang mannerisms and music-show dancing of the 1930s in the "Rubies" section of *Jewels*, with its jaunty sexuality and muscular flaunting, and, in *Union Jack*, of the Scottish folk dance, military marches, and English music-hall turns Balanchine first saw when he lived intermittently in London between 1929 and 1933.

Balanchine was a classic American genius because he wanted to make it new while knowing, as some adherents of that phrase do not know, that inherent in its very grammar is a paradox not to be evaded: the "it" already exists, or we wouldn't be able to refer to "it," wouldn't be able to see "it," hear "it," or make "it" anything at all. The injunction can only mean that the artist must try to reveal possibilities in language or dance movement or nature that were already there even if not heretofore visible. The illusion that it is possible to make a new thing, or even to disengage a thing wholly from earlier usage, always begins with an assertion that the past can be evaporated by fiat. "A rose is a rose is a rose, is a rose" is in one sense a dizzy proposition by which Gertrude Stein hoped to restore roses to a reality long ago encrusted by poetic associations. Of course there are no such things as roses until we so name them. Their reality depends upon some sort of poetic impulse to begin with; and it is an amusing indication of the impossibility, not to mention undesirability, of splitting off things (or one's self) from the past that Stein apparently didn't know she was echoing Emerson's "Self-Reliance": "These roses under my window make no reference to former roses or to better ones; they are for what they are. There is simply the rose."

The American, by which I specifically mean the Emersonian, genius, of which Balanchine was an example, feels no less enlivened by an artistic than by a biological inheritance. In either case the genius is compelled to an emulative creativity, convinced that what is created will somehow represent the truth that the material and historical conditions impinging on it are importantly different from any that existed before. A genius doesn't choose to imitate any more than to deny the past; he recognizes that he is himself at once an inescapable and inimitable creation of it. He creates without ego, and for the reason that he knows that whatever genius he may have is a mysteriously, perhaps even accidentally, transmitted gift. Creation is all at once a gesture of gratitude and a gesture of competition. And it needn't involve anxiety or usurpation with respect to any precursor. Balanchine was without anxiety as a creator because he always satisfied himself that his creative will was at work within a cultural situation markedly unlike any encountered by his classical predecessors. The results therefore would be different in the very nature of things.

Balanchine made the decision to wed himself to America in 1933, to create in America a classical ballet company using American dancers and whatever else America might throw his way. But it was not his decision alone. It might never have been made without the initiative of Lincoln Kirstein, who can be thanked for bringing him here. It was Kirstein who first conceived the idea, against the taunts of Pavel Tchelitchev, who thought ballet by that time had ceased to be in any way tied to a country. Dismissing the compromise of importing a European company to the United States, Kirstein and Balanchine went on to create what is now the New York City Ballet with the clear determination that it should be an American ballet. One of the richest bequests of European court culture was thus to become naturalized.

America gave Balanchine the opportunity to discover a European musical and dance heritage that not many Europeans even now can recognize as their own. Being the most musically trained of all choreographers, with the capacities to be a professional pianist and conductor, he found choreographic possibilities in music that no one had thought to look for. And also being the most heterosexually vibrant of choreographers, he was astonishingly intuitive about the resources locked into the bodies of particular dancers, especially American women dancers, whose shape pleased him from the beginning. Speaking to the National Press Club in Washington, he described with affectionate amusement the kind of women dancers he knew in Russia, with their "little feet, little hands, little necks—like brioche."

It could therefore be said that he didn't really invent at all, but only discovered. In a metaphysical sense this is true, but so is nearly anything else. Besides, it is true of any genius. A great poet doesn't invent a language; he finds under the pressures of historical needs and opportunities combinations and rhythms that are both latent and original. "Language is fossil poetry," Emerson said, implying among other things that the poetry existed before it gave shape to the words we commonly use. The words refer us to a prior impulse, and it is that impulse, in a most radical sense, that constitutes the vitality of tradition. So, too, with music before notation, with dance before choreography.

A work of art is not a monument, not an invitation to reverence; it is an inducement to some equivalent work, on our part, of combination, imagination, recognition. Nearly always, however, a large segment of Balanchine's audience idealizes itself as a cultural elite. Probably they are, but the self-consciousness makes them far more aloof and fastidious than their master. Few of them would be capable of the imaginative leap downward from the Stravinsky Festival of 1972 to an emphatically and delightfully eccentric piece like *Variations Pour une Porte et un Soupir* in which, to Pierre Henry's *musique concrète* of recorded sounds, creakings, and sighings, Karin von Aroldingen, assisted by a wind machine and pulleys, maneuvered a black gown so vast it covered the stage and the walls, while John Clifford writhed, flopped, rolled in front of and eventually through her.

Perhaps, as I suspect, the piece was meant as a teasing com-
munication from Balanchine to the woman he once called his
muse, Suzanne Farrell, then in exile with Ballet of the 20th Century, a company founded by Maurice Béjart, who had choreographed a ballet to the same music. It was, as it were, a sample of
how easily Balanchine could do the Béjart sort of thing, a
reminder that he had already done something like it decades ago
in *Errante.* It was outrageous and funny and extravagant, the
show-biz side of Balanchine unleashed. Above all, it was evidence, if any were needed, that he was so little afraid of being
taken for vulgar that when someone dismissed the piece with
that word, I heard one of his closest associates reply by pleasantly agreeing: "Of course it's vulgar. He is the Prince of Vulgarity!" Votaries of Balanchine aren't usually capable of that
reaction. But wasn't his second ballet in America, *Alma Mater,*
about a football hero and a coed?

As I've been intimating, one of the most significant aspects of
Balanchine's genius was his relaxed insistence that he was free to
be a popular entertainer, to experiment with any kind of material, and to do so not only when he worked in film or in show
business, but specifically when he was being a classical choreographer within the repertoire of the New York City Ballet and in
the French and Russian traditions.

Peculiarly, the characteristic clue to defensiveness about popularity or popular culture, when it besets a repertory company, is
not the exclusion of certain materials but rather the segregation
of them within a program, along with a kind of idiotic determination that the classical numbers should be totally cleansed of
any contaminations having to do with sex or show biz. Some time
ago I wrote about the Joffrey Ballet, which to its credit performed some Balanchine works and more by Ashton than any
company in the world except the Royal Ballet, but which lamen-
tably decided to offer the following program: their own version
of a classical ballet, Joffrey's *Remembrances,* a stuffily dressed,

badly danced, tedious, and elevated piece about Wagner; a second piece that would have gone nicely in *Oh, Calcutta!,* choreographed by Margo Sappington, who had done some work on that musical; and a Big Think mythologizing ballet by Gerald Arpino called *Relativity of Icarus.* This last was said to be about the journey of escape each of us tries to make from paternal and earth-dominated existence—I paraphrase—but it obviously had far less to do with the Cretan labyrinth than with a gay bath. A little something for everyone. It's unfair to compare a Joffrey mélange to the Balanchine repertoire, but I do so to make the point that with the latter no such segregation of material or of effects is possible. The erotic, the mythic, the classical, and the jazzy are all inextricably mixed in any single piece, and in the interests of a total design that prevents us from separating out any of the elements.

For example, a program that brings together *Serenade,* to Tchaikovsky's Serenade in C, *Apollo,* to Stravinsky's score, and *Who Cares?,* to some songs of Gershwin, would seem structurally no different from the Joffrey program I have mentioned: a sedately classical, a mythic, and a show-biz number. And since I'm arguing that an enterprise like Balanchine's is not afraid of anything, let it be conceded that Balanchine and Kirstein were influenced no less than is Joffrey by the practical desire to have what is known as a balanced program. What is markedly different is that to schedule together any three works choreographed by a genius is automatically to create without willing, intending, or even expecting it a marvelous kind of echo chamber, flashes of similarity, reflection, reverberation, and allusion that pass from one work into another, until it seems as if every so often they all share some hidden, barely articulated community of meaning. Repetition within a field that includes works of enormous variety and dissimilarity is a natural expression of the obsessive nature of genius, its indefatigable interest in what it is about or compelled to be about. Genius is always to some extent mystified by its own workings because the mystery resides at last and utterly in the basic, elemental, and resistant materiality of the art itself, be it words or paint or, as here, the materiality of a musical score, of bodies, of the traditional codes of dance, even the very curriculum of the dance school.

So when the curtain rises on *Serenade* and reveals a line of girls poised, with a kind of sequestered simplicity, in the first position, anyone may recognize an allusion to a class recital about to begin, a demonstration of newly acquired competence. And it's especially beautiful if you happen to know that this ballet, the first work by Balanchine after he came to the United States, actually originated quite casually one day in 1934 with his first group of American students in Hartford, Connecticut. He began with the seventeen girls in his class, still the same number that we now see. Their standing in this initial position signals their basic commitment to classical dance, and as they peel off the line into further movement they discover—and it was of course Balanchine who was himself once again discovering as he created—what that commitment entails. Because of the evident modesty of the group, the simplicity of dress, and the bareness of the surroundings, there is something tender, poignant, and eventually even frightening in the gradually accumulating demands to which the dancers are exposed. There are demands on the body, which make one of them fall, or momentarily collapse. There are demands on the ego: though some are given solos, no one of the aspirants is allowed to emerge as the star. It is a way of suggesting that everyone is to learn the difficulty of moving so as to express, not the self, but the whole work, the music, the other dancers. And there are, finally, the demands on the emotions, as the dancers discover possibilities of meaning and story in the music and in their movements to it.

Balanchine is teaching them, himself, and us that in response to the vibrant surgings and recessions of the Tchaikovsky score, the pirouettes, adagios, and duets will for brief moments reveal

glimpses, fragments, shadows of old stories and themes, of significances already credited to these dance movements by the
great ballets of the past, long before these young women and the
few young men who join them decided on a career in dancing.
There are only fleeting, fractured hints of stories that of course
do not even need to unfold here and now; they have already
been unfolded, already belong to us. But they are also left in gestural code because Balanchine wants to say that whatever the
feelings generated by these movements, whatever sad or happy
story they encapsulate, the choreography is not obligated to the
externality of a story line or a line of feeling. It is instead responsive to the line of bodies and to the phrases of music in all their
volatility. Gestures of youthful delight and the discovery of physical power and beauty, responses to the shock of the unexpected,
the recognition of love, separation, chance, and fate—these are
momentary possibilities only. As when a young woman on the
floor, reclining on her right arm and looking back at a man standing, bending slightly over her, his arms stretched out and curved
forward in a prelude to an embrace that is never completed, also
sees directly behind him the figure of another woman, her arms
similarly arched—is she seeing a guardian angel behind her
potential lover? a figure of parental restraint? a competitor? dark
possessiveness? Phrasings from *Giselle,* from Petipa's *Swan
Lake,* from *Sleeping Beauty* suggest themselves and then dis-
solve into the larger, central narrative of the work. And that,
again, has to do with the marvelous, frightening, demanding
acquisition of an inheritance and of the physical and emotional
power to deserve it and to renew it.

Serenade is a signature work of Balanchine's, a dramatization
of what he was to make of classical dance, as well as classical
dancers, in America. It is as inquisitive about the mythologies of
classical dance as is the earlier, directly mythological *Apollo.*
There, it is Terpsichore, the muse of dance, who—in a seeming
quotation from Michelangelo's fresco where God touches the

finger of Adam—touches Apollo's finger and signals the beginning of dance, especially of duet, when a man discovers in his
movement with a woman not only a new kind of pleasure but a
new infusion of power that submits, nonetheless, to the civilizing
influence of music.

In *Serenade,* Balanchine indicates in the provenance of the
ordinary—a classroom recital situation—some of the mythologies inherent in classical dance movement; in *Apollo,* to the
quite different measure of Stravinsky, he proposes that direct
mythological representation has to include the clumsily human,
the ordinary, which, by tradition, also belongs to mythology. As
if to emphasize this admixture, the productions of *Apollo,* over
the years, progressively simplified the dress of the God and
the Muses, and removed the trappings, including the stairs
on which Apollo used to ascend, bathed in light. But even when
the ballet was first conceived, according to an early Terpsichore, Marie-Jeanne, "He wanted an unformed, unmajestic
Apollo." "You are," Balanchine told Lew Christensen, the first
American to dance the role, "a woodcutter, a swimmer, a football player, a god." Balanchine thereby revealed a more learned
and sophisticated awareness of Greek myth, where being a god
meant also being a shepherd, warrior, or swimmer, than did
those critics who well into the 1950s objected to what they considered the ballet's sometimes indecorously casual or graceless
movements.

Apollon Musagète was the first of the three ballets on which
Stravinsky and Balanchine directly and minutely collaborated.
The music offers exciting and strenuous opportunities for intentionally awkward movements, for steps that remain unfinished,
all of which contribute to the characterization of a god who is in
the process of discovering that he *is* one while also learning to
cope with his bodily shape. Apollo isn't the entire ballet, however, but only one figure in it, and what the ballet itself means to
express is that within the nobility of classical dance, what

Stravinsky himself has called "the beauty of its *ordonnance* and the aristocratic austerity of its form," there can be articulated an idiomatic bodily vocabulary not before included in the classical dictionary. Dancers appear to shuffle, the feet turn inward, and as Alexandra Danilova, of the original cast, remarked, "Sometimes instead of going on the toes you went on the full feet . . . everything was new."

It looked new once again during the season I'm writing about, partly because it had been stripped down still further by Balanchine, who omitted the prologue as well as the final ascent, partly because of the freshness brought by Kyra Nichols dancing Polyhymnia, and especially because of the dispassionate, elegant mastery of Suzanne Farrell and Peter Martins in the principals' *pas de deux*. They were particularly suited to this duet because each found in the other a partner of such strength and resourcefulness that they could move with a grand mixture of confidence, competitiveness, respect, and, on Martins's part, a cool wariness of Farrell's extraordinarily powerful independence of movement.

It also looked new, as if it had been more recently conceived, because of its proximity on the program to *Who Cares?*, a work that invigorated several evenings. It's frequently been noted that Balanchine's choreography to seventeen of Gershwin's songs, including "Fascinatin' Rhythm," "'S Wonderful," "The Man I Love," and "I'll Build a Stairway to Paradise," alludes to *Apollo* and other classical precedents, as one way of celebrating the claim that for all its jazz rhythms *Who Cares?* is still a classical ballet in an incontrovertibly crisp American mode. "Dry, frank, refreshing, not syruped by nostalgia," as Kirstein said of the music, the Gershwin tunes make us, as a classic should, anxious not to recapture the period in which they were written but to find some equivalent to it in our own. The second half of the ballet, with Jacques d'Amboise and an incomparable trio of Patricia McBride, Merrill Ashley, and Wilhelmina Frankfurt, had some of the same configurations and sequences as *Apollo,* where the god, like his Manhattan counterpart, watches each of the three women dance alone, then has a duet with each of them, and then dances with all three at once, in configurations that remind us of the earlier ballet. Balanchine intends more than merely choreographic quotation, however, and the similarity between the two works is a way of pointing to the echoes in Stravinsky's music that he had heard in Gershwin's.

Balanchine loves to do this sort of thing, as when he makes a concluding duet in *Symphony in Three Movements* an imitation close to parody of the "Dance Maroc" in *Don Quixote,* to the music of Nicolas Nabokov. I half suspect he is slyly directing our attention to Nabokov's unmodified borrowings from Stravinsky—and others. Balanchine guards the Stravinsky musical heritage and can track the movements of any of its beneficiaries. Thus, when he quotes a dance movement from *Apollo* in *Who Cares?,* he asks us not only to visualize a connection between the two ballets, but also to hear "how comradely the links are," as Arlene Croce puts it, "between the Gershwin of 'Lady Be Good,' 'Tip-Toes,' 'Oh Kay!' and 'Funny Face'" (not all of which are included in *Who Cares?*) "and the syncopated Stravinsky of *Apollon Musagète.*"

Allusions and cross references can be merely cute when they do not allow some larger inference. But what they allow us to infer, as they play across a configuration of *Serenade, Apollo,* and *Who Cares?,* is nothing less than the American aspects of Balanchine's genius. These echoes, and one could locate equivalents of them almost anywhere in his work, conspire to suggest that there are essential connections between classic myth and those mythic evidences that emerge in a classroom recital in Hartford or a ballroom theatrical dance in Manhattan, connections between soft shoe and dancing on points, between jazz and classical phrasing both in music and in dance. Balanchine affirms, as have America's great classic writers, that the classic can be inferred from the vernacular, the vernacular from the classic. To see and hear this demonstrated with such authority and delight by the New York City Ballet, now securely under the direction of Ballanchine's chosen successor, Peter Martins, is to witness a veritable act of democratic civilization.

5

THE HIDDEN T. S. ELIOT

※

In 1922, T. S. Eliot sent to a friend and patron in New York, the lawyer John Quinn, a leatherbound notebook, along with some loose leaves, containing about fifty pages of miscellaneous poems and fragments of poems transcribed by the author between 1909 and 1917. Eliot never wanted most of these poems to be published, and until now they haven't been. The Notebook, as it is called, eventually found its way into the Berg Collection at the New York Public Library, where scholars could inspect but not directly quote from it. It has at last been edited and annotated, with the permission of Valerie Eliot, the poet's widow, by the accomplished British critic Christopher Ricks, now at Boston University. He has called the volume *Inventions of the March Hare,* the self-ironic Lewis Carrollian title Eliot had written in black ink on a front page of the Notebook and then canceled.

The core of the book includes about thirty-nine hitherto unpublished Notebook poems, some very good and all immensely interesting to anyone who cares about Eliot's poetry, and Ricks's voluminous annotations of them. There are in addition four appendices. One of these is given to the texts, with lists of variants, of seven poems, as they first appeared in the Note-book or the loose leaves, that were published as *Humoresque* (1910) or in *Prufrock and Other Observations* (1917). Another appendix includes the texts, as they originally appeared on the loose leaves, of eleven poems that were published in Eliot's *Poems* (1919), *Ara Vos Prec* (1920), and *Poems* (1920). A third appendix consists of selections from Eliot's criticism, mostly on the subject of literary influence and indebtedness. These were chosen in part because they appear to lend support to Ricks's own annotative obsessions on this occasion.

Included in a fourth appendix are what Ricks calls "ribald verse," though in their childish and sordid sexuality they have lit-tle to do with one of the root meanings of *ribald*, which is amorous. These were found on leaves that Eliot had excised from the Notebook. They were written over an extended period of close to fifteen years, and Eliot tried unsuccessfully to per-suade Wyndham Lewis to publish some of them in *Blast*. Included are "The Triumph of Bullshit," where each stanza, addressed at the outset to "Ladies," ends with the refrain "For Christ sake stick it up your ass." There is also "Ballade pour la grosse Lulu," one of the poems Lewis wouldn't print, which imagines an interview with "Booker T./Entitled 'Up from Pos-sum Stew!'/Or 'How I set the nigger free!'" And then, presum-ably the prize entry, there are seventeen brief poems that Eliot referred to as "King Bolo, and His Big Black Kween" in a letter to Ezra Pound, in whose papers they were discovered. Featured are descriptions of huge penises, defecations, buggeries, and group masturbations.

Eliot circulated copies of these poems among his male friends, and they represent, it seems to me, a flip, pseudo-jock side of the thwarted sexuality evident in all his poetry and in some of his crit-icism. This same sexuality gets expressed, for instance, in the nightmare images of such a Notebook poem, and quite a good one, as "The Love Song of St. Sebastian," or in the sexual dead-

ness of the many male speakers in other of Eliot's poems, and in
the abdications from human sexual love in *Four Quartets,* including what has been taken to be a celebration of heterosexual cere-
monial courting in "East Coker." There Eliot borrows lines from
the writings of a sixteenth-century forebear, Sir Thomas Elyot, to
extol, as if they needed to be protected by Elyot's spelling from
the contaminations of more contemporary expression, the ancient
virtues of "The association of man and woman/ In daunsinge, sig-
nifying matriomonie." But by the end of the verse paragraph
this gives way to Eliot's characteristic sense that now and always
human sexuality, even under the auspices of the sacraments, yields
to beastliness and to scatology:

> The time of the seasons and the constellations
> The time of milking and the time of harvest
> The time of the coupling of man and woman
> And that of beasts. Feet rising and falling.
> Eating and drinking. Dung and death.

Sex is dung, and dung is death. This is close to the definition
of pornography in the great essay "Pornography and Obscenity"
by D. H. Lawrence, about whom Eliot harbored a settled hostil-
ity, including the charge that he was "sexually morbid." Pornography, according to Lawrence, is almost always "underworld," an
area vividly depicted in early Eliot, wherein sexual excitement
becomes an essentially masturbatory playing with dirt, so that
"any sign of sex in a woman"—or a man—"becomes a show of
her dirt." Sexuality in all of Eliot's poetry is in that sense porno-
graphic. So it is, of course, for countless millions of other people
and their partners, but none of these is also endowed with Eliot's
distinctive poetic genius. What he sought was a creative commu-
nion not with persons but only in his intercourse with poetry
itself and at last with a mother and a God imagined in Dantean
visionary modes, though without Dante's devotion also to human
bonding. The King Bolo poems reveal nothing of that poetic

genius, and the poems could have been written by any number of dirty-minded boys.

As the editor of this volume, Ricks is intent on displays of scholarly recall, with an indefatigable capacity to summon, in response to any word, phrase, or sound pattern in Eliot, some corresponding call from the vasty deeps of world literature. Of the volume's 414 pages, not counting the index, barely ninety are given to unpublished poems from the Notebook and to the ribald poems excised from it. These are the only poems which Ricks annotates as to sources, allusions, echoes, and the like. Devoting more than twice those ninety pages, indeed more than two hundred pages, to his annotations, Ricks risks suggesting that the title, *Inventions of the March Hare,* befits his contribution more than Eliot's. There are real discoveries in some of his notes, and many are informative and useful to an understanding of the poems. But in large measure they turn out to be tenuous at best, in some cases irrelevant, and others actually require that Ricks substitute words of his own for Eliot's so as to proffer one or another unduly confident "find."

A few examples before returning more fully to Eliot. Two of these occur conveniently in the four pages of notes, when even a full page would be plenty, for the fifteen-line poem "Mandarins." The mandarin figure in the first of four such poems is an anticipation of Eliot's lifelong fascination with the figure of Coriolanus. With the crowd huddled at his feet, the mandarin

> . . . merely stands and waits
> Upon his own intrepid dignity;
> With fixed regardless eyes—
> Looking neither out nor in—
> The centre of formalities.
>
> A hero! and how much it means;
> How much—
> The rest is merely shifting scenes.

Ricks decides to comment on the phrase "neither out nor in," but in this instance he doesn't choose to cite or quote a related passage. Instead, he indulges in a chummy confidence, especially unwarranted for American readers, that his lead will be enough: "'neither out nor in': compare the grand old Duke of York, his men 'neither up nor down.'" As it turns out, those who can recall the English nursery rhyme about the "grand old Duke" are no luckier than those who can't recall it. Nor is "neither up nor down," except syntactically, significantly related to "neither out nor in." The mere syntactical or structural similarity of phrasing between "neither out nor in" and "neither up nor down" is scarcely sufficient evidence that this nursery rhyme is of any relevance whatever to Eliot's poem. Language overflows with such syntactic coordinates, like left/right, front/back, top/bottom. Or as we used to say in the Army when signing off, over/out. Further, "the grand Duke" is not a "mandarin-like" figure at all. He is a pleasantly eccentric figure of fun:

> The grand old Duke of York,
> He had ten thousand men.
> He marched them up to the top of the hill
> And marched them down again.
>
> And when they were up they were up.
> And when they were down they were down;
> And when they were only half way up
> They were neither up nor down.

Ricks inspires no greater confidence when he gets round to annotating the last line of this short but interesting poem: "The rest is merely shifting scenes." For this he offers: "'The rest is': compare *Hamlet* V,ii,350: 'The rest is silence.'" In justification for proposing this connection, he mentions that the immediately preceding poem in the Notebook is "Silence" and then proceeds to cite three French poets, including Verlaine: *Et tout le reste est littérature.*

Such annotative energies are generated not out of Eliot's need in this line or that to be explained or by the reader's need to be informed. They result primarily from Ricks's evident need to dazzle. And in the interest of doing so, he often willingly ignores or distorts the plain evidence. No one has ever had any trouble, so far as I can discover, with the famous lines from "The Love Song of J. Alfred Prufrock": "I should have been a pair of ragged claws/ Scuttling across the floors of silent seas." This image, which occurs also in the Notebook version of some parts of the poem, is of two protuberances large enough to appear to be separated from the body, and therefore to some extent out of touch with any of the body's motivating or sexual energies. These are, I take it, most likely the claws of a New England lobster, famous as a delicacy in coastal towns on Cape Ann, like Gloucester, Massachusetts, where Eliot summered in his youth. He often went sailing out past the clutter of lobster pots set close to shore, and came to revere the fishermen and the seascapes, which figure importantly in his poetry. (The "dry salvages" are a group of rocks off the Gloucester coast.) Eliot might be referring, stretching it a bit, to crab claws, but there is no compelling reason to suppose that he is. Crabs, unlike lobsters, are endowed only with rudimentary claws when they have them at all, and with rather stocky bodies from which it is not easy to picture the claws as a separable "pair" operating by themselves.

Why, then, does Ricks insist in his notes on referring exclusively to crabs? For the reason, I guess, that he is in possession of some prize catches on the subject of "crabs"—but not of lobster claws—and is determined to display them. In more than a page of addenda, he offers in evidence a passage marked by Eliot in his copy of Darwin's *The Descent of Man* on the sexual characteristics of crabs, an OED entry showing that as early as 1861 there was in use the phrase "crab lice," and a passage from Turgenev's story "Smoke," which refers to a crab at a lavish dinner party, in which Ricks ingenuously locates a series of words used consecutively also in the poem: smoke, claws, long fingers.

Besides the tedious irrelevance of the claims themselves, it turns out that while the lines from "Prufrock" were copied by Eliot into the Notebook in 1911–12, the edition he marked of *The Descent of Man* is the edition of 1913. Moreover, the letters in which Eliot first reports an enthusiasm for Turgenev are dated late December 1917.

Ricks is a seasoned academic, an eminent and learned scholar, and he would not so freely engage in this sort of annotative adventurism only on his own authority. Encouragement for such efforts as his can be found in Eliot's early criticism and in decades of precedent among interpreters of Eliot. Their Talmudic zeal was fed increasingly by Eliot's own Notes to *The Waste Land,* not to mention the allusive schema Joyce liked to hand out about *Ulysses.* Eliot's early criticism was his most influential—it included "Tradition and the Individual Talent" of 1919, the essays and reviews published in *The Sacred Wood* a year later, and, in 1923, "Ulysses: Order and Myth"—and these provided much of the theoretical underpinning for the dominant kinds of close reading that swept the American academy in the 1940s and 1950s under the banner of the New Criticism and, in England, in the pedagogy of F. R. Leavis, one of Eliot's first and best champions. These early critical pronouncements exhibit the sweeping dogmatism of a young man determined to be heard and desirous of being taken as a sage. They are full of deferential hints to the effect that he regrets having to reveal the painful historical inevitabilities that he is required, as a sage, to urge upon us.

The critical writing was wonderfully supple and persuasive, unencumbered by the contradictory pomposities of the later works like *Notes Toward a Definition of Culture* or by the hateful and repellent crudities about literary contemporaries or near-contemporaries and about Jews in the infamous *After Strange Gods* of 1934. And the strategies of the early prose

worked. Among other things he was able to persuade most critics (except those who knew him best like I. A. Richards or Virginia Woolf, or, in America, Edmund Wilson) that his poetry was
not personal, even while it hints everywhere that it is.

It is one of the most remarkable performances in the history
of literary public relations and literary careerism. Eliot contrived
to preserve his impulses toward lyric self-exploration under
cover of allusive patterns that loudly insist on the poetry's historical consequentiality, on its large Significance. Thus, in the 1921
essay "The Metaphysical Poets," Eliot remarked:

> We can only say that it appears likely that poets in our civilization, as
> it exists at present, must be *difficult.* Our civilization comprehends
> great variety and complexity, and this variety and complexity, playing
> on a refined sensibility, must produce various and complex results.
> The poet must become more and more comprehensive, more allu-
> sive, more indirect, in order to force, to dislocate if necessary, lan-
> guage into his meaning.

Eliot's decision to link allusiveness to "difficulty," when it could
as easily be thought of as a mode of clarification, was essential to
his larger intention. And that was to claim, as Wordsworth had
done for his own age and in much the same terms, that the
period in which Eliot was living, the first quarter of the twentieth century in the United States and Western Europe, was an
unprecedentedly bad one.

Wordsworth and Eliot were not the first greatly ambitious poets
(nor will they be the last) to boast of the heroism of writing in the
worst of times when language is itself threatened with loss of
meaning. The same special pleading was even more pronounced
when, in 1923, Eliot credited Joyce with achievements in the so-
called mythical method, which is necessarily an allusive one, and
did so in a way designed to praise his own achievement in *The
Waste Land,* published the year before. The method involves
"manipulating a continuous parallel between contemporaneity

and antiquity," he said, and this manipulation (which may be found in English literature, as he must have known, at least since Spenser's *The Faerie Queene*) is compelled by a contemporary degeneration which was unprecedented in degree. "It is simply a way of controlling, of ordering, of giving a shape and significance, to the immense panorama of futility and anarchy which is contemporary history."

As a matter of cold fact, allusiveness in poetry, even this portentously sounding "more and more" of it, has nothing whatever to do and has never had anything whatever to do with worsening cultural and historical conditions. Neither has the "mythical method." Furthermore, there's no way of telling if Eliot's period of time was worse than any other, or for that matter that the twentieth century is worse than any other. As Frost elegantly put it in 1935, with Eliot in mind, I suspect, "It is immodest of a man to think of himself as going down before the worst forces ever mobilized by God."

Eliot's portentous comments were, rather, a calculated effort at self-promotion. They were designed to intimidate his readers, to make them assent to what he was trying to exhibit by his allusiveness, which was that he was a great poet working directly in the idiom of other poets known to be great. Besides, he was suggesting that any failure on the part of readers to appreciate the allusiveness, comprehensiveness, and difficulty of his poetry was evidence that they had themselves succumbed to the "futility and anarchy" which that same poetry, along with Joyce's *Ulysses,* was unique in recognizing.

Very often what strikes us first in Eliot's early poems is precisely their allusiveness, in the form of epigraphs, and with *The Waste Land* it's also what strikes us last in the form of Eliot's appended Notes. A notorious example is the epigraph to the 1919–20 "Burbank with a Baedeker; Bleistein with a Cigar." The epigraph is a hodgepodge of six quotations, starting with a rather supercilious "Tra la-la-la-la-la laire," this being the call of the gondolier—the setting of the poem is Venice—taken from a poem by Théophile Gautier, whose highly accelerated stanza form Eliot was imitating. This is followed by "nil nisis divinum stabile est; caetera fumus." The first word ought to be "nihil" and the Latin phrase means "only the divine endures; the rest is smoke," an inscription in a painting by one of Eliot's favorite painters, Mantegna (1431–1506), found in a church in Venice, on the subject of the martyrdom of St. Sebastian. (There is also a sadomasochistic poem in the Notebook entitled "The Love Song of St. Sebastian.") The next four allusions are, respectively, to Henry James's *The Aspern Papers,* Shakespeare's *Othello,* both of which are also set in Venice, and then to Robert Browning and the Renaissance dramatist John Marston.

Eliot could hardly have expected, nor would he have preferred, even his most recondite readers to catch all these allusions. It has been pointed out that thirty years after the first publication of the poem three of the quotations still remained unidentified until one interpreter sought help from Eliot himself. Fun and games on the old Rialto! With a little ingenuity each of the allusions can be made pertinent to the poem, though hardly essential to one's reading of it. But something besides pertinence is at work in Eliot's teasing display of erudition, and fun and games oughtn't to be ruled out as one possibility.

Nor can they be ruled out when we get to the Notes to *The Waste Land.* Ricks's mentions of them have a reverential seriousness that misses, I think, part of what Eliot is up to. Many of the Notes are straight enough—like "Line 20. Cf. Ezekiel II, i"— and Eliot later mentioned that he wanted the notes both to prevent a resurgence of charges that he was wont to plagiarize some of his best phrases and also to reassure readers who might recognize an allusion to, say, Dante, that they are on the right track. But in several of the longer notes there is a charming and insidiously significant element of camp, especially when Eliot poses as tour guide with a Baedeker or other such manual. Thus, to some lines in the poem that by themselves adequately identify St. Mary Magnus Church in London (". . . where the walls of Mary Magnus hold/ Inexplicable splendour of Ionian white and gold"), Eliot offers the following: "The interior of St. Magnus Martyr is to my mind one of the finest among Wren's interiors. See *The Proposed Demolition of Nineteen City Churches*: (P. S. King and Son, Ltd.)."

Still, the levity in Eliot's allusive practices ultimately points to a serious and interesting purpose. The Notes, like the show-off allusiveness in the epigraphs, should be read with the same alertness as to tones of voice and placement that the poetry asks of us. They are best thought of as part of the poem to which they are appended. In the note to the lines about St. Mary Magnus, for instance, the tour-guide neutrality and pedantic aloofness of tone, as in the imparting of the book title, give a macabre twist to the information that this church and others like it are threatened with destruction, the same fragmentation represented in the veritable structure of the poem itself.

A far more devious intention, and an important clue to Eliot's efforts at this time to define his status as a world poet and not just as an American one, can be found in a note that has caused considerable speculation, especially about the influence on his poetry of Whitman, which later becomes unmistakable in the *Four Quartets.* The note concerns a line in the last section of the poem, which Eliot once identified as his favorite, and which Pound left practically untouched, the so-called water song in "What the Thunder Said." The line in question is "Where the hermit-thrush sings in the pine trees." This has often been cited as an echo of some lines in Whitman's "When Lilacs Last in the Dooryard Bloom'd": "Solitary the thrush/ The hermit withdrawn to itself. . . ." Eliot claimed that he didn't read Whitman till "much later in life," after he had composed his early Laforgean poetry, whatever *read* here means with respect to a poet he could not have failed to come across in his youth in St. Louis, Cambridge, and Cape Ann.

But if Eliot was merely avoiding mention of Whitman out of some reputed anxiety of influence, then he could easily have cited any number of other loftier names, loftier at least in 1922, on the roster of poets who have used the familiar trope of solitary birds in the trees for the poet and for poetic song. Why, instead, does he choose only another, loudly banal American source, and a non-poetic one at that? He refers us to a decidedly real North American bird and, what's more, to its Latin name, the first word of which sounds scatological enough to delight the author of the Bolo poems. He identifies the bird: "This is *Turdus aonalaschkae pallasii,* the hermit-thrush which I have heard in Quebec Province. Chapman says (*Handbook of Birds of Eastern North America*), 'it is most at home in secluded woodland and thickety retreats. . . . Its notes are not remarkable for variety or volume, but in purity and sweetness of tone and exquisite modulation they are un-equalled.' Its 'water-dripping song' is justly celebrated."

John Hollander, in his brilliant *The Figure of Echo: A Mode of Allusion in Milton and After,* offers the lines from Eliot about the hermit thrush, along with the related lines in Whitman, as an example of the differences among quotation, allusion, and echo, only the last of which does not depend on conscious intention. He remarks that in Eliot's note, which mentions Chapman but not Whitman, it is "as if a kind of suppression were at work in the texture of recognition and avowal, a nod to allusion but not to echo." I would want to go a step or two further, and repeat that if there is in Eliot's note a suppression of Whitman's presence in this poem, then it is so conspicuously done, by his reference instead, not to other poets, but to an American ornithological handbook, as in fact to call attention to his refusal to acknowl-edge the one American poet he might have mentioned. And if Whitman is passed over for someone named Chapman, so then is every other American poet.

This is Eliot's way of emphasizing that while there may be auto-biographical sources for his poetry rooted in his personal Ameri-can experiences, those sources emphatically do not include any experience of American poetry. The implication is that no "song birds" are to be found in American poetry, no precedents or models, that is, for Eliot's poetic voice. He enjoyed bird-watching and liked the Chapman manual. It was given to him, in fact, by his greatly revered mother on his fourteenth birthday in 1902, and he kept it in his library for the rest of his life. But when it comes to his career in poetry (which he was desperately anxious for his mother to appreciate), he will acknowledge only those poets in whose company he prefers to belong, the great poets of European civilization.

When Eliot gets around to making one of his rare mentions of Whitman, he says in 1935 that he first saw him, and Edgar Allan Poe, "through French eyes." Even when, still later, and by then not wanting to leave *any* bases unoccupied, he does begin to claim that his poetry is more American than English in its sources, he means only in its autobiographical sources. What he always affirmed was what he had discovered for himself while an undergraduate at Harvard avidly reading French poetry and Arthur Symons's *The Symbolist Movement in Literature*: that he could turn his American experience into poetry only with the help of European models. Of his lovely and very early "Preludes," for example, which have always seemed evocative of the run-down glamour of London and Paris neighborhoods, Ricks's edition of the Notebook versions shows that "Prelude I" ("The winter evening settles down/ With smell of steak in passageways") was titled originally "Prelude in Dorchester" (a town in Massachusetts), while both "Prelude II" ("The morning comes to consciousness/ Of faint stale smells of beer") and "Prelude III" ("You tossed a blanket from the bed") were titled "Prelude in Roxbury" (another town near Boston). Even before his first visit to Europe in 1910, he was seeing his native cityscapes through Laforgue and Baudelaire. "Without Baudelaire, Corbière, Verlaine, Laforgue, Mallarmé, Rimbaud—I should not have been able to write poetry at all," he said in 1933 and, in 1940, that the kind of poetry he needed "to teach me the use of my own voice did not exist in English at all." He was doubtless thinking of the "Preludes," "Rhapsody on a Windy Night," and some of the passages written in 1909–10 that found their way into "The Love Song of J. Alfred Prufrock" when he made the additional admission, in his 1950 essay "What Dante Means to Me," that from these French poets, among other European writers, "I learned that the sort of material I had, the sort of experience an adolescent has had in an industrial city in America, could be the material for poetry; and that the source of the new poetry might be found in what had been regarded hitherto as the impossible, the sterile, the intractably unpoetic."

The "unpoetic" might include "the yellow fog" of St. Louis that in "Prufrock," as well as in the second of the Notebook poems, "First Caprice in North Cambridge," "rubs its back upon the window panes," and the seascapes of his Cape Ann boyhood that begin to appear as early as the Notebook poem "Embarquement pour Cythère," where he mocks his "knowledge, nautical complete." He is already aware of the perils and power of the sea that will manifest themselves metaphorically in "Gerontion," the "Death by Water" section of *The Waste Land,* "Ash Wednesday," "Marina," and of course "The Dry Salvages." And at every stage of his poetic career he returns to a haunting image from childhood that includes a passageway, footsteps along it, a garden, a small door, the sound beyond the door of children's voices and of some elusive presence of a girl or a woman. This recurrence deserves a closer look, which I'll give it shortly, but it should be mentioned that it existed first outside the poetry in a childhood experience Eliot described in a talk at the Mary Institute, in his old neighborhood in St. Louis, in 1959. At seventy-one, he recalled that the schoolyard of the Mary Institute "abutted on my father's property," and went on:

> There was at the front of our house a sort of picket fence which divided our front yard from the schoolyard. This picket fence merged a little later into a high brick wall which concealed our back

garden and also concealed the schoolyard from our back garden. There was a door in the wall and there was a key in the door. Now when the young ladies had left the school in the afternoon and at the end of the week, I had access to the schoolyard and used it for my own purposes of play. . . . I remained extremely shy with girls. And, of course, when they were in the schoolyard I was always on the other side of the wall; and on one occasion I remember, when I ventured into the schoolyard a little too early when there were still a few on the premises and I saw them staring at me through a window, I took flight at once.

But while images from his American childhood are obviously compelling to his imagination, they don't of themselves constitute poetry. Such images would yield some of their mysteries, some of their at least potential significance, only to the extent that he could take them from life and, time after time and each time with some slight variation, find a place for them in a recurring pattern of metaphors that draws upon the already composed but forever self-transforming life of great poetry. This is how his otherwise curious comment on tradition in "Tradition and the Individual Talent" of 1919 needs to be understood: "Tradition cannot be inherited, and if you want it you must obtain it by great labor." Can any comparably ambitious French or English poet be imagined saying such a thing? His caution that "tradition" requires a lot of hard work, like the degree of allusiveness to which it gives birth, is meant to warn and intimidate any reader who aspires to understand his poetry, particularly any American reader. It's going to be hard work, but it might save your soul. W. H. Auden was to remark in his 1956 introduction to *The Faber Book of Modern Verse* that no real European would think of tradition in this way. He would not need to "acquire by great labor" something he regarded as a birthright. Auden's perception had in fact already been anticipated by Eliot in an essay of 1918, "In Memory of Henry James," where he used it further to exalt his own anticipated apotheosis as a great international poet: "It is the final perfection, the consummation of the American, to become not an Englishman, but a European—something which no born European, no person of any European nationality, can become."

Most of Eliot's self-promoting critical formulae involving tradition, impersonality, objective correlative, and the difficult allusiveness supposedly unique to modernist writing were for several decades treated with ridiculous solemnity in the academy. This persisted even after Eliot himself, when it served his purpose, disavowed many of them. The formulae and pronouncements deserve to be taken seriously, of course, but only in the way that the language of poetry itself deserves to be, as so many metaphors or adjustments of voice that the poet can then freely turn in some other direction, including the opposite direction, if they begin to obstruct rather than enable the reading that the poet wants to receive. Eliot was describing himself better than he knew when he originally wanted to call *The Waste Land,* borrowing a phrase from Dickens's *Our Mutual Friend,* "He Do the Police in Different Voices." In "The Frontiers of Criticism," a lecture delivered when he was sixty-eight years old to an audience of more than 14,000 people at the University of Minnesota, he warned against some of the very critical habits which he once helped to promote, source hunting and "the lemon squeezer school of criticism," and remarked, with that sort of deferential beg-your-pardon which is a sure sign of high vanity, that a "few notorious phrases" of his own "have had a truly embarrassing success in the world."

In particular his use of the term "impersonality" or depersonalization has often been taken to mean that he intended to deny to his poetry anything confessional, personal, and private, anything that might adulterate or raise questions about the poetry's greater historical and universalizing urgency. Here, too, he tried to redress a balance for which he was originally responsible. In her edition of the facsimile of the original drafts of *The Waste*

Land, Valerie Eliot gives a prominent place to her husband's reported assertion that "various critics have done me the honour to interpret the poem in terms of criticism of the contemporary world, have considered it, indeed, as an important bit of social criticism. To me it is only the relief of a personal and wholly insignificant grouse against life; it is just a piece of rhythmical grumbling." These self-reversals and unpersuasively excessive recantations are themselves evidence that he was, as Edmund Wilson noticed earlier than most other critics, a deeply incoherent personality, and, as Wilson put it in a review of Eliot's *Poems 1909–1925,* his "real significance is less that of a prophet of European disintegration than of a poet of the American Puritan temperament." What Wilson and I. A. Richards were both responsive to early on is the enormously powerful personal presence everywhere in Eliot's poetry. However fragmented it might be, there is a self, titanically struggling, before our eyes and ears, to put itself together. In her diary, Virginia Woolf, who was always strikingly perceptive about Eliot, appreciatively records the comment of a close mutual friend that *The Waste Land* is "Tom's autobiography—a melancholy one."

Eliot's "impersonality" is only a way, a method, of being authentically personal. Indeed, for him as for any poet of large artistic ambition, being personal means being a poet. It is not at best only a profession; it is a way of being in the world, of placing yourself in its language. He says as much in writing not about himself, but about Shakespeare. Again, in "Tradition and the Individual Talent," he referred to "the struggle—which alone constitutes life for a poet—to transmute his personal and private agonies into something rich and strange, something universal and impersonal." Being personal obviously requires as much, even more, "great labor" than does the attainment of tradition. And it is the more difficult because it is never possible to be sure that you have actually succeeded in being truly personal. In making the effort, you are required to use words that are not, to repeat, your own, that are by nature devious, and that can betray you, and not simply in the sense of revelation. In a particularly affecting moment in "East Coker" he describes his personal dilemma as a distinctly and forever poetic one:

> So here I am, in the middle way, having had twenty years—
> Twenty years largely wasted, the years *l'entre deux guerres*—
> Trying to learn to use words, and every attempt
> Is a wholly new start, and a different kind of failure
> Because one has only learnt to get the better of words
> For the thing one no longer has to say, or the way in which
> One is no longer disposed to say it.

All poetry, to that degree, is "impersonal" because, as the not always ingratiating Sweeney repeatedly complains to Doris in "Fragments of an Agon": "I gotta use words when I talk to you." Poetry constantly enriches itself on the imprecision of words. And it is the consequent varieties of interpretation that can be elicited by any given poem that can keep it alive for many generations to come. The same poem will of necessity mean different things to different people at different times. In a radio broadcast in 1951 entitled "Virgil and the Christian World," Eliot said:

> . . . if the word 'inspiration' is to have any meaning, it must mean just this, that the speaker or writer is uttering something which he does not wholly understand—or which he may even misinterpret when the inspiration has departed from him. This is certainly true of poetic inspiration: and there is more obvious reason for admiring Isaiah as a poet than for claiming Virgil as a prophet. A poet may believe that he is expressing only his private experience; his lines may be for him only a means of talking about himself without giving himself away; yet for his readers what he has written may come to be an expression both of their own secret feelings and of the exultation or despair of a generation.

In his poems he is forever talking about his self in the hope only of getting closer to it, of seeing it anew in some different

poetic context: "A poet," says Yeats in the opening sentence of
"A General Introduction for My Work," "writes always of his
personal life, in his finest work out of its tragedy, whatever it be,
remorse, lost love, or mere loneliness; he never speaks directly
as to someone at the breakfast table, there is always a phantas-
magoria." Over time every great poet or novelist begins consciously to repeat himself, specifically to repeat certain metaphors
that he can't be done with, always with slight alterations. Just as
he has all along taken pains to repeat other poets, or done so
unwittingly, with inflections and modifications, so Eliot's later
poetry is a self-echoing, an interpretation, a reading, a rewriting
of his own earlier ones. And as in Yeats and Stevens, this often
involves very direct citations of images that have preoccupied
him from the beginning of his career.

After *The Waste Land,* Eliot's poetry became noticeably less
pushy in its allusion to other poets but correspondingly more
allusive to his own. It was as if his own oeuvre came to constitute
in itself a tradition, a body of work that represents a pastness
which is his own personal and literary past and which contains a
still bewildering and bewitching power over him. Part of the
value of Ricks's edition of these hitherto unpublished early
poems is that for the first time it is possible to measure the full
extent of this development in Eliot's writing.

One of his most revelatory repetitions has to do with the same
images he referred to at the Mary Institute, that cluster about
"the hyacinth girl." The figure appears in the opening section of
The Waste Land:

> "You gave me hyacinths first a year ago;
> "They called me the hyacinth girl."
> —Yet when you came back, late, from the Hyacinth garden,
> Your arms full, and your hair wet, I could not
> Speak, and my eyes failed, I was neither
> Living nor dead, and I knew nothing,
> Looking into the heart of light, the silence.

The phrase "the heart of light," a pointed reversal of Conrad's "the heart of darkness," marks a moment of ecstasy that is close to a departure from bodily life. A very poignant, personal moment was erased from *The Waste Land* when Eliot assented to Pound's cutting of a line in the next section. The cut was made from the heated marital exchange, in "The Game of Chess," characteristic of what is reported to have gone on between Eliot and Vivienne. She herself wrote in the margin of the manuscript where the conversation occurs, "wonderful." To her mind-numbing question "Do/ You know nothing? Do you see nothing? Do you remember/ Nothing?" Eliot had allowed himself the ghostly answer "I remember/ The hyacinth garden."

Traces of that garden are to be found throughout his poetry, even before the exquisite "La Figlia che Piange." They make an appearance, for instance in the retrospectively haunting and untitled Notebook poem that is identified by its opening line:

> Hidden under the heron's wing
> Or the song before daybreak that the lotos-birds sing
> Evening whisper of stars together
> Oh my beloved what do you bring—
>
> With evening feet walking across the grass
> And fragile arms dividing the evening mist.
>
> I lie on the floor a bottle's broken glass
> To be swept away by the housemaid's crimson fist.

Why, when a flesh-and-blood woman does manage to intrude into these goings on, must she be said, as against the visionary woman with her "fragile arms," to have a "fist," and a "crimson" one at that? Disgust need not be the only alternative to decorporealized idealization. Everywhere in Eliot, human sexuality is either displaced by "mist" or associated with violence, pain, and animality. In the early poems the disgust is unabashed and lurid, showing the dark side of the adolescent bawdiness of the Bolo poems. The results can be startlingly graphic, given what one had learned to expect of the prematurely "aged eagle." In one of his relatively becalmed states, as in the poem "Opera," which is about a performance in Boston of *Tristan and Isolde,* Eliot portrays himself as "the ghost of youth/ At an undertaker's ball." But on other occasions he is busy keeping the undertaker in business. After giving himself a preliminary flogging in "The Love Song of St. Sebastian" at the foot of the stairs to his lady's bedroom, he is ready to mount, assured that now she "would take me in/ Because I was hideous to her sight." He then assures himself of his love for her by strangling her: "And I should love you the more because I had mangled you/ And because you were no longer beautiful/ To any one but me." In "First Debate between Body and Soul" he writes of "masturbations," "defecations," and "The withered leaves of our sensations."

Along the same lines is the weird little poem "Ode," the only poem Eliot suppressed after having published it. It is particularly hair-raising because as the bridegroom inspects the lamentable spectacle of the bloodstained bed of his honeymoon night—his first wife Vivienne, besides her many other disorders, was plagued by menstrual problems—he is all the while smoothing his own hair, as was Eliot's habit:

> When the bridegroom smoothed his hair
> There was blood upon the bed.
> Morning was already late.
> Children singing in the orchard
> (Io Hymen, Hymenæe)
> Succuba eviserate.
>
> Tortuous.

The young man here, exhibiting some of Eliot's own obsessions with the decorum of personal appearance, might remind us of the Pateresque young artist in Joyce's *Portrait,* who describes himself as foolishly trying "to build a breakwater of order and elegance against the sordid tide of life without him and . . . the powerful recurrences of the tide within him." Another version of this figure in Eliot's earliest poetry is the "mandarin," whom we've already glanced at in the poem of that title, a figure who aspires to be "the center of formalities." And this in turn might refer us to Eliot's many evocations of Coriolanus. These begin early on, including an easily missed one in the aforementioned "Ode." Since "Ode" counts as a previously published poem, it is in a category of the Notebook poems that Ricks does not annotate. This means that he doesn't comment, any more than have other interpreters, on the importance of the epigraph included with the first and until now only publication of the poem. It is Coriolanus addressing his enemies: "To you/ and to all Voscians/ Great hurt and mischief."

Eliot's intense interest in Coriolanus made him a frequent listener to borrowed recordings of Beethoven's Coriolan Overture, and is clear from his many references in his criticism to Shakespeare's play. Coriolanus is depicted in the play as both a great warrior and, at the same time, a great mother's boy. Of his exploits the First Citizen remarks that "he did it to please his mother and to be partly proud." He is a man of prowess, and an emotionally crippled child.

Like the inwardly despairing, tortured bridegroom smoothing his hair, the hero-dictator in each of the two parts of Eliot's "Coriolan," written the year after his adored mother's death in September 1929, also carefully contrives a public image of control and imperturbability. All the while, like the figure in "Hidden under the heron's wing," he secretly yearns for oblivion, a sort of death in life, a suspension of all desire, especially as it may involve others, and even if they ask no more than to give him, as Eliot by this time was being given in considerable measure, power and adulation. In expressing this, the poetry achieves a distanced, inquisitive focus, as if in emulation of the staring crowd, only then, and suddenly, to reveal that the public image is in part a reflection of the man's benumbed remoteness both from what he publicly represents and from his deepest emotions:

> There is no interrogation in his eyes
> Or in his hands, quiet over the horse's neck,
> And the eyes watchful, waiting, perceiving, indifferent.
> O hidden under the dove's wing, hidden in the turtle's breast,
> Under the palmtree at noon, under the running water
> At the still point of the turning world. O hidden.

Among other things, what is hidden is the terrifying suspicion that perhaps there is nothing to hide. There is only a yearning for something that cannot in this life find for itself any "objective correlative," to use Eliot's term for what he found lacking in *Hamlet,* yet another play about a mother-obsessed character.

Of only one love other than the love of God is it sometimes said that it surpasseth all understanding: the love of a mother for a child to whom she has given birth, a love which may be so all-consuming as to prove emotionally disabling for the child. This is a fate that has concerned other great poets from Whitman to Lawrence to Stevens. Eliot was nearly always contemptuous of Lawrence's writing, to a point where E. M. Forster had publicly and effectively to deride him when he chose to carp in print about the wording of Forster's obituary for Lawrence in 1930. And yet Eliot is reported to have said to undergraduates he taught on a visit to Harvard—and this, again, was after the death of his mother in 1929—that in *Fantasia of the Unconscious* Lawrence had written better than any psychologist had managed to do about possessive mother love and how it might assist in a son's intellectual development while preventing him from entering into any reciprocally full, emotional-sensual relationship with another woman. It led, correspondingly, to the idealization of spiritual relationships with more or less desexualized substitutes.

Such a substitute may be the mother herself, of course, or "Mother," as Eliot calls out to her in "Ash Wednesday." Pictured in the by now familiar context of visions, gardens, and roses, she is both given the physicality of an actual mother, "Exhausted and life giving," and associated with the Virgin Mother, who also had a memorably powerful son with a hidden side. Jesus was for Lawrence and for Emerson representative less of human victory than of defeat. "He did well," Emerson writes of him in his journals in 1842, and yet, "This great Defeat is hitherto the highest fate we have. But he that shall come shall do better. The mind requires a far higher exhibition of character, one which shall make itself good to the senses as well as to the soul; a success to the senses as well as to the soul." Eliot's visionary woman-mother in "Ash Wednesday" is once again in that garden Eliot will not enter. It is she who makes all physical love, not just when unconsummated but especially when it *is* consummated, into a "torment":

> The single Rose
> Is now the Garden
> Where all loves end
> Terminate torment
> Of love unsatisfied
> The greater torment
> Of love satisfied. . . .

The most beautifully articulated moment in Eliot's poetry when he calls out to "mother" occurs in the second of the Coriolan poems, "Difficulties of a Statesman," written in close proximity to "Ash Wednesday." Here, in the evocations of family heritage, and a self-identifying reference to Eliot's prominent nose, the poet, who has by now acquired some of the poetic authority and power equivalent to the man in the poem, seems

directly, and in magnificent Whitmanian cadences, to address
his own recently dead parent:

What shall I cry?
Mother mother
Here is the row of family portraits, dingy busts, all looking
      remarkably Roman,
Remarkably like each other, lit up successively by the flare
Of a sweaty torchbearer, yawning.
O hidden under the . . . Hidden under the . . .
      Where the dove's foot rested and locked for a moment,
A still moment, repose of noon, set under the upper branches of
      noon's widest tree
Under the breast feather stirred by the small wind after noon
There the cyclamen spreads its wings, there the clematis droops over
      the lintel
O mother (not among these busts, all correctly inscribed)
I a tired head among these heads
Necks strong to bear them
Noses strong to break the wind
Mother
May we not be some time, almost now, together,
If the mactations, immolations, oblations, impetrations,
Are now observed
May we not be
O hidden
Hidden in the stillness of noon, in the silent croaking night.
Come with the sweep of the little bat's wing, with the small flare of
      the firefly or lightning bug,
"Rising and falling, crowned with dust," the small creatures,
The small creatures chirp thinly through the dust, through the night.
O mother
What shall I cry?
We demand a committee, a representative committee, a committee of
      investigation
                    RESIGN RESIGN RESIGN

The complex interplay here of allusions and echoes that reach
back to Eliot's earliest Notebook poems—of the "hidden" and

barely articulable, of gardens, mothers, figures of authority who are emotionally fragile—these repeated figurations are a poetic representation, in the word patterns of his poetry, of a lifelong effort. It is an effort at conversion, and poetic conversion was his subject long before, and also after, his conversion to the Church of England. Poetic turnings and tropings, initially of the poetry of the past and then, increasingly, of his own earlier poetry, are efforts to bring into a sort of focus something forever hidden from him in his own past and in the literary past, the past of words themselves. When he wrote in "East Coker" in 1940 that "The poetry does not matter," he can be taken to mean that any finished poem, any oeuvre, matters less than does the effort that went into the making of it, this effort of conversion, "the intolerable wrestle/ With words and meaning." With "Burnt Norton" of 1935, the first of what were to be *Four Quartets,* the reader is directly solicited to partake of this activity of poetic conversion. Eliot can now assume that we are reading his lines the way he is writing them, that we are hearing the echoes that reverberate back to his earliest poetry. So much so that he allows the familiar passageways and visionary gardens to become also metaphors for passages of poetry, for poetic feet, and poetic echoes:

> What might have been and what has been
> Point to one end which is always present.
> Footfalls echo in the memory
> Down the passage which we did not take
> Towards the door we never opened
> Into the rose garden. My words echo
> Thus, in your mind.

6

ALLUSIVE POP:
BETTE MIDLER IN CONCERT[°]

✦

It was clear from the beginning that Midler's Broadway extravaganza in 1975 was a specialized event for a specialized audience.
By the time it closed, its very specialness—its remarkable
dependence on listeners who would have to be almost scholarly
in their appreciation of the conventions of popular song and
entertainment—had become for Midler a barely tolerable burden. It seemed literally to weigh on the shoulders of a star who
must by then have given up expecting any large Broadway audience who could share with her the knowledge that she was up to
subtleties worth the trouble. The cognoscenti, always in a minority even in the first weeks, had left her to a mass of eager illiter-
ates. By the fifth week, she was delivering a fair number of her
songs and lines facing only her cast—the three funny and outrageous Harlettes, Lionel Hampton and his jazz orchestra, a score
of black singers—and with her back to the audience. In the last
three weeks she became rather desperately condescending, bla-
tantly signaling her parodistic intentions.

° Without the assistance of my friend and companion the late Richard Santino, with his
extraordinary knowledge of American popular song and singing styles of the 1940s,
1950s, and 1960s, this article could not have been written.

The very title of the show should have been a clue to inherent contradictions. *Clams on the Half Shell* was only in part a justification for the exuberant fun of her entrance—a clam shell was hauled onstage by some minstrel-show dockside darkies. It then opened, to reveal her, arms raised triumphantly, her beautiful skin and breasts straining against the chic, flouncy, tattered streetwalker's dress; her smile, big-toothed and gleaming radiantly, sweetly expectant, confident of the energies behind it, obviously hopeful, and therefore a little poignant, about any answerable energies in the audience she was about to confront. "With no one to deride me," as she later phrased it in what could be called her theme song, "Friends." But to some who would know, "clams on the half shell" alludes to jazz musicians' slang—"clams" means wrong notes. We were looking at a romp, but we were also listening to a parody, and if the show was in some respects a direct appeal to sentiment, as in "Hello in There," or raunchiness, as in the great opening song written by her friend Elton John, "The Bitch Is Back," it was also full of indirections, hints, modulations, and allusions contrived to redirect our responses and sensitize them by satire and stylized teasing. As the weeks went on and the hints got lost or went stale because so few of them were picked up, Midler became parodistic about the show itself. One night the clam opened and it was empty. Midler was missing, until she came crawling on in its wake, spouting water.

Midler's parodistic predilections shouldn't be mistaken, as they usually are, for camp. Behind them is an eager receptivity that is the reverse of camp; many of her jokes derive from sentiments that are nearly embarrassing in their self-exposure. It is this quality that softens her toughness. She is completely open to the half-trashy, half-beautiful, always totemized world of the recent past, which seems to include everyone's teens, whether of the 1940s, 1950s, 1960s or 1970s. She gives people the courage of their nostalgias because she seems herself to have been resistant to nothing that has ever come close to touching her. More often than not, her spoofing is a form of exuberant exorcism, as of that New Jersey group of the 1960s, the Shangri-Las. Doing their famous "The Leader of the Pack" on her first album, she rendered all the parts of an utterly shameless dialogue about high-school love to the sound of revved-up motorcycles, the girls' voices very Marilyn Monroeish, redolent of the physical and psychic pains of virginities lost, and well lost, only the night before. "Hey, Jay, is that Jimmy's ring you're wearing?" "Uh, huh." "Oh, it must be nice driving on that motorcycle after school, huh." "Uh, huh." Trash. No doubt about it. So are parts of the revue, like the Harlettes' "toilet medley," delivered as from Midler's own Hawaii high school—"picture if you will three algebra majors in the ladies' room at Commonawanalaya High School." Trash—yet, as Midler knows and feels, also endearing—and also a kind of neglected history, the history of American adolescent consciousness, which is mostly available only in song, the bitter versions of which cascade out of Bob Dylan's early work. It is Midler's special appeal and inimitable strength of personality that she can let herself satirize *and* be moved by what most of us are ready to leave behind.

Her whole stance is therefore precarious, at once proud and self-deprecating, sad and zany, and it calls for the subtlest kinds of response. Unlike Lionel Hampton, with whom she shared the second half of the revue, she couldn't be sure of a well-managed evening. She worried about and commented anew on every song every night, while his commentaries were predictable even when extemporaneous. His superb work on piano, drums, and vibraphone was always on cue. His performance over the ten weeks could never be less than efficient and polished.

Midler by contrast was all agitation, her control the more exciting for her flirtations with chaos, her momentary lapses the result not of carelessness but of her own honesties of mood. She asked you to worry about her; she also asked you to worry about yourself and your adequacies in relation to what she was offering—in some degree a sexual proposition—and some nights some of the audience was up to it. Her awesome energies were persistent, making you wonder if she'd be carried off by them, until you noticed underneath the expenditures of energy a strange kind of monitoring going on, a kind of resentment even at having to put out so much for an audience only sporadically up to the mark. Built into the show from the moment she began to speak was a degree of impatience, coarsely expressed but fine-tempered nonetheless—"shut up," she told the Harlettes in the first number; "you shut up too," she told the orchestra, "I wanna talk to my friends," looking past the front rows toward the balcony. But a half hour later she was after the audience as well—or, rather, the square majority who laughed as if she'd succeeded in *being* what she was trying to satirize. Suddenly a wonderful Carmen Miranda–Martha Raye smirk, then a gloriously loud Long Island nasality: "Harry, did she really *say* that? Did she say what I *thought* she said? I don't *get* it"—pronounced "gedded." Pause. "And the reason you don't get it . . ." Pause again. And if the audience doesn't laugh at the innuendo, she'd then clarify it for them in a tone contemptuous enough to be an accusation, "is because you don't get it. Get it?" Whether she would leave the sequence in the middle was a barometer of how much she had come to trust or like a given audience and usually a sign, too, of whether her energies would begin to flag.

Her direct appeal to and dependence on the audience was in no sense merely a call for support, or the corny sharing of inner joys and sufferings (really the cheap pretense of sharing) that for me sometimes sullied the brilliance of Judy Garland and Edith Piaf. Rather, what Midler wants to say to the audience is that she, no less than they, is in a critical relationship to her material and her performance. She is inviting us to participate in her artistries more than in her feelings. Throughout she signals her intention to do the unexpected, to break out of situations framed by producers, directors, other performers, and certain recalcitrant elements in the audience. She invites us into a kind of complicity with her *against* the revue as a prepared and rehearsed occasion. Part of our feeling that Midler has an excess of life is a result of her success in making us aware she is one of us but more—a person able to be simultaneously star and critical witness.

If there had to be a single word to describe Midler, it would be the word "haunted." She has the vocal resources to sing in the style of any woman vocalist of the past thirty years, and many of these styles can be heard at one moment or another in her performances or recordings. In "Drinking Again" there are echoes of Dinah Washington, not the genteel Washington who did the song, but the later, more bluesy and raspy one; in a song like "Breaking Up Somebody's Home" there's a lot of Janis Joplin, but Joplin surpassed by the wonderful mellowness Midler brings to the hectoring, driving, sassy sounds; there's a bit learned from the jazz singing of Sarah Vaughan and much more from Billie Holiday, especially in Midler's vast improvement of the classic Lambert, Hendricks and Ross rendition of "Twisted."

Midler doesn't imitate or parody a specific singer through an entire song. Rather, like a person truly distracted by proliferating recollections, she will suddenly veer off from one coloration into another. This sometimes happens with an air of true discovery. As with most great jazz singers, she therefore never does a song exactly the same way twice. The avenue of experimentation is always left open. There are little bits of Martha Raye in the "I love, I love/I love, I love" sequence of "Back in the Bars Again," or of Monroe, when Midler announces "a toilet medley" for the Harlettes, who then proceed into 1950s songs touching everyone from The Chiffons to Sam Cook to the ubiquitous do-ron-ron sounds of the period. Then a switch to the Andrews Sisters and the 1940s, a straight and lovely "Sentimental Journey." The evocations aren't always of women, and in some of the louder pieces, like "The Bitch Is Back," she momentarily slips into Dylan's rapid, snarling, sputtering of words, each precisely articulated. Many times there's a slightly preoccupied air about her, part, again, of her being outside and inside the show all at once, but part, too, of her being the kind of performer who is all the while inquiring into the historical resonances of what she's doing at the moment.

The extraordinary fluctuations of Bette Midler's performance bring up a central problem which has always beset high arts but which popular art has only recently confronted. What are the uses, misuses, and dangers of nostalgic evocation, especially when the material for nostalgia is sometimes only a few years old? Midler's nostalgic predilections are part of a trend in popular entertainment, but her expression of it, compared to the nostalgia of a group like The Manhattan Transfer, is perhaps unparalleled in critical awareness. The degree to which such a performer responds to the pressures of repetition is a measure, I suspect, of the fact that popular culture cannot really feed on itself as high culture has conspicuously been able to do—witness the pastiche of a Joyce, an Eliot, a Pynchon—without getting thinner as a result, and without losing the audience. Finally the audience is as dense about pop as about high culture if it cannot feel the historical as distinct from merely sentimental or campy significances.

Midler's nostalgic strain is as original, culturally suggestive and powerfully entertaining as anything now going on in the theater. She has included the kind of nostalgia familiar enough in pop entertainment—like the emulative allusions to Billie Holiday's latter-day jazz style in "We'll Be Together Again," along with vocal glances at Ella Fitzgerald and Louis Armstrong; or the put-downs of Helen Reddy in her version of "Delta Dawn"—but her nostalgia moves beyond imitation. More important, and with little precedent except in the work of certain rock groups like the Beatles,* are the amalgamated allusions to a number of different singers and musical styles that can

---

*Whom I have discussed at length in an essay entitled, "Learning from the Beatles," in *The Performing Self* (1971).

occur in a single number, as in "Back in the Bars Again" at the end of the first half of her 1975 revue. The setting, a drab, unhappy, anonymously located bar, finds Midler standing there like an eager single on her one night off, looking into a juke-box—"Oh, what a hot box." In tones of sweet but deadly enthusiasm she mulls over her choices, talking as if to herself about the list of attractions: Jerry Vale (who did "Shadow of Your Smile"), Domenico Modugno (who inflicted "Volare" on the Western world for most of the 1950s), Wayne Newton (the chubby hermaphroditically voiced singer of the country-western songs for which Midler has a particular loathing), Tammy Wynette (another country-western singer, known especially for "Stand by Your Man"). "You do that, Tammy," says the disingenuous Midler. Here, as throughout the show, her detestation for the mediocre in pop culture, including a more recent example like Olivia Newton-John, is surpassed only by her beautifully rendered affections, however teasing at times, of the likes of Fanny Brice or Martha Raye or again and always Billie Holiday.

Midler is a pop artist whose whole tendency is classical. Very little of what she does is a direct expression of personal feeling. Rather, it is meant to reveal her place in a tradition about which she is fully, critically, impersonally aware. The evolution of the classical tendency and of impersonality in popular music generally is as yet an uninvestigated phenomenon. It's mostly lost on an audience, high or low, which hasn't learned how to listen to what the performer is really doing. Midler's kind of compacted, accelerated commentaries on other performers and on certain kinds of musical style began, I think, in the mid-1960s, and had a corollary development in Ronald Tavel's *Theater of the Ridiculous.* Such developments were direct results of a new kind of expert minority audience for film and, especially, popular music. Thanks to the enlarged capacities for electronic recording, there developed a taste for the overlappings of stylized sound, the kind of thing one can hear on certain cuts of the Beatles' *Magical*

Mystery Tour, like "All You Need Is Love," which passes from the French National Anthem, through an echo of Charlie Chaplin, then through sounds of the blues and boogie-woogie, until at the end it seems to be swept up and dispersed into the musical history of which it is a part and into the electronics by which that history has been made available: at the end of the piece, we hear what can only be the sounds of a radio at night, fading and drifting among the signals of different stations.

Midler is remarkable because all by herself she can make her voice the locus for the pop music of the last three or four decades. With her voice she does what certain writers have attempted on paper—Allen Ginsberg and William Burroughs, for example, with their experiments in cutting out passages from different places and randomly assembling them into collages of meaning; or Norman Mailer, who offers in *Why Are We in Vietnam?* passages meant to duplicate electrified disc-jockey talk, a jigsaw of various American speech styles and of the social portraiture that goes with them; or Gore Vidal, with his cinematic collages in *Myra Breckenridge*; or Thomas Pynchon, who has the capacity to dislocate us in one sentence from a mood appropriate to, say, Captain Marvel into another, more appropriate to an elegy for lost American signs and signatures. All these writers are, finally, quixotically patriotic—and so is Midler; they are haunted, as she is, by the overwhelming and grotesque admixtures of American objects, American sounds, swamped by nostalgia for so many things that they can't neatly sort them out.

What this means is that a revue like Midler's—including massive stage machinery of such American artifacts as jukeboxes and a huge plastic figure of King Kong on his skyscraper, holding Midler in his paw—is given less to comments on life, though there is an abundance of these, than to comments on styles of life, styles which have affected (and often cheapened) the life of ordinary people who grew up since World War II. Style is to the fore, and whether the media really are the message,

Midler's message is about media. It is a brilliant, precarious, and necessarily flawed expression of a relatively new but general self-consciousness about the objects of pop culture, especially about the way these have possessed our imaginations all the more for being wholly commercialized, mostly electronic, and therefore extraordinarily ephemeral. We get nostalgic about very recent things simply because they are so quickly snatched from us and replaced by something new.

At a moment both funny and sad, as the songs in "Back in the Bars Again" race by her, Midler could be heard shouting in mock-adolescent anguish, as if to stop the process of accelerated loss, as if to preclude the nostalgia creeping over her, "That's my fay-vor-rit pah't." A lot of feeling, however shabby some might suppose it to be, is stored up in the stuff of pop culture, as it is in the toys of childhood, particularly in America, because American youth have been able to afford the machines which are the instruments by which much of this stuff has come into existence as sight or sound. What old tattered photographs were to earlier generations, recordings and film—neither old nor tattered—are to present ones. That is why Midler's particular way of expressing nostalgia needs to be taken as seriously, as studiously, as some of the literary manifestations I've mentioned, though this does *not* mean that we should think of it as equivalently good or satisfying.

And why not? Because the vogue of nostalgia in the popular arts is the result less of the inherent strengths of old materials, old songs and artifacts, than of the technologies of commercial entertainment. The persistent fame of certain old stars like Mae West or W. C. Fields is a result of the stubborn memory and taste of people who are disposed more to higher than to pop culture, but the fantastic restitution to popularity of many others, including some of those parodied by Midler, is the result of the commercial need continually to drag up from the bottom whatever might even possibly be resold. A lot of this kind of junk was in Midler's show, and she knew it. She also knew that it ceases to be interesting after the first time it's heard, if it's interesting even then, and after that either bores or sickens the listeners, which forces the performers into even more blatant expressions of self-consciousness, catering only to that part of the audience who "don't get it." A moment of enormous consequence—and a dividing line in the history of culture high and low—occurred when it became possible for kids, or anyone, to sit at home and create a medley of sights or sounds, splicing together in film or tape whatever they chose from whatever year or decade. But only certain highly intelligent people have taken advantage of this great change, by which anyone coming to consciousness after 1950, like Midler, could become scholars, so to speak, of every performer from Humphrey Bogart to Baby Snooks. Television and hi-fi thus became, for aficionados of low or pop culture, the equivalent of the *Oxford Book of English Verse* for high.

New technologies did for low or mass or pop culture what the techniques of Pound and Eliot and Joyce had done for literary culture. It made what Eliot calls "a simultaneous order," and this is the very thing one hears in Midler's songs. It's easy to be misunderstood in these matters by high-cultural paranoids, so let it be said carefully. To wit: structurally—not in quality, not in so-called contributions to Western culture, not in what it does to the traditions of art, but structurally—there is no difference between the juxtapositions of style in sections of *The Waste Land* and the juxtapositions in sections of *Clams on the Half Shell.* "Did he really *say* that?" Yes, I did, but scarcely to suggest that Midler is T. S. Eliot. It is to suggest, rather, that by her achievement she lets us see how pop and high culture in this century partake of some of the same characteristics, especially when it comes to nostalgic allusiveness. And having said that, and found reasons for it in the technology of commercialized mass media, we can then see why the enterprise of pop culture can be so difficult to sustain, particularly when carried out by someone as special as Bette Midler, so nervous, so easily demoralized.

Unlike the nostalgic materials brought forth in *The Waste Land*, those in pop culture are seldom as deeply rooted in the human imagination, in the myths which have possessed that imagination for centuries. Instead, the materials of pop culture are intricately subservient to a form of commercialism intent on built-in obsolescence. That was the special burden which Midler faced every night and which most of her audience were unable to share with her. They really "don't get it." But how could they be expected to? The very resources of pop culture Midler explored and exploited were transmitted, after all, by a technology which at the same time habituates all of us to inattention. It teaches us to say "hello" to old people, old things, but not to say, as this altogether admirable performer asks us to, "hello in there."

7

ERASING AMERICA

⁘

I. Baudrillard's America Deserta

"I think, therefore I am." This wasn't meant to apply only to those for whom thinking is a line of work, though that appears to be the operating assumption of the celebrated French sociolo-gist-philosopher Jean Baudrillard in *America* (1988), now trans-lated into English. At first the reader might wonder why a prose as dense as his should be made more so by having it, in the American edition, stretched across pages of a width and gloss more appropriate to an otherwise agreeably produced and illus-trated coffee-table book. But if not actually initiated by the author, the design must have been done to please him, intent as he is on the primacy of the visual image. The design is probably meant to be a comeuppance for the credulous, any American or Parisian, who might harbor a sentimental preference for the cul-tural supremacy of the printed word, even while this is actually the hidden preference of the author himself. At several points, such people are objects of the author's scorn for not having yet achieved his own fascinated horror and elation in response to the United States, "the great hologram" where "cinema is true because it is the whole of space, the whole way of life that are cinematic." In this "tactile, fragile, mobile, superficial culture," he wants to discover the destiny that lies in wait for Europe.

His America is a country without persons—not one is introduced—and for that matter without people, these having been absorbed into his theories of hyperreality and simulation. Seventeen thousand runners in the New York Marathon move him to tears because, "collectively, they might seem to be bringing the message of catastrophe for the human race." Since the European discovery of this continent, Americans have gotten used to being treated in this way, as mere shadows on a blankness asking to be inscribed with images about the world's "future," especially catastrophic ones. Baudrillard thus joins a grand tradition of European imperialism, intellectual imperialism, that is, though intellectual imperialism is not a problem that seems ever to have occurred to him.

His most lyrical descriptions are of the deserts, evidence that the country as a whole consists in its very landscape only of space waiting to be filled with thinking of his own. Using a terminology that I'll explain in a moment, he says that the deserts have denoted "the emptiness, the radical nudity that is the background of every human institution. At the same time they designated human institutions as a metaphor of that emptiness and the work of man as the continuity of the desert, culture as a mirage and as the perpetuity of the simulacrum." Or, later, "the whole of America is a desert. Culture exists there in a wild state; it sacrifices all intellect, all aesthetics in a process of literal transcription into the real."

D. H. Lawrence, with Tocqueville one of the most intuitive of all foreign writers about America, was able in a work like *St. Mawr* to see the actual pathos of American figurations of "desert" and "space" as Baudrillard can't, the pathos of desire that wants to free itself from submission to the objects, or signs, conventionally provided for it. This is a preoccupation found everywhere in American writing, from James Fenimore Cooper to Emerson, from Mark Twain to Whitman and Henry James, from Theodore Dreiser to Willa Cather, on to Norman Mailer and Thomas Pynchon. Lawrence's two Englishwomen, Lou Witt and her acerbic mother, are to be found at the end of the story in the deserts of New Mexico, where the younger woman, like the New England woman who occupied the ranch before her, expects to find "another world" in a space where "man does not exist," and has hopes of "living through the eyes into the distance." The story is a tough allegorization of an American-Romantic transposition of desire into spaces wiped clear of complicating human presences; and as in his *Studies in Classic American Literature,* Lawrence shows, no less than have American writers of the past, the heroic impossibility of the venture. Baudrillard, who refers vaguely to the Puritans, in fact knows nothing whatever of American history or American literature, and therefore has no difficulty in declaring the United States has neither. *"America is the only remaining primitive society"* (his italics) because it is "lacking a past through which to reflect" on itself.

This attempt to make America into the "future" of Europe by erasing any evidences of its own cultural past is only preliminary to the larger and more personal ambitions of the book. And these are to show that the "future" cannot be understood or even perceived by anyone who remains stuck in the kinds of thinking to which Baudrillard, as a European, admits to being indebted, the thinking particularly of the Frankfurt School and of Walter Benjamin. America, both the place and the book as he has conceived them, is invented to demonstrate that any theories that have not evolved as Baudrillard's have done are now, no less than persons and people, an encumbrance.

In several previous works, a number of which have also been translated into English, Baudrillard places himself at the revisionary end of a line that begins with Marx and his commodity law of value and was later variously transformed by Benjamin, as in his most famous essay, "The Work of Art in the Age of Mechanical Reproduction," by Herbert Marcuse in *One-Dimensional Man,* a major text for the 1960s, and by the writings of Marshall McLuhan on the semiology of an electronic environment in which "the medium is the message." Together and in different ways, these writers gradually dislodged Marx's commodity law of value, a development Benjamin had predicted, and replaced it with codes of signification the ceaseless permutations of which make value itself increasingly elusive and indeterminate.

These codes govern what Baudrillard calls "simulation" and the production of "hyperrealism." That is, just as commodities ceased to refer directly to value, so signs have ceased to refer to things. They have come to refer only to other signs, in endless proliferation. "The signs no longer designate anything at all," Baudrillard says in *The Mirror of Production,* "only other signs." Because signs refer to nothing of substance, nothing you can put your hand on, they create desires and demands that are insatiable, a situation for which Baudrillard reserves the word "obscenity." And because the perpetuation of the process depends on the creation of needs that cannot be satisfied, the production of signs must be continuously accelerated in order to produce new realities, none of which can be verified outside the process itself. This is what he calls "hyperreality." While all this has become prophetic gospel to its adherents, it is of course only a hypothesis, like any other. The degree of assent you give it may depend on how little or how much the process is complicated by bringing into it the possibilities of human resistance and discrimination with respect to signs. Or it may depend on the degree to which the process is or is not considered unique to this century. Is the production of needs and desires any more dependent now on electronic media, for example, than it was in the past on, say, parades, religious rituals, insignia of rank, architecture, the superstitions that attend certain natural occurrences?

These are only some of the factors that ought to produce skepticism, and therefore a more moderate tone in which to discuss the electronic proliferation of signs. Instead, the tone is nearly always hyperbolic and apocalyptic. When, as is often the case, this rhetoric is directed at America, as it has been in recent decades by Marcuse, Mailer, Pynchon, DeLillo, and others, it tends to make workaday accounts sound hopelessly complacent.

The problem with the crisis rhetoric that accompanies theories of simulation and hyperreality like Baudrillard's is not merely that it flouts what he himself calls the "general code of abstract rationality." More important, it fails to take account of the, to me, obvious fact that "reproduction" has always and forever been the only way in which human beings have been able to acknowledge reality and to talk about it. For much longer than electronic forms of reproduction have existed, language itself has been a form of reproduction. And not just in embossed Bibles: reproduction is part of the very inflections of daily speech. The so-called shock of modernity is a vastly overstated one, and since Benjamin coined that phrase it has come to mean almost entirely a scowling and jowling about the frightful consequences of television or, for that matter, photography. Televisual images, so it is alleged, have made human beings themselves into simulacra, into hyperreal and encoded figments, models of simulation to a point where they can no longer know what simulation is. "The Americans for their part," says Baudrillard, "have no sense of simulation. They are themselves simulation in its most developed state, but they have no language in which to describe it."

Why is it, then, that any moderately bright American undergraduate can tell you the same thing—about other undergraduates, of course? The hyperventilations about the televisual in Baudrillard's *America* are finally little different, to digress into politics for a moment, from most analyses of Presidential elections bandied about by television anchormen. With reference only to the election campaign closest to the publication date of this translation—between George Bush and Michael Dukakis in 1988—most press reports ascribed Bush's victory, in good part, to a brutal Republican media blitz in August and September, in which Governor Dukakis was ridiculed as a mushy liberal opposed to the pledge of allegiance, held responsible for garbage found floating in Boston Harbor, and made complicit with a conspicuously black figure named Willie Horton, a convicted murderer let out of jail by the Governor on weekend passes, the better, presumably, to do his thing. This sort of hype was supposed to have duped the public.

It is just as likely that most viewers were sufficiently aware of what the footage was designed to do to them and were able to assess it with a by now well-trained and wary eye for the techniques of advertising. Bush may well have lost as many votes as he gained by the negative commercials. If they were effective, it was not because people believed them but because, as the Bush staff had hoped, Dukakis did not give voters anything else to believe in. Wasting precious weeks early in the campaign on squirish visits to town meetings in western Massachusetts, none of them worth national coverage, he failed to define himself or the issues in such a way as to make the charges against him merely trivial. It was he who wanted the campaign to turn on the issue of competence, and his conduct of the media war was a fair test of his competence, especially since as President he would need to face the potentially devastating coverage meted out almost daily to Presidents Nixon and Carter, to the beloved great communicator himself, President Reagan, and, notably, to President Clinton. Dukakis had all the money he needed, media people easily as tough as Bush's, and the advice of another liberal Governor, Mario Cuomo of New York, who had managed to brush off similar mud-slinging. But through some combination of insularity, rigidity, and an immigrant's son's desire to appear well-bred (Bush had only to appear less so), he flunked.

My point is that the image made by a candidate on television is one of the perfectly valid and telling "reproductions" that voters can go on. It is as good and perhaps more reliable than "reproductions" of the kind that existed before the advent of television. Thus, in response to a horrendous first question in the second debate between the presidential candidates—how he would feel about capital punishment if his own wife were raped and murdered—Dukakis gave an answer worthy of a mechanical mouse. He was rightly judged on this occasion as someone who in a crisis probably could not bring to his decisions a trustworthy range of human feelings. He didn't even manage to say that the killing of his wife would of course make him feel murderous, as indeed the question itself should have, but that besides being a husband he was a public servant charged with enforcing the law dispassionately, and would do his best to meet these different and conflicting obligations. The media told some unattractive truths about Dukakis while giving a none too flattering image of Bush, who won a small majority of the only 50.4 percent of eligible voters who went to the polls, the smallest percentage since 1924. He won because he appeared—quite accurately, I think—as marginally the better of two weak candidates.

Many Americans, but not in Baudrillard's book, are quite capable of using the media and of not being used by them. They make complicated and sensible decisions on the basis of images, a fact that intellectualists, blind to the fact that *their* language is also media, are usually loath to concede. To do so would be to put at risk those platitudes of the anti-technologists that are as old as literature itself, and manifest in, say, Henry Miller's view of America as an air-conditioned nightmare, in Mailer's attacks on plastic, in the brilliant fictional exploration by Don DeLillo and Gore Vidal of how television images get confused with life, and now in Baudrillard's hopped-up vision of America as the place where one can witness, in the form of apocalyptic orgy, "the disappearance of history and the real in the televisual."

The kinds of power over the viewer of which electronic media are capable need to be better understood, no less than does the power exercised in and by literature. Baudrillard's self-promoting rhetoric only frustrates such efforts, as in his use of words like "real" and "history." Are we to assume that, in some better world than ours, "history" and some concept of the "real" existed in a pure state, uncontaminated by mediation? Behind literary-intellectual histrionics about the unprecedented dangers of modern technology, there almost always lurks a soft idealization of a prior literary culture and of earlier times, as in Marcuse. Literature itself, often more tough-minded than interpretations of it, treats these idealizations for what they are—pastoral mythologizing. *The Faerie Queene* was indicating as much four hundred years ago. What, then, can it mean when Baudrillard says that "'the marketing immunity' of governments is similar to that of the major brands of washing powder" when, without the hip references, an identical observation could be made of almost any government since the beginning of time?

Though anti-technological pastoralists are too politically devious to admit it, the vital difference for them between our own and earlier centuries is simply, and I think very insidiously, this: that the "immunity" of which Baudrillard speaks needs no longer to be purchased by governments from educated courtiers like himself, but can be gotten from the masses. That is, the virulence of the attacks on electronic media can be understood as expressing the fear that the media empower people in the mass as never before and dispel the aura that still attaches to the literary culture from which these people feel excluded. This is a possibility worth considering, because it brings attention to issues that cannot fail to discomfit die-hard populists no less than anti-technological pastoralists. The issues include the worldwide resurgence over the last twenty years of religious fundamentalism, for example, a phenomenon that shows the extent to which people in the mass are stubbornly and perhaps forever possessed of ancient superstitions whose strength and political utility have nothing significantly to do with the use of electronic media. Indeed, it might have been expected, especially in videoland America, that some unappeasable desires of the kind supposedly created by Baudrillard's proliferating images would have emerged long since to put such superstitions out of mind once and for all. It seems instead that their terrifying persistence depends on cultural, racial, religious, and attendant sexual dogmas that are transmitted generation to generation, through circuits and images that are stronger, more complicated, and more insidious than technological ones.

Was authority, including political authority, any more beneficent in the sixteenth century, when some of these same dogmas were particularly strong, or was government then any less clever at "marketing" itself, especially when it wanted support for foreign military adventure? Only the blindness of a literary cultural conservatism not importantly different from Allan Bloom's in *The Closing of the American Mind*—a book as ignorant as Baudrillard's of American history and American writing—can explain the heedless complaint that, thanks to the land of hyperreality, "no one keeps count of the mistakes made by the world's political leaders any more, mistakes which, in days gone by, would have brought about their downfall . . . The people no longer take pride in their leaders and the leaders no longer pride themselves on their decisions."

The version of a European past which we can infer from this passage, and throughout this book, is created by a writer who likes to couple the words "real" and "history," a fabrication born of the need to say something more fabricated still about the televisual future of Europe as represented, he believes, in the United States. It is this same United States, be it remembered, that has the media to thank for bringing the Watergate revelations into the

open, even while President Giscard d'Estaing used French law
and tradition to block the media's reports about his own and his
government's dealings with Jean Bedel Bokassa, the French Army
stooge who became the cannibal emperor of the Central African
Republic.

   Baudrillard's book is an example of the extraordinary extent to
which West European writers feel free to treat America nearly
as shamefully, for ideological purposes, as, in Edward Said's brilliant dissections, they have treated the Orient. "America" is their
inevitable metaphor for "modernity," in opposition to the
metaphoric past called "Europe," and just about anything at all
can be said about it. This is apparent enough even in a recent
and unnecessary little gathering of Albert Camus's *American
Journals*, two-thirds of which concern his trip to South America
in 1949. The comments on a trip he made to the United States in
1946 deserve the consideration duly accorded a postcard from
someone who feels compelled to send it. We are told that "no
one ever has change in this country" and that "everyone looks
like they've stepped out of a B-film." Camus was no luckier in his
conversations, as when he hears from someone identified simply
as Tucci (probably Niccolo) the utterly numbing observation
that "human relationships are very easy here because there are
no human relationships." In that case he should have gotten out
on the town immediately, I would think. A half century later
Baudrillard is also bothered by evidence that "relationships" are
one of the few scarcities in the New World. He complains several times that people do not look at him or at one another—not
only in New York City but in California, which just happens to
be the cruisiest of all the states. I suspect he is not reporting
what happened to him in either place but remembering what
happened to Baudelaire in the streets of Paris: only unreturned
glances, according to Benjamin's *Illuminations*. "The expectation roused by the human eye," Benjamin writes, "is not ful-
filled." As we all know, that does sometimes happen.

Any book is in some ways an act of self-promotion, and if the self is sufficiently imposing this may work greatly to the book's formal and stylistic advantage. The style of the later Henry James, omnivorously determined that nothing be lost, is a case in point; another is the show-off technical brilliance of Joyce's *Ulysses,* where the author exults in being a master of the novelistic forms he intends to put out of commission. Baudrillard would like similar benefits to accrue to his efforts to expropriate America in the service of his theories. This expectation explains why there is so much tempestuous energy in the writing of *America.* Baudrillard wants it inferred from his style that he has escaped academic inertia, of the New World or Old, "these Californian scholars with monomaniacal passions for things French or Marxist." He confesses at one point that he wants "to excentre myself, to become eccentric," and to do so "in a place that is the centre of the world." Toward the end of the book, he even shows some uneasiness about his own heated perceptions: "perhaps Americans are quite simply vulgar, and the meta-vulgarity is merely something I have dreamt up."

There are hints, in other words, of his being as watchful of his own as of America's performance, conscious of the effort of language by which he hopes to register his momentary transformations from European savant to new American mutant and back again. His style therefore tries, far too energetically, to catch the tempo of "this spectral form of civilization which these Americans have invented" and which he finds by turns appalling and amazing. The prose is filled with sudden disjunctions of tone ("a form realizing itself in its pure operation and in pure circulation [hello Karl!]"); it is given to obtuse assertions ("the jogger commits suicide by running up and down the beach") which are supposed to redeem themselves as metaphor; it is full of heavy terminological breathing ("the general cryogenization of emotions") which in the same paragraph expires in banalities scarcely meant to be comic in a book where comedy is in very short supply indeed ("Americans have no identity but they have wonderful teeth"). Despite moments in Wistful Vista ("where are the days when girls used to wear bracelets on their ankles?"), he sounds more often like an irate and tired parent at meetings of the local school board ("just look at the child sitting in front of his computer at school: do you think he has been made interactive, opened up to the world?"). This is more the specter of Thornton Wilder than the "spectral America where everything depends on the existence of the ray of light bearing the objects."

And so it goes, replete with patent absurdities ("there are no cops in New York"). The result is a more than average demand on the reader's leniency, as if surely the author must mean much more than he is saying. Modernist texts have accustomed readers to persevere in spite of rebuffs of this kind so long as there are eventual rewards. Ideally, these consist not of meanings withheld but of glimpses into those risky, often embarrassing moments when a writer is most urgently involved in the difficult task of finding out for himself meanings that can only be discovered in his way of handling the subject. Baudrillard, alas, pushes his luck. His appreciation of authors who pull off this sort of thing is evident in his *"Oublier Foucault,"* a monograph translated into English as "Forgetting Foucault" (*Humanities and Society*, Winter 1980). Foucault's discourse, he says, duplicates the operations of power which it also proposes to trace. In illustration, he describes how "the smallest qualifiers find their way into the slightest interstices of meaning; clauses and chapters wind into spirals; a magistral art of decentring allows the opening of new spaces (spaces of power and of discourse) which are immediately covered up by the meticulous outpouring of Foucault's writing." By means of such analyses he hopes to show that "Foucault's is not therefore a discourse of truth but a mythic discourse"—a distinction that must allow for the fact that mythic discourse can itself produce truths, or why would anyone care about it? The real targets of his distinction are those academics who end up taking from Foucault "the truth and nothing but the truth."

Baudrillard would like to create a mythic discourse for himself, and *America* is a failed effort to do so. For him America is the place and now is the moment at which the signs of the future are being produced in an irresistible flow of heat and light. His style is correspondingly hot, an effort to mimic the cinematic, televisual, kinetic processes by which the mass media, like the acceleration of heat in the desert, bring about "a barely perceptible evaporation of meaning." Equivalent to Foucault's myth of power would be his own myth of desire, produced by the acceleration of signs. Desire is more ubiquitous than power, more immediately visible, full of more obvious blandishments. Naïvely, he intends to use language in a manner approximate to the grotesque mixtures of effect and abrupt distortions of electronic media, all in the service of that frantic self-referentiality which produces, as he says of video-stereo culture, "a sure intensity and deeper meaninglessness."

II. *Martin Amis's Inferno*

I write this in the veritable crunch of Martin Amis's "moronic inferno": the weekend of July 4 in New York City. The date marks the independence of the colonies from British rule, and in this year of 1986 it includes an extravaganza honoring the restoration of the Statue of Liberty on its hundredth birthday. There are Liberty T-shirts, Liberty charcoal briquettes, Liberty dry-roasted peanuts, along with the greatest fireworks display in the nation's history and the greatest massing of ships, including tall sailing ships from around the world, since the Second World War. Besides President Ronald Reagan ("Here's Ronnie: On the Road with Reagan" is the title of one of Martin Amis's essays), there is President François Mitterrand of France and an unidentified elderly woman who, when asked by a television interviewer why she, too, loved the Statue of Liberty, responded that she loved it because it looked so much like Elvis Presley.

All the better that the woman didn't intend to be subversive or satirical. Her remark is typical of the liberating inflections that can be heard all the time from unassuming people. They suggest that America and Americans are not yet as bad, or as flat-minded, as they have positioned themselves to be. Amis is oblivious to little touches of this sort, to a degree that makes unfortunately true of him a characterization he unjustly offers of Joan Didion: at no point does he "think about the sort of people who [he] would never normally have cause to come across" in his journalistic duties. The essays collected in *The Moronic Inferno: And Other Visits to America,* with some added links and post-scripts, were written over the past several years for various newspapers and journals, particularly the London weekly *The Observer.*

They include mere snippets, like a note on the resurrection of *Vanity Fair,* or on William Burroughs ("most of Burroughs is trash"), or on Kurt Vonnegut. There are more extensive review-interviews of writers such as Gore Vidal ("I cannot get through Vidal's fiction") and of film directors such as Brian De Palma (his films "make no sense") and Steven Spielberg. There are news-story commentaries, on "The Case of Claus von Bülow" and on "The Killings in Atlanta," where Amis discovers that the Peachtree Plaza Hotel is "a billion dollar masterpiece of American efficiency, luxury, and robotic good manners." And there are predictably disapproving reports on Jerry Falwell's evangelical Right and on Hugh Hefner and his Key Clubs, which have since been banished from the Playboy empire. The best items are the sensitive and well-researched "Double Jeopardy: Making Sense of AIDS" and "Gloria Steinem and the Feminist Utopia." The book begins and ends with obsequies to Saul Bellow. "Saul Bellow," we are assured, "really is a great American writer."

The "really" is quite unnecessary, since, so far as Amis's reading has taken him, all other American writers are more or less bush-league. The book's title is taken from a phrase in Bellow's

Humboldt's Gift (Bellow himself found it in Wyndham Lewis), and Amis's use of it, which is much broader than Bellow's, is a clue to his rather awkward, retrospective ambitions for this collection. The title encourages one to suppose that a reportorial assignment has somehow been transformed into a cultural one without any intervening effort at rewriting or rethinking. And yet he admits that nearly all the essays "were written left handed"— not by choice, that is, but at the request of various editors. No wonder he himself betrays some uncertainty about the results. We're told first that he had been asked on a couple of occasions "to write a book about America"; then, that in going over his selected journalism, he discovered that "I had already written a book about America"; then, that he is giving us merely "a collection of peripatetic journalism"; and finally, that the portentous title does not in fact refer to America: "The moronic inferno is not a peculiarly American condition. It is global and perhaps eternal. It is also, of course, primarily a metaphor, a metaphor for human infamy: mass, gross, ever distracting human infamy."

Amis is an OK writer, but he shouldn't expect his prose to carry that kind of baggage. He tends to chug and wheeze with incremental repetitions whenever it occurs to him that he ought to be solemn. He has been made anxious over the years, I suspect, by such experiences as the one he reports in "Diana Trilling at Claremont Avenue." In response to an "incautious remark, illiberal in tendency," made by him at their first meeting in London's Connaught Hotel, Mrs. Trilling in the company of her husband, Lionel, "cracked her teacup into its saucer and said 'Do you really mean that? Then what are we doing here? Why are we sitting here having tea with this person?'" Amis, who prefers not to be respectful to very much, is nonetheless enthralled at any hint that there are Standards and that the Standards are at work, so that when he again sees Mrs. Trilling for tea, this time in her Manhattan apartment, he describes the end of their meeting on a half-plaintive and wholly exalted note:

"'But there aren't many people like you,' I said cautiously. 'You're a clear thinker.' 'That's right. Too clear perhaps,' said Mrs. Trilling." He has learned when to pass the cookies but has forgotten, as Mrs. Trilling seldom does, when to be amused.

The trouble is, Amis doesn't seem to have much fun on his visits. One reason is that he has yet to master a requirement of good cultural reporting: that you must learn how to enjoy a lot of things you disapprove of, and that you have to find out why some other people seem to enjoy them instinctively. There are, inevitably, figures whose delight in themselves is contagious, like Gloria Steinem, Truman Capote, and Gore Vidal, though even in these cases Amis has to be pulled into the party, and he manages so successfully to resist the charm, energy, and audacity of Norman Mailer that he is left only with personal abuse: "In the United States, provided you are Norman Mailer, it seems you can act like a maniac for forty years—and survive, prosper and multiply, and write the books. The work is what it is: sublime, ridiculous, always interesting. But the deeds—the human works—are a monotonous disgrace." Why so heavy a hand? The fact that the "human works" conspicuously include nearly a dozen bright, healthy, and happy offspring, all of them devoted to a father who remains friendly to their various mothers, is the kind of factor Amis is so determined to miss that he shouldn't have brought the matter up in the first place.

Bellow might have told him that it is always dangerous to try to be interesting when you are insufficiently engaged in a personal way with your subjects. In one of his good moments (*Salmagundi,* No. 30, Summer 1975), Bellow allowed that, "if I were terribly moralistic I would scold everyone about this: that people do feel that there's something wrong, unappetizing, unappealing in the ordinary—that they have to do something supererogatory, make themselves appeal; that the world is very boring, that they, themselves, are very boring and that they must discover some way not to be." While Amis the journalist cannot

afford to be boring or bored, he never wants to let himself go, to
risk the self-exposures of an unguarded liking for something
other than the monumental. Deeply hostile to artists who willingly put themselves forward in their work, like Philip Roth,
Woody Allen, and Mailer, he is a sort of neoclassicist manqué,
distressed by a force of monstrosity, appetite, and vulgarity
which he calls "America." In Florida he boasts, "Drop me down
anywhere in America and I'll tell you where I am: in America,"
while in the New York of Gloria Steinem he complains, "As soon
as you leave New York you see how monstrously various, how
humanly balkanized America really is."

Nice thing about America, you can say anything you want
about it, even if it's contradictory. "American novels are big all
right," he tells us in the opening piece on Bellow, "but partly
because America is big too," a bromide discarded long since by
anyone who has bothered to ask himself why, in that case, *Mid-
dlemarch* and *Ulysses* are not small. On his visit to Palm Beach
("Never in my life have I seen such clogged, stifling luxury"), he
drives inland and discovers himself "immediately confronted by
the booming chaos of middle America," a transition achieved
less, I suspect, by driving than by typing. If wearing name tags
has to be mentioned in the essay on Ronald Reagan, what can be
said about them? Obviously, that this is "something that Americans especially like doing," and if nothing else can be made out
of the conviviality of the news cameramen on the campaign
plane, then why not propose that "their laughter, like so much
American laughter, did not express high spirits but a willed
raucousness." Enough, I say, of this willed raucousness! If,
as he proposes in "Mr. Vidal: Unpatriotic Gore," "humorless
people . . . include a great many Americans" who nonetheless
obligingly laugh a good deal, then Amis's style seems to me better suited to them than to his compatriots, with their cagey risi-
bility. Anyway, Americans "tend to reduce argument to a babble
of interested personalities." And so it goes. Hugh Hefner's

alleged confusions of money and sex, consumerism and need, are "a very American mix," while euphemisms represent "a very American dishonesty." And when evocations of America are not put to work in place of a more personally engaged attentiveness, the function is just as glibly assigned to the easily maligned 1960s: the usual rag bag of "Sixties sophistries" or "the Sixties, that golden age of high energy and low art," though, as it happens, it was a triumphant decade in American painting (which is mentioned not at all), in fiction (notably with Thomas Pynchon, who is referred to once), and in poetry, with Elizabeth Bishop, John Ashbery, and Robert Lowell, to name only a few artists who are not mentioned anywhere in the book.

I'm not suggesting that a survey is the answer; rather, that Amis's rhetoric and buzz words exist in default of a willingness to find what he might have looked for. There is instead a kind of tightness and huffiness, issuing in such phrases as "our present permissiveness about turning tragedy into entertainment"— even though to some of us that is what a lot of literature tries to do—in the course of making a quite misleading point about "non-fiction fiction." The trouble, so he opines, is that "what is missing . . . is moral imagination, moral artistry. The facts cannot be arranged to give them moral point."

When Amis drums on a word like that, you know he's winding up for a not very effective delivery. "The facts" come into existence only when someone recognizes them as such, which is a human arrangement to begin with. And even assuming, which no historian or reporter in his or her right mind ever would, that in non-fiction "the facts" cannot be arranged to make a moral point, it is always the case that these "facts" are nonetheless arranged and rearranged by the style in which they are rendered, as a moralist like Gibbon would have shown Amis long before Truman Capote's *In Cold Blood.*

Except at points in the articles on Steinem, on AIDS, and on Vidal, it is mostly impossible to find in Amis's style those local, intimate, inquisitive reactions that might complicate the settled opinions of the communities for which he writes. He would like to suppose himself exempt from the criticisms he makes of Joan Didion, and for the reason that he assumes that what he calls "literature" is on his side, though I'm afraid he has a way to go. "Probably all writers," he remarks, "are at some point briefly under the impression that they are in the forefront of disintegration and chaos, that they are among the first to live and work after things fell apart. The continuity such an impression ignores is a literary continuity. It routinely assimilates and domesticates more pressing burdens than Miss Didion's particular share of vivid, ephemeral horrors."

This is the familiar voice of a contemporary cultural conservatism trying to enlist a literature whose inner turmoils it fails or does not want to comprehend. There is, besides, a conspicuous inability to elicit such literary continuities as might have allowed Amis a better sense of the American scene and the American writers he visits. It isn't necessarily that he needs to read more, though that wouldn't hurt, but that he needs to discover *how* to read the complicated inflections I mentioned at the beginning. This is true especially of Bellow's novels. Their distinction resides not in what Amis calls their "High Style . . . and exalted voice appropriate to the twentieth century," a formula not only at odds with the actual experience of reading Bellow but so gaseous as to be applicable to any ambitious writer of any time. Bellow is most alive precisely in his capacity to extemporize a style in which ordinary slang, coterie usages, vulgarities, provincialities, and waywardness of speech continually work against the pontifications of characters like Mr. Sammler and Herzog, and in a manner contrived to redeem them. This is the sort of responsiveness, nuance, and play that Amis has not yet made his own.

III. Peter Conrad's Confusions

When the Redcoats first encountered colonial revolutionaries, they were quite unexpectedly beaten, and according to an anecdote in Harold Rosenberg's *The Tradition of the New,* they were beaten because they were the best-trained infantry in Europe. They had been so well trained that when they looked at the rough American terrain on which their opponents had chosen to meet them, they could not see it. Instead, what they saw was a European battlefield on which they expected to march in formation to meet and overwhelm a similar formation of enemy, rather than uncouth renegades shooting from behind trees. A gridiron of style, a trained mode of perception, preceded them into battle, creating the illusion that in front of them was only what they intended to find.

Though he doesn't mention Rosenberg, or any other critic for that matter, Peter Conrad, Fellow of Christ Church, Oxford, is convinced that a similar destiny was in store for the English writers of the nineteenth and twentieth centuries who "imagined" America during their visits to it. They imagined it not freely but in obedience to various preexistent notions both about the continent and about themselves. He locates these imaginative metamorphoses of America in the writings, in turn, of Frances Trollope, Anthony Trollope, and Charles Dickens (gathered under the heading "Institutional America"); Oscar Wilde and Rupert Brooke ("Aesthetic America"); Rudyard Kipling and R. L. Stevenson ("Epic [and Chivalric] America"); H. G. Wells ("Futuristic America"); D. H. Lawrence ("Primitive America"); W. H. Auden ("Theological America"); Aldous Huxley ("Psychedelic America"); and Christopher Isherwood ("Mystical America").

As the chapter titles suggest, each of these writers is alleged to see America as if it were shaped by literature or in conformity to a cluster of images. America for Trollope and Dickens becomes, therefore, a failed novel: in place of a society, it has institutions that destroy any possibility of "character." Wilde, and in a slightly different way Brooke, delighted in what displeased their predecessors: the failure of America to create any semblance of European private life meant for them the absence of domesticity, and a corresponding opportunity for the workings of perverse and decadent theories of aesthetic reform. Brooke is said to be different from Wilde because, whereas Wilde tried to "ally art with the muscularity of sport" during a visit to the Harvard gym, Brooke, reporting on a baseball game between Yale and Harvard, "more decadently turns sport into ballet," though why myth, religion, or Shakespeare are not also made "decadent" by being turned into ballet goes unexplained, unless for Conrad ballet itself is "decadent."

At first, Stevenson and Kipling were happy that America was an alternative to the Victorian novel, Conrad believes, since they were looking for the epic or chivalric romance. H. G. Wells was also happy at first—nearly everyone in the book eventually comes to think of the place as "hell"—since America represented "the novel's logical successor, science fiction." Lawrence expected to discover yet another answer to the moribund European novel in a mythological past existing beneath the institutional enterprising or technological surfaces.

Subsequent English visitors praised America for the very reason that it failed to live up to these earlier literary expectations. Because America has become a public "hell," it all the more affords, out of some benign neglect, a private haven for anyone's "thing." Auden, Conrad claims, could satisfy his infantilism while subscribing to the theology of Reinhold Niebuhr; Huxley could freely investigate the subliminal gods with the assistance of drugs; Isherwood can commune with Swami Prabhavananda along with any number of sun-tanned meditators and/or boyfriends. There is therefore a sequence to the "discoveries" or, rather, a progressive contraction, moving from institutional life that destroys individualism, through the promise of free exploration and rebirth, to the blank acceptance or celebration of self-extinction.

In the act of "discovering America," Conrad tells us in the introductory chapter, these writers were "discovering" themselves. Really? All of them were known to be what they were, for good or ill, before they even got to America. What happens in this book is that Conrad uses writers as he alleges they used America—as a *tabula rasa* on which freely to project what he prejudicially wants to report. But while it is obviously possible to think of America as a *tabula rasa,* it is not possible to think that way of the printed page—unless, that is, you are Mr. Conrad. The persons he describes are caricatures, often scurrilously drawn, of figures who can be otherwise known or accounted for. Where facts or what was actually written stand in his way, he blithely ignores, changes, or distorts.

An early example appears directly after his statement that in "discovering" America these writers were "discovering" themselves. Of Oscar Wilde's lecture tour in 1882, Conrad says, "America for him was a theatre, a place in which he could play at being himself and be handsomely paid for doing so. Wilde enjoys America because he can merchandize a self there, turn existence into gratuitous performance. America liberates him from the pieties of the society into which he was born, and changes his outlawry into celebrity." Wilde was not, of course, born into English society, whose "pieties" he satirized, but into Anglo-Irish society, and as a student at Trinity College, Dublin, he had already famously "played at being himself." Why would a man already cartooned in *Punch* and burlesqued by Gilbert and Sullivan in *Patience,* which had opened in New York and other American cities months before his arrival, still "need" America to "liberate" him or to make him celebrated? In what sense is a man, not convicted of any crime until 1895, who was to marry in 1884 and proceed to father two children, an "outlaw" in 1882? If Wilde had by then even come out of the closet, which he hadn't, it would have been at most into some private hallway protected from Conrad's or anyone's view. And what is "gratuitous" about a performance still crucial to an understanding of the history of literature and of cultural styles? Should he not have been "handsomely paid"? Should he have been paid less? At the other end of the book Conrad makes a remark about two of Wilde's later associates that adequately disposes of the issue of American income: Auden's admonishment of Isherwood for his work in Hollywood, he observes, combines "existential reprimand with a philistine's envy of the rewards."

Wherever you turn in this book Conrad sounds brisk, assured, giddy in his confident marshaling of terms and patterns; brisk, assured—and misleading. He is anxious always to be dazzling, outrageous, "brilliant" in adducing connections. The sentences move with a metronymic regularity never deflected by recalcitrant textual or historical evidence, and lest we choose to look at any of the works from which he takes his many quotations, he is careful not to supply page references, bibliography, or even the exact date of letters. Dickens, according to Conrad, decided that "America mortifies its victims by depriving them of their characters," so that *Martin Chuzzlewit,* which began to appear serially a year after Dickens's *American Notes,* has as its meaning that "promotion to institutional status is death as a character." There's no point arguing here against so flat a reading of either book, since it is offered merely as a windup to one of Conrad's bravura follies. At the end of the chapter he tells us:

> America revenged itself on Dickens by making him the victim of his own prophecy. It first made a public man of him, and then it killed him. His second trip there, between November 1868 and April 1869, ruined his health and hastened his fatal heart attack in 1870, and it did so because he allowed himself to become an institution, a commercial property freighted about the country by a lecture agency. . . . Selling himself to a delirious public, killing himself in order to bring his novels alive in dramatic readings, Dickens was suffering a morbid

American institutionalization. America exacts a penalty of those it celebrates and enriches: it had made a classic of him, and was urging him to confirm his immortality by dying.

Anyone who knows anything about Dickens is aware that he can be credited, more than any other figure in the history of literature, with institutionalizing the business of writing. America was only one of his lucrative territories, and a reason for the controversial nature of his first trip, in 1842, was his outspoken remarks on copyright protection for his own work. America did not "make a public man of him" any more than it made a "celebrity" of Wilde, and it had no responsibility for his business ventures as a public reader. Dickens undertook three major lecture tours in the British Isles (1858, 1861–65, 1866–67) before his second tour in America. Contrary to the allegation that this American tour "ruined his health" is the known fact that he was so sick before his departure that some of his friends asked him not to go. Still better known, and more important to the issue at hand, are the correct dates of this second American tour. It did not take place between November 1868 and April 1869 but a full year earlier; he therefore died two years after it—in fact, while on a final lecture tour in England, collapsing after a reading in St. James Hall in March 1870.

Nor is Conrad any less misleading about Dickens's first trip to America. Having served up some ersatz fare about *American Notes* ("in Dickens's nightmarish America, there is emptiness: panic has driven away even the houses"—whatever that means), Conrad then takes us to the oyster bars. They sound sinister indeed—if you haven't read Dickens, that is:

> The oyster bars of New York are doubly fugitive, both subterranean and cellular. They are excavated beneath the ground, approached by "downward flights of steps," and constructed to reflect the ungregarious nature of the oyster eater, who has something to hide. Dickens imagines "the swallowers of oysters . . . copying the coyness of the

thing they eat," recoiling into the protective casing of their guilty privacy. Hence cubicles are erected to barricade them from one another, and they sit apart indulging their solitary vice "in curtained boxes, and consort by twos, not by two hundreds."

In the relevant passage, however, Dickens is quite charming about oysters, oyster eaters in New York, and oyster-houses.

> At other downward flights of steps, are other lamps, marking the whereabouts of oyster cellars—pleasant retreats, say I: not only by reason of their wonderful cookery of oysters . . . but because of all kinds of eaters of fish, or flesh, or fowl, in these latitudes, the swallowers of oysters alone are not gregarious; but subduing themselves, as it were, to the nature of what they work in, and copying the coyness of the thing they eat, do sit apart in curtained boxes, and consort by twos, not by two hundreds.

Conrad seems to do everything with the material except read it. In the chapter "Aesthetic America," where everything is honed to fit his parody version of Aestheticism, we learn that Rupert Brooke's description of Niagara Falls "is entirely self-referring, austerely unconnected with human affairs," even though, when Conrad has other purposes in mind—a contrast between Wells and Brooke at the Falls—he claims that Brooke's description in 1913 constitutes "a political premonition" of the war which was to change him from "an aesthetic weakling into a warrior." Of course, poor Rupert had no more premonition of the war in 1913 than did Henry James, Henry Adams, or anyone else. That is, he had none at all. His description of Niagara Falls can best be understood not as political premonition but as literary derivation, and if Conrad ever listened to prose or poetry instead of scanning it for images, he would have heard in Brooke's language not "a rebuff to the safe Victorian piety about nature" but a rather confused indulgence in Victorian sage-grandiosity. Not a glum indulgence, however, as is clear from a letter he wrote, during the trip, to A. F. Scholfield, a friend from

King's College days. Admitting with pleasant eagerness that "I'm so impressed by Niagara. I hoped not to be. But I horribly am," he goes on:

> I am a Victorian at heart, after all. Please don't breathe a word of it: I want to keep such shreds of reputation as I have left. Yet it's true. For I sit and stare at the thing and have the purest Nineteenth Century grandiose thoughts, about the Destiny of Man, the Irresistibility of Fate, the Doom of Nations, and the fact that Death awaits us All, and so forth. Wordsworth Redivivus. Oh dear! oh dear!

If anyone can make mistakes, then by the same token anyone, even accidentally, ought to get things right more often than Conrad does. There are so many errors and misinterpretations tumbling over one another that it becomes impossible to trust anything he says. What can be done with a critic so coarse and inattentive that he can refer to Lawrence's *Studies*, a masterpiece of exploratory criticism, as a "sulphurous denunciation of 'classic American literature'"? In support, he claims that Lawrence in a letter of July 1918 reports that "even his typist transcribing them collapses, as if after exposure to their contagion." The letter says nothing of the sort. It in no way suggests a cause-and-effect relationship, and instead indicates that the typist never even got to the work: "I sent the American essays to a friend in London, who was going to put them with a 'safe' friend to have them typed. The friend collapsed and they are hung up. I don't want to go to an ordinary typist," he wrote to Cecil Gray.

Peter Conrad's readings of Lawrence are utterly tone-deaf, and not to be able to listen to Lawrence, to move with the cadences of his voice, is not to know what he is saying. As a characteristic example, he asserts that, in Lawrence's essay "Pan in America," "Pan escapes from Wordsworth's tame lakeland to America where, Lawrence announces, he is reincarnated as Walt Whitman. The lustful goat-god becomes the tutelary spirit of American transcendentalism, and is renamed 'the Oversoul, the

Allness of everything.' In America, Lawrence declares, 'Pan is
still alive.'" As it happens, Lawrence's brilliantly supple and
funny essay turns Conrad's argument on its head:

> "Oft have I heard of Lucy Gray," the schoolchild began to repeat, on
> examination day.
>   "So have I," interrupted the bored instructor.
>   Lucy Gray, alas, was the form that William Wordsworth thought fit
> to give the Great God Pan.
>   And then he crossed over to the young United States: I mean Pan
> did. Suddenly he gets a new name. He becomes the Oversoul, the
> Allness of everything. To this new Lucifer Gray of a Pan Whitman
> sings the famous "Song of Myself": "I am All, and All is Me." That is:
> "I am Pan, and Pan is me."
>   The old goat-legged gentleman from Greece thoughtfully strokes
> his beard, and answers: "All A is B, but all B is not A." Aristotle did
> not live for nothing. All Walt is Pan, but all Pan is not Walt.
>   This, even to Whitman, is incontrovertible. So the new American
> pantheism collapses.

Lawrence can be made to "announce" or "declare" crudities only
by someone deaf to the extraordinary mobility of his writing, his
play with and against polemical assertion, his exuberant wit.

But Conrad can hold together his dreary and flat-minded
schematizations only if the writings he uses are made inert,
deprived of the modulations of humor, which is no mean accomplishment when the roster includes Dickens and Lawrence,
Oscar Wilde and Auden. Conrad is particularly severe about the
last two and also about Rupert Brooke. It might well be unfair to
suggest that this constitutes fag-baiting, especially since his mis-
treatments extend by calculation and miscalculation to everyone
in the book. He is no less misleading about Dickens's tour of
America than about Wilde's. And yet it's worth asking why he
gets so much more exasperated by Wilde's fur coat than by Dickens's oysters or, for that matter, by Kipling's fur coat. Comparing
the coats worn by Kipling in Brattleboro, Vermont, 1893, and by

Wilde on arrival in New York from England in 1882, he remarks: "Kipling's furs are the animal's defenses against an inimical climate. To survive the cruel Vermont winter, he had to grow a furry second skin. Wilde's coat, on the contrary, symbolizes nature sacrificed to art: seals and otters have been flayed merely to adorn his precious body." In what sense Kipling has an "animal" body while Wilde has a "precious" one, or Wilde has a "symbolic" coat while Kipling has a real one, will not bear sorting out. That both were mightily cold *Homo sapiens,* to take a larger generic view for a moment, would be obvious had Conrad bothered to note, or discover, that Wilde arrived in New York on January 4, that if Vermont has severe winters so does New York, and that on this particular day the reporters who waited for his ship complained of especially frigid winds and temperatures. If Kipling can wear a fur coat under such circumstances, why can't Oscar Wilde? Doing a bit of Conradian analysis of Conrad, the reason for Wilde's ineligibility becomes obvious: because of Wilde's later-to-be-committed crimes against nature (1886 is the usual date assigned to the first transgression), his "precious" body is not worthy of the natural protections allowed "animal" bodies like Kipling and your average raccoon, ocelot, or skunk. No furry second skin for *that* one, flayer of seal and otter!

If Wilde is to be left out in the cold, Auden, whose crime against nature is compounded by his becoming a naturalized American, is deep-sixed altogether. Although the chapter devoted to him is called "Theological America," it has almost nothing to do with theology. There are some references to Auden's association with Reinhold Niebuhr, presumably because it occurred in New York, but there is nothing at all about the central "theological" influence on Auden—Kierkegaard—presumably because it did not occur there. Essentially the chapter is an extended diatribe, strictly adhering to the recipe used throughout the book: split the American episodes from the author's life, garble them more or less completely, add a pinch of salt, whip to frothy peaks, and serve immediately. Be sure to overheat. A sample: "New York, rigidly laid out in space on a numbered grid of streets, monitored in time by those flashing clocks on the tops of buildings, encouraged the punctilious ritualism of Auden, who didn't know whether he was hungry unless a clock instructed him, and invariably left dinner parties at 9 P.M. to go home to bed." Or: "Auden looked forward to senility and did his best to advance it, behaving like an ungovernable, finicky baby, organizing his regime around regular mealtimes and early nights, re-creating in his apartment in St. Mark's Place the squalor of the nursery." And one last, summary example: "Auden's rebarbativeness, which became progressively fouler and nastier over the years, was the sign of his refusal to allow himself to feel at home anywhere. Prizing his own precious"— that word again—"freedom as an alien, he set about systematically alienating other people . . . he declined to visit Japan because he was convinced that the toilet seats would be too small for his sagging rump."

The only questions raised by writing of this kind have to do not with Auden but with Conrad, and can only be inquired into by him, with a little help, perhaps, from his friends. But in recoil one might have the pleasure of recollecting the many affectionate and funny reminiscences by Auden's friends, notably in the *Conversations* of Robert Craft and Igor Stravinsky, hardly sentimental, inexperienced, or patient observers of the human scene. Conrad's comments on Auden display only in an extreme form the mentality at work here, with its incapacity for understanding, accuracy, or minimum attentiveness. Allowing for the fact that just about anything mediocre can get into print, how, nonetheless, does a book so positively bad as this one survive even the most primitive and slipshod editorial attention? To give a few more examples at random, did no one point out the folly of trying to adduce similarities between Wells and Henry James against the evidence of *Boon* and of James's responses to it? Or that if Lawrence "rates killing highly as a mode of knowledge," isn't it strange that he finds the picking of flowers sometimes abhorrent? Or that Mark Twain cannot be said to "embody the epic" since he never wrote anything corresponding to one? Or that if you say that "jazz is anxious music, rhythmically frenetic and emotionally unbalanced," it only means that you have never heard Louis Armstrong or Sarah Vaughan or any other jazz musician?

To whom can the blundering and blustering of this performance be addressed? Not to anyone who knows anything, and not, God forbid, to anyone who doesn't.

8

VIDAL'S AMERICAN EMPIRE

※

With *Empire,* Gore Vidal further buttresses his vast chronicle of American history from *Burr* (1973) to *Lincoln* (1984) and *1876* (1976), then on to *Washington, D.C.* (1967), and the onset of World War II. *Empire* fills in the turn of the century, from 1898, with William McKinley's administration, to 1906, when Theodore Roosevelt, who came to office after McKinley's assassination in 1901, had reached the middle of his first elected term. Roosevelt had already helped set the course of American empire as McKinley's Assistant Secretary of the Navy. Presiding in that capacity over the buildup of the American fleet, he was strongly persuaded by the views of Captain Alfred Thayer Mahan, author in 1890 of *The Influence of Sea Power upon History,* and those of his friend Brooks Adams, who argued in *Law of Civilization and Decay* in 1895 that political supremacy depended largely on the control of trade routes.

Roosevelt did not need much persuading. He had reached similar conclusions in 1882 with his own *The Naval War of 1812.* An ardent supporter of American expansion, he agreed with the Brooks Adams of *America's Economic Supremacy* (1900) that "supremacy has always entailed sacrifices as well as triumphs, and fortune has seldom smiled on those who, besides being energetic and industrious, have not been armed, organized, and bold." "Bully," as Roosevelt is apt to say several times too often in this novel, clicking his ever visible "tombstone teeth."

Roosevelt had a large element of the ridiculous in him, but as Presidents go, he was unusually intelligent. Because of him America was "armed, organized, and bold" at the right time and place. So that while the American people may have been taken by surprise on February 15, 1898, when the battleship *Maine* was blown up in the harbor of Havana, Cuba, then a Spanish possession, Roosevelt and the fleet were ready. The fleet had already been positioned so close to the Philippines that William James, one of the teachers exasperated by Teddy's loquacity at Harvard, and later an officer of the Anti-Imperialist League—he is absent from Vidal's glittering cast of characters—was among those who wondered just how surprised anyone had a right to be. James could not then have known that Roosevelt, while briefly replacing his superior at Navy, had secretly ordered Admiral Dewey to assemble his ships at Hong Kong, from which they could steam into Manila and destroy the Spanish armada.

In a mere ten weeks America had come into possession of a world empire that included Cuba (to which independence of a sort was granted), Puerto Rico, Guam, and the Philippines. The Philippines resisted for a time, requiring the brutal suppression of an independence movement originally armed and inspired by the islands' new conquerors, and at a cost in lives, fortune, and honor greater than the cost of the war with Spain. All told it had been, in John Hay's phrase, "a splendid little war."

Empire opens with a house party at Surrenden Dering, deep in the English countryside, a day after the war has ended. The hosts are a recently retired senator from Pennsylvania, Don Cameron, and his wife, Elizabeth, niece of General Sherman, the hero of an earlier war (though not a hero if you lived in Atlanta). Elizabeth is the adored confidante here, as she was in life, of another house guest, the historian and novelist Henry Adams. The opening is in the mode of Henry James, who in fact drops by for lunch. Vidal's James is more convincingly portrayed here than he is even in Edith Wharton's *A Backward Glance* or in Simon Nowell-Smith's invaluable compilation of reminiscences, *The Legend of the Master.* And while Vidal may have depended on such sources for help in catching the great novelist's manner and cadences of speech, he greatly enriches these by qualities of sharpness, worldly perception, confidence, and toughness, which he has inferred from James's fiction and critical writings.

Vidal's James is a figure of benign, alert majesty who will prove more than a match for the effusive conversational aggressions of President Roosevelt at a White House dinner (such a dinner did actually take place). How appropriate to James's life, and signally to the theme of Vidal's novel (though outside its time frame), that a novelist who brought two continents under his authorial sovereignty should, in the delirium of his final illness, have begun signing his letters with the name "Napoleone," using, as Leon Edel points out, the old Corsican spelling. With his relaxed, receptive, skeptical style, James in these opening chapters gives an early indication of how Vidal's novel will itself deal with its powerful and famous characters. James is allowed gently to demolish the assertive pomposities of Brooks Adams, who on this as on other occasions manages to irritate his brother Henry, and to deride affectionately the patriotic, sentimental dialect poems composed by another guest, John Hay, the ambassador to the Court of St. James's, the former Assistant Secretary to Lincoln, and soon to be called back to Washington as McKinley's Secretary of State.

Also introduced in this first chapter is the fictional heroine of the book, Caroline Sanford. Like Isabel Archer in James's *Portrait of a Lady,* Caroline intends to be a "free" woman. But where James's heroines have an unfortunate habit of renunciation,

Caroline will have none of it. In her own mind she doesn't rule out sleeping with a woman as readily as with a man; she will manage to seize the inheritance that her brother Blaise tries to deny her; and she determines on a career in Washington, as yet unheard of for a woman. She transforms a respectable but impoverished newspaper into a sensationalist and politically powerful one, while acquiring an illegitimate daughter during her (and the book's) one extended sexual affair—an emotionally cool one—with a married congressman named James Burden Day.

It will be obvious that in *Empire* Vidal manages to mix inextricably the fictive and the historical, the social and the legendary. These elements are so fused in his style that none can be differentiated from the others. All partake of the same issues of inheritance, legitimacy, rivalry, deception, and ambition. Such mixtures can of course be found in many good historical novels, but in Vidal they are brewed in a particularly potent way. He means to suggest that the historically great figures, their position and achievement notwithstanding, are no different from the fictive persons with whom he surrounds them. Part of Vidal's originality derives from the attendant assurance that he can create and command the American history of his novels all as much as any imaginary components. No other twentieth-century American writer has Vidal's sense of national proprietorship, and his presumptions work marvelously well for both his novelistic intentions and, for reasons I'll get to, the political point he wants to make.

Taking any position involves limitations, however, and these include for Vidal a reluctance to confront anything that he can't bring within the control of his high urbanities. He has none of the humility claimed, for example, by Henry James in *The American Scene*, of 1907, the very period of this novel. Speaking of New York City and its awesome differences from the New York of his youth, James admits that "the reflecting surface of the

ironic, of the epic order, suspended in the New York atmosphere, have yet to show symptoms of shining out, and the mon-
strous phenomena themselves, meanwhile, strike me as having,
with their immense momentum, got the start, got ahead of, in
proper parlance, any possibility of poetic, of dramatic capture."

There are similar evidences that America is beyond "capture"
in Mailer, Bellow, Roth, or Pynchon when they try to express the
obscure nature of the national identity as it exists in poor, mar-
ginal, or inarticulate people. So far, Vidal has relegated such
scenes and human types almost exclusively to the series that
includes *Myra Breckenridge, Myron,* and *Duluth,* novels that
reveal how, parodistically at least, he chooses to invent an American unconscious. In *Empire,* as in other novels in the chronicle,
he limits himself to highly self-conscious people of the governing and dominant classes. And from the first exchanges among
Hay, Henry James, and the Adams brothers, with Caroline and
her fiancé Del Hay listening in, the implication is clear: it is to be
assumed that polite conversation can fully account for national,
international, or geopolitical reality.

While such an approach might easily foreclose "any possibility
of poetic, of dramatic capture" of those elements that yield only
to more exploratory ones, the danger is mostly outweighed, I
think, by the political and literary benefits that accrue to Vidal's
directness, clarity, and purposiveness of style. It is as if he shares
in part at least the perception of Hay, who, he writes, "thought of
the [White House]—the city, too, and the republic beyond—as a
theater, with a somewhat limited repertory of plays and types."

The positive accomplishment of Vidal's style is that it proves
an effective instrument to clear away the verbal mumbo jumbo
that often accompanies the idea of "empire," to dispel any metaphysics about the kinds of power necessary to imperial acquisition, and to expose the mythologies that have made "empire"
glamorous and palatable, especially to a country that recoils
incredulously when that word is applied to itself. Even the

admirable McKinley wants to believe that only on his knees and in prayer could he convince himself to annex the Philippines. We had a duty to Christianize it, he said of a country already eighty percent Christian.

On the subject of "empire," Vidal is writing outside the dominant stylistic traditions in which imperial power is usually represented in English. Melville, Conrad, and, later, Faulkner, Mailer, and Pynchon write about the imperial quest as if its source, movements, and results are necessarily concealed. It is evoked by them as a mystery, something which calls for a style correspondingly elaborate and suggestive, which cannot ever be fully exposed to view. By contrast, Vidal's prose is intended to strip American imperialism of any shrouded majesty and to erase from the American political landscape the "hieroglyphic sense of concealed meaning" that Pynchon finds even in a configuration of California city lights seen from afar.

I confess a preference for a prose that carries a greater sense of the inexpressive, of the imponderable, than Vidal's characteristically does, and for the reason that it not only allows for Vidal's quizzical sense of politics and history but can carry it to even greater lengths than Vidal is able to do. *Moby-Dick,* arguably the greatest novel written by an American, is also a critique of nineteenth-century capitalistic imperialism, especially toward colonial people. And yet Melville's critique is inseparable from the density of his style, suggesting as it does that imperialism is concealed in a rhetoric of mystification even from its main actors. An offhand comment Vidal has made in an article on Anthony Burgess—that people do not find Ahab nearly comic enough—is not so much wrong as myopic, an indication of how resolute he is in opposing anything less than the clearest possible exposure of a betrayal of the country's purpose which, as he sees it, began with the Founders themselves and was intensified with the Louisiana Purchase.

However, a fact often lost sight of is that, like Santayana, Vidal refuses to treat American imperialism as if it were something that shouldn't have happened. I mean the Santayana who in *Persons and Places* referred contemptuously to William James's bellyaching about the American seizure of empire from Santayana's native Spain, complaining that James

> cried disconsolately that he had lost his country, when his country, just beginning to play its part in the history of the world, appeared to ignore an ideal that he had innocently expected would always guide it, because this ideal *had* been eloquently expressed in the Declaration of Independence. But the Declaration of Independence was a piece of literature, a salad of illusions . . . The American Colonies were rehearsing independence and were ready for it; that was what gave their declaration of their independence timeliness and political weight. In 1898 the United States were rehearsing domination over tropical America and were ready to organize and to legalise it; it served their commercial and military interests and their imaginative passions. Such antecedents and such facilities made intervention sooner or later inevitable. . . . James's displeasure at the seizure of the Philippines was therefore, from my point of view, merely accidental. It did not indicate any sympathy with Spain, or with anything in history that interests and delights me. On the contrary, it was an expression of principles entirely opposed to mine; much more so than the impulses of young, ambitious, enterprising America.

Santayana is here expressing Vidal's hard-nosed worldliness, along with an appreciation, which Vidal's fiction also shares, of "young, ambitious, enterprising America." Myra Breckenridge is herself a thwarted evidence of this appreciation, and Caroline Sanford is a historically earlier, more respectable version of Myra. Caroline will have her way and do the best she can for herself despite those who try to crush her. (She is no less charmingly Luciferian than Aaron Burr, another aspirant to empire outside the officially sanctioned one.) Pregnant by Congressman Day, she gets herself a husband—a hapless lawyer who is her cousin and whose bed she will never share—by agreeing to pay his debts; threatened with a takeover of her newspaper by her half- and only brother, Blaise, and guessing that he is secretly of her own same-sex inclinations, she gets Congressman Day to seduce him, thereby giving her the leverage of blackmail over both of them. And yet Vidal's Henry Adams endorses the author's high opinion of Caroline. This is the Adams who in his own *The Education of Henry Adams* is charmed by Clarence King as "the ideal American" whom all his acquaintances aspire to be: someone with the energy and knowledge equal to the accelerating demands of a new age, while persevering in the ideals of the old. Neither Adams nor Vidal asks that so capable a person should also be a nice one.

Vidal is not in any simple way against American "empire." He has spoken nostalgically about the ten-year period after World War II, when the United States was the most powerful empire the world has ever known, calling it "the golden age," the promised title of the summary volume in his American history chronicle. "What potential there was for the Republic and how we blew it," he lamented in *Interview* (June 1974). Rather, he opposes his country's often brutal and self-defeating ways of getting and managing an empire, one example of which was the McCarthyite brand of anti-Communism that helped to bring "the golden age" to an early end. Nor is he complaining that America, like other countries, creates fictional apologias for expansion. It is not the fictions themselves, but their proliferation, mechanization, and shabbiness, that, in his view, have sickened and corrupted the nation. *Empire* locates this process of corruption in the conjunction, at the turn of the century, of Roosevelt's jingoism with William Randolph Hearst's yellow journalism, a term derived from the yellow ink used in printing a cartoon strip called *The Yellow Kid,* in Hearst's *New-York Journal.*

By the end of the novel, Roosevelt and Hearst are the leading contenders for control of the new "empire," and in the meeting that brings the novel to its close, the President must, grotesquely, shove his rival aside in order to secure his own designated chair at the head of the cabinet table. There are several such exquisitely managed scenes between peoples of immense personal force, as when Hay and the supercilious Elihu Root gradually bait the aspiring Roosevelt into the admission, "I hate irony." But perhaps the best such scene is the final one, in which Roosevelt and Hearst each claim to have invented the American empire. Hearst says at one point that "the future's with the common man, and there are a whole lot more of them than there are of you." "Or you," Roosevelt replies.

Who is the "common man"? Once Roosevelt and Hearst have used this exhausted rhetorical expression, the issue is dropped. By letting it pass, Vidal probably means to suggest that in the nation dominated by these two, "the common man" is effectively passing out of existence, about to disappear into the combination of mass press and governmental brainwashing that, having to some extent shaped "the common man," now largely produce him. This, I think, allows us to read *Myra Breckenridge,* along with *Myron* and *Duluth,* as post-Hearstian comedies, in which people have devolved into grotesque assemblages patched together out of images created by television series and B movies. The three novels are comic-nightmare versions of Vidal's more realistic historical novels.

Is history fiction? Is fiction history? Roosevelt jeeringly remarks to Hearst at the end of *Empire,* "I was aware of your pretentions as a publisher, but I never realized that you are the sole inventor of us all." "Oh, I wouldn't put it so grandly," Hearst replies with impressive calm. "I just make up this country pretty much as it happens to be at the moment." The two are clearly not practiced in analytic philosophy—what does it mean to "make up" something if the something already "happens to be"?—but Hearst brings as much discrimination to the issue as it deserves. Fiction-making is and always has been an essential part of history-making, essential, that is, even to the decision that something, and not some other thing, deserves to be called "history." The fictionizing occurs not only retrospectively but on the spot, as in Greek myths, allusions to which are frequent in this novel. The ancients themselves needed the mythologies they gave themselves before handing them on to us for our eager adaptations. In life fiction is no less inseparable from history than it is in Vidal's historical novels. He confirms this with a technical brilliance the more impressive for being nearly invisible, especially in his characterization of McKinley.

Along with recent revisionist historians, Vidal regards McKinley as the first great President since Lincoln. In *Empire,* the revisionist process is transferred from later historical interpretations and given to the actually engaged figures in McKinley's own circle. Driven by events and by their own quest for historical importance, the men around him feel compelled to displace one fiction about the President—that he is a pawn of Mark Hanna, the Ohio millionaire who helped him to the White House—with another, in which he is, as Vidal has Brooks Adams describe him, "our Alexander. Our Caesar. Our Lincoln reborn." Meanwhile, McKinley, in Vidal's portrait, is quietly occupied with his wife, with food in great quantity, and with small-town musings on "whether we are really going to set up in the empire business or not." He is an endearing rather than a grand enigma, and becomes enigmatic only because he is involved in a new political situation that asks him to be more than he knows himself to be. Events require a figure commensurately imposing. For Vidal, McKinley's true greatness consists in his modest but crafty demurrals, and the space his modesty allows him for sanity, flexibility, and independence. What better "empire," the novel seems wistfully to suggest, than that?

9

THE CASE OF
ARTHUR INMAN

On December 5, 1963, a man in Boston named Arthur Inman, having made several earlier attempts on his own life, managed to put a bullet through his head. A variety of chronic ailments and complaints had made him an invalid for nearly all of his sixty-eight years, and except for brief excursions in his ancient chauffeur-driven Cadillac, he had since 1919 confined himself to an apartment building in downtown Boston named Garrison Hall. For as many as sixteen hours of a normal day he would stay in bed, when not sitting or reading in the bathroom. The rooms he frequented were kept shaded for the same reason his car was painted a dull black: to protect his eyes from glare. He suffered periodically from nosebleeds, hay fever, arthritis, influenza, a slipping rib cage, migraine headaches, pain in the testicles, pains in the neck, collarbone, and shoulder, chills, cold sweats, canker sores, skin rashes, trouble with his stomach, which required frequent pumping, trouble with his throat, which required ultraviolet treatments, trouble with his coccyx, which was ministered to by a succession of osteopaths. He was especially dependent on Dr. Cyrus Pike, who much of the time was having an affair with Inman's wife, Evelyn.

Inman was visited daily by an assortment of doctors, nurses, prescribers and quacks, and by people off the street, easily a thousand of them over the years, who answered his advertisements in the newspaper for anyone willing for a fee to talk or read to him or otherwise make themselves useful. One such was Eddie Simms, chauffeur, manservant, confidant, and raconteur, who claimed to have been a professional ice-skater and a baseball player and to have driven for Diamond Jim Brady and Lillian Russell. Many of those who answered the advertisements became for periods of time a part of Inman's extended household, charmed into telling their stories to a man who listened eagerly in the half-light, gave them straightforward advice, and was clearly in no position to be moralistic or condescending about anyone else's confessed behavior, however bizarre. Pubescent girls and young women particularly appealed to him. He took a shine to Alma Bush, for example, because "her feet, those subtle indicants of a woman's character, were exquisitely kept." He would invite them to undress, admire their finer parts, fondle them, and often as not cajole them into bed. Some nearby colleges did not approve, but his wife, who had attended Wellesley, not only befriended but recruited some of his female attendants.

Such a household required a sizable yearly income, which was supplied, not without grumpy conditions, by his wealthy family in Atlanta, where he was born, and later by trust funds. It also required a lot of space. He rented five apartments in Garrison Hall, which, though run-down, was inexpensive and cozy, with a generally tolerant management. One apartment was occupied by Evelyn, who, with her need for independent space and her taste for travel, often incensed him. She left for good on several occasions and came close to divorce, but remained his wife for forty years, until his death. Another apartment was used by his secretaries and handypersons; and still another was occupied now and again by some favored girl, like Kathleen Connor. He met Kathleen in 1958, when she was sixteen, and sometimes thought of adopting her. A fifth apartment, in addition to the one occupied by Inman himself, was rented and then sublet on the floor below, so as to ensure quiet. He was hysterically sensitive to noise, which was a strong factor in his attempts at suicide. The horrendous noise, dirt, and certainty of disruption became especially acute in the early 1960s with the construction of a building complex in the nearby Boston and Albany railroad yards. This spelled the end of the elaborately buttressed existence he had meticulously set up for himself, and, like one of his heroes, Adolf Hitler, he took his life in his own "garrison" as the enemy closed in.

Kathy was able to spend an hour alone with Inman's open casket in the funeral home, and even though as an Irish girl from the nearby town of Charleston she had witnessed a number of wakes, she was appalled at his appearance, as we learn from the editor's coda to Arthur Inman's diaries:

> "Joseph, Mary and Jesus," she says she said, "what have they done to you?" The Arthur who loathed perfume and powder and who more than once had ordered his girls to scrub the paint off their faces was gussied up with cosmetics. It made her laugh and cry. She told him he looked terrible. She reminded him of her promise not to abandon him and straightened his tie. As she got ready to leave, she spied a bit of blood in his ear and removed it with a moistened corner of her dress.

We sense in such reportage, with its easy modesty and directness, almost no distance between the words and the things they describe. It is as if there were no style interceding between us and life, as if the writing were produced by the experience, and not the other way around. It is thus an especially appropriate ending to Daniel Aaron's edition of the *Inman Diaries* and evidence of the deftness, imagination, and tough economy which mark everything he has managed to do with this amazing sprawl of a document.

During those forty-four years in Garrison Hall his diary was Arthur Inman's obsession, day and night. Every ride he took, every tiff with his father about money, every stock and real-estate manipulation, all his tenacious involvements in the lives of people who worked for him or visited him, the personalities and public events of the interval from the great crash of 1929 to World War II and the emergence of the American empire— everything found its way into his writing. Everything existed in order to be written down. In the end the diary totaled 155 volumes with as many as 17 million words. Proust's novel *A la recherche du temps perdu,* in the Moncrieff/Kilmartin translation, runs to about one and a half million words, or 11 percent of the Inman. He left instructions with his trustees—for some reason, no more detailed information about his will has been disclosed—that they should show the diary to Harvard University in the hope that, with financial support from the Inman estate, some version of it might be published. The historian David Donald read the manuscript—he is quoted on the dust jacket as saying that it is "the most remarkable diary ever written by an American"—and recommended it to Harvard University Press, along with the suggestion that the distinguished critic and Professor of English in the Harvard English Department, Daniel Aaron, be invited to edit the document. It took seven years, and involved the reduction of the 17 million words to less than one-tenth of that, and of a thousand "characters" to about forty-five.

Very late in life, and then only reluctantly, Inman faced the fact that in its original form the diary was unpublishable, and that all he could hope for was "a sensitive and judicious editor" who might do for him what had been done for Thomas Wolfe. "Without the large editing of Thomas Wolfe's work," he asks, "would he have achieved a place in American letters?" Most of the time he had enormous ambitions for his diary. How could he not when it was the only excuse for living which he could make to himself and to others? Under these circumstances, it is impressive that he was not particularly bothered by his failure to get anyone to publish excerpts in his lifetime, that nearly all those to whom he showed parts of it were only politely enthusiastic, and that he himself was often severely critical. Aaron shrewdly prints parts of the diary in which Inman precedes, by what seems to me only a few seconds, the complaints a reader is ready to make: that it is "shapeless" and "formless," that much of it is "'filling,' boring, complaining." Though not an especially witty man, Inman refers at another point to "a worthless, unfruitful business, this writing, like knitting off-size socks for children without feet."

The editor's interpolated commentaries are invariably useful, and he mentions several ways in which the diary might be read: as the story of a "son of the south" transplanted north and obsessed with his ancestors; as a social history, an autodidact's story of life in America from 1919 to 1963; as a "non-fiction novel"—an idea that appealed to Inman—about real people and happenings, punctuated by dramatized occasions and epistolary narratives. It could be argued, however, that these extemporized alternatives only prove that Inman did not in fact know what form his writing should take or how the reader might be asked to take it. Without Aaron's interventions the diary would not exist as a book, and its unique virtues are to be ascribed not only to Inman's persistence but to Aaron's literary skill and intelligence. Reading over some of his pages in 1945, Inman admits:

> I sometimes reflect that this diary is one of the strangest documents of autobiography ever written by anyone. In its pages is an agglomeration of subject-matter only a catholic taste will wish to absorb—or so it seems to me. There is virtually no physical motion to sustain interest through shifts of environment. An unwilling celibate pens it. Philosophy and pages of history walk side by side with emotional outbursts and sentimental encounters. There is some beauty now and again, a facility of expression, a vehement earnestness but likewise not a little crassness here and there, much awkwardness of concept,

as much juvenility as sapiency . . . Hate living I may, disdain people I may, long for oblivion I may; nonetheless I find existence exciting, people stimulating, oblivion not near. If I pass on to a small section of posterity the excitement, the tension, the bewilderment, the suspense, the confusion of these years, I shall be satisfied. The people in the chronicle are not great people, save certain of those in the historical background; the events close to me are not startling events; my days are passed, as it were, behind plate glass. Yet it may be that in this strange document I will have succeeded in perpetuating the beating pulse of an era.

When this entry was written, World War II had just come to a close in Europe, and the "beating pulse" of the era, of the last "good" war, was felt by everyone. But scarcely in synchronization with Inman. For while at the time a good many of his countrymen shared his antipathy to Jews, Boston Irish, and Negroes, they would have found offensive, if not disloyal, his admiration for Hitler, Mussolini, and the Japanese. So too, by then, his detestation, tinged with envy, of Franklin D. Roosevelt—Roosie the Rat, as he called him. Not surprisingly, he later became a fan of General Douglas MacArthur and Senator Joseph McCarthy. His opinions about public figures and events are for the most part so loony as to be harmless, and this, along with his more general oddities and his willingness to modify his prejudices when he has to deal with individual Jews, Irish, or blacks, helps take the curse off the diary as "public confession." His hatreds are, besides, usually softened by self-condemnation, as when in 1943 he says: "I hate Jews, English, Roosevelt, life, myself."

Inman's social and political rantings tell us very little of consequence about the period, but a great deal about Inman's curious obsession with power. There are hints throughout of a remarkable person who early on became afraid of his own intensities and of the dangerous transgressiveness into which these might lead him. He disguised himself to himself and to others, notably his father, by induced fears of persecution that necessarily verified

themselves by his success in finding persecutors, and it is sympto-
matic of his confusions that his loathing of persecuted minorities
gives way now and then to far more interesting associations of
himself with them. He welcomed the circumscriptions of his life
because these precluded any public test of his feelings or of his
desire for power, even while he projected these onto autocrats,
rabble-rousers and conquerors. He created a safe and wholly
controlled environment in which to express his immense energies. The diary itself, like Garrison Hall, gave his life whatever
form it had.

Little glimpses of his life before the onset of his illnesses offer
some clues to his peculiar nature, as in his recollections of a
night when he went to the river behind the Donald Fraser
School for Boys near Atlanta, where he says he spent "the best
winter of my life":

> A very bright moon. Moonlight running down the roof of the big
> house. Fences, dark. In black silhouette the big water tank. The old
> stable empty, mysterious. Utter silence, myself, alone, moving in an
> otherwise motionless world. Beautiful.

This was written in 1937, thirty years later, and in a sense it
describes the singularity of his lifelong ambition: to move unim-
peded in an otherwise motionless world, or to imagine a world
that could be made to move at his bidding while he remained
motionless. How appropriate that he envied and at times grudg-
ingly admired Roosevelt, an immensely powerful President in a
wheelchair.

Garrison Hall and the diary were evidences of power that
depended paradoxically on invalidism, and it is characteristic of
his writing, too, that when it becomes most assertive or hyperbolic it almost immediately tapers off into disclaimers or concil-
iatory expressions, just as in his treatment of those around him
he is often simultaneously peremptory and pleading. It is impossible to dislike him because it is impossible to know him, even

after 17 million words. It is impossible to determine, for example, if he was really ill, and to what extent. Aaron invited a medical report based on the diary from Dr. David Musto of Yale University School of Medicine, and prints it as an appendix to the second volume. Musto is of the opinion that Inman's life was "cruelly complicated by medical maltreatment and by excessive, chronic ingestion of bromides, alcohol, and other powerful chemicals. These attempts to cure had almost without exception a destructive effect on his emotional stability, judgment, and physical health." He concludes his findings with the speculation that

> his illness in late adolescence allowed him to create a secure environment in which he was able to be productive along the lines he chose. Whether his initial illness could have ended without a life of invalidism is difficult to say. The secondary gain was so great and solved so many of his emotional problems that he had little incentive to change his style of life. He persisted in his goal to write a response to the times in which he lived, and he succeeded. Under the envelope of illness Arthur Inman had an indomitable will; it is in this interplay between sickness and creativity that his fascination lies.

I think Inman is an instance where we can afford to go beyond Dr. Musto's familiarly benign notion of the "interplay" between sickness and creativity. Literary ambition, the ambition to *be* a writer, seems to me in most cases to involve an attitude toward life which is usurpatory, autocratic, and brutal, all under the mythology of literature as a source of redeeming value. One reason Inman's diary is remarkable is that by being essentially formless, being without the mediating effects of an elaborated style or of set patterns, it brings us flatly face-to-face with Inman the writer, or rather with the appetites and connivances, the willfulness and the pathos of his literary ambition and its effects on those around him. He never disguises that he is dedicated not to the free exploration of life but to certain highly structured and

regulated provisions for the reception only of such life as will
serve his diary. The diary went on for 17 million words because
there was no limiting discipline of form operative in it—any
more than there was in the writing of Thomas Wolfe—no principle for modulation, subordination, highlighting, suspense, none
of the things that would allow us to call this by as fancy a name as
he wished for it: a "novel diary." The important point is this: that
the only form for the diary, before Aaron's redaction, was
antecedent to the writing of it: the setup at Garrison Hall and
the blank volumes waiting to be filled.

Inman might have become the writer he dreamed of becoming—he admired John Dos Passos, F. Scott Fitzgerald, and
Francis Parkman, the great historian of France and England in
North America who also had a number of debilitating illnesses—
and he had good taste in poetry, though his own verse was quite
bad. He might even have written the kind of diary he sometimes
envisaged: "to do in non-fiction what Balzac did in fiction." But
to do any of this he would have had to take the risk of sacrificing
the very conditions he contrived, conditions that allowed him to
receive the materials to write about in a manner that gave him a
flattering sense of power over them. He exercised his writerly
power merely in this provision of materials, not in their disposition. Without Garrison Hall and its entourage he would have
had to exercise power through the contrivance of formal literary
arrangements, which in turn would have given him at least a clue
as to who or what he was. But this he would not do.

My point is literary, not moral, since we should all by now
have accepted the evidence that "life" in any work of literature
exists thanks only to a murderous economics of exclusion and
inclusion. Inman was able to be unfair only in the preparation,
not in the execution, of this work. For all his manipulations of
people, his outrageous opinions, his flirtations with dictators and
toughies, Inman paid such a high price, psychologically and spir-
itually, and set for himself such conditions that he forfeited the

power to do much more than record what came along, excusing even that process in constant oscillations between praise and dismissal of it.

Some of the best-written and shaped parts of the diary are not his at all, but letters from his correspondents. This is especially true of Patricia Caffree, who started as one of his readers and talkers in 1931. She wrote to him at length about her brief career as a Broadway dancer, about Hollywood and her disastrous marriage there to a man whose boyfriend, whom she quite liked, spent every Saturday night with them, about Germany and army camps where her second husband was stationed as a military policeman. There are good letters from Evelyn, when she was sent by her husband to report on conditions in the Midwest, and from Anthony Abruzzo, a sometime hobo, thief, drunkard, and Communist Party organizer whose remarkable accounts Inman solicited and paid for. These, along with transcripts of conversations with many other equally colorful figures, are filled with the minute details of quite ordinary daily existence, and they make Aaron's edition of the diary an invaluable *annaliste* history of life in America during the middle third of this century.

10

IS THERE AN AMERICAN
MANHOOD?

There is a species of literary criticism flying high in the academy which ought eventually to come to roost in the Food and Drug Administration. The FDA is that part of the United States government charged with assessing the safety of products and labeling them. Do they meet the minimum daily requirements of ingredients that are good for you? Are there dangerous additives or local colorings that need to be exposed by analysis? This is just the sort of thing students are being encouraged nowadays to ask of the literature they read. Criticism in the spirit of the FDA is intended to reduce your consumption of certain of the golden oldies, to reveal consumer fraud in books that for these many years have had a reputation for supplying hard-to-get nutrients.

Illusions as to the value of revered works of literature do need every so often to be dispelled. Some people may swear off the canon altogether as a result, but for most of us, the results aren't likely to be so decisive or long-lasting. Like the warnings issued about cigarettes, the cautions about eggs, alcohol, and chocolate, or the recurrent scares about apples and raspberries, the warnings being sounded about literature—that narrativity is biased toward violence, that novelistic composition is a form of

imperialism, that characters we've learned to trust are ideological plants—won't long dissuade the hearty reader from going
back to the classics as to some plate of infamous goodies.

Meanwhile, FDA criticism will probably earn a few more
adherents, thanks to books like David Leverenz's *Manhood and
the American Renaissance* (1989). It is better than most such
books because, for one thing, Leverenz is at times a competent,
if constricted, close reader, even while at heart he is resentful
about being required to be one at all. For another, the fifty-four
pages of notes provide an instructive review of critics and historians of gender ideology. He thereby places his arguments
within ongoing debates about American literature, especially on
how best to situate it in relation to other writing. In this instance,
the other writings are mostly American works of an historical or
non-canonical kind. In discussing other critics Leverenz is not in
the least combative—evidence, I take it, that he is cleansed of
the competitiveness of his profession and of any infections of the
aggressive masculinity he may have picked up from reading the
likes of Emerson or the ever devious Hawthorne.

His contentions are that in the Northeastern United States
before the Civil War "the reigning ideology of manhood ori-
ented itself toward power, not feeling" (such dichotomies
abound, alas); that the ideology took hold less because men were
afraid of women or of the feminine components in themselves—
a feminist argument that has always seemed to me persuasive—
than because men were afraid of being humiliated by other men
in the perfervid economic enterprise of the time; and that this
fear was disguised, even from those who felt it, by publicly
accredited rhetorics of self-reliance. Like the new historicists he
admires, Leverenz has decided that self-fashioning is animated
by forces outside the individual, that these are only superficially
situated in specific historical events (for example, the financial
crisis of 1837, when Emerson noted in his journals that "the
land stinks of suicide") and are to be traced instead in insidious

gender formations as they move into economic arrangements and class-consciousness.

When Leverenz says that "manhood" was "a reigning ideology," he is momentarily simplifying his own arguments. His emphasis is not on any single idea of manhood. It is on the struggles among various factions, each of which wanted to define the term, to appropriate and represent it. These competitions were as ferocious as any that occurred in the marketplace. Entrepreneurial males of the 1830s and 1840s posed an implicit challenge to the manhood traditionally reserved to the older class of genteel patriarch, and both factions were being challenged in turn by independent artisans. Meanwhile, in novels, poems, and essays, it was being suggested that only the "poet" ("he who stands," said Emerson, "among partial men for the complete man") could sufficiently imagine a nation that was still in need of being imagined. "America is a poem in our eyes," to quote Emerson again, and if so, who else could bring it into focus? Businessmen cannot control even the terms in which they do business. Didn't the punning Thoreau say he had "walked over each farmer's premises"?

The quotations I've volunteered here would probably strike Leverenz as so much literary footwork. He looks to language for some combination of social brainwashing and psychological trauma, the latter being the fault of father-figures who induce shame and resentment. For the former slave Frederick Douglass, about whom and Harriet Beecher Stowe he writes his best criticism, the father is obviously White Master, though there is also White Mistress, in whose capacity to read and write, and in whose willingness to teach them both to a young slave, Douglass begins to discover the instrument of both freedom and revenge. For Hawthorne, fear of domination resides in the specter of homosexual rape carried out by an older man—specifically, a domineering uncle-guardian named Robert Manning, whose bed and board the fledgling author shared before he left for

Bowdoin College. (Manning also happened to be, for those who might want to make something of it, the most renowned pomologist in the United States and author of *The Book of Fruits*.) Leverenz believes that Emerson's fear of humiliation presumably began even earlier, in the alleged bullying of an exacting father when the boy was eight. Whitman's father was, in the poet's words, "manly, mean, angered, unjust," and Melville's was driven to suicide after failures in the market. The novelist's rage was only increased by his supposed inability to mourn his father's death, and this gets transfigured into Captain Ahab's monomaniacal vengefulness, compulsive penis envy, and desire to be whipped. Only Richard Henry Dana in *Two Years Before the Mast* and Francis Parkman in *The Oregon Trail* (Parkman's homosexual proclivities are scarcely mentioned) come forward as relatively standard cases of the urge to "be a man." Leave it to the genteel types—William James being another and later example—to mistake manhood for the capacity to endure prearranged physical hardship. Their version, no doubt, of the English public school.

It will be obvious that Leverenz likes to stay close to home—with father-fixations in one section of the United States, during three or four decades, as represented in American works only. There is no attention whatsoever to the possible impingement on those works of English or classical works wherein manhood is at issue—as it is in Homer, Spenser, Marlowe, the Shakespeare of *Coriolanus*, the Milton of *Paradise Lost*, Byron, Shelley, Fielding, or Scott. Most of these writers were more widely read in pre-Civil War America than were any male American writers. With some notable exceptions, like F. O. Matthiessen and Marius Bewley, some decades ago, and, more recently, in the criticism of Leslie Fiedler, in Harold Bloom's admixture of Emerson and Wilde, and in the work now being done by a few young Americanists, this sort of oversight has been par for the course in American studies, where making English–American connections is suspected, it seems, of diluting the obligatory task of making connections between American literary works and domestically produced documents that have historical importance but are at another level of literary competence.

The bustling historicism that goes on in American studies is probably a compensation for the fact that relatively few works of great literary accomplishment were produced in America during the first half of the nineteenth century. While some of this literature is astonishing by any standards, there simply isn't enough of it for any extensive course of study without the inclusion of other materials; and if the subject is to keep its American title, these must perforce include home-grown items from historical archives and popular culture. The result is a stifling parochialism exactly where there is most need for comparative studies involving other literatures of much longer duration. Principally, this has to mean literature in English, which just happens to be the language in which American literature is written. Those like Leverenz who refuse to inquire into "the Atlantic double cross" (to recall the title of an exceptional book by Robert Weisbuch) are not able in any effective way to speculate on a phenomenon of immense consequence to Leverenz's subject. I refer to the evidence that nearly all the writing that has ever been done over several centuries has predominantly been an exercise, very often self-conscious, of male prowess and competitiveness. This has left its mark on gender formations everywhere, no matter how locally they may show themselves in American culture.

Like writers of this century in some Third World countries, American writers early in the nineteenth century found themselves in an essentially gendered relation, as son or daughter, to the language of the parent country, the syntax of which had already revealed its susceptibility to male domination. All the writing produced in the pre-Civil War period in America carries trademarks from the Old World. The very idea of a new world and of a new American continent was shaped by imported literary tropes, as Myra Jehlen's *American Incarnation* has shown. Images of liminality became images of frontier, and I have suggested elsewhere that the way the speech of American characters alternates between idiomatic-commoner and grandil-oquent "over-soul" looks for credibility to analogous manipulations wherein Shakespeare projects the double nature, human and divine, of kings and other exalted figures.

When Leverenz writes that "if women writers portray manhood as patriarchy, male writers from Melville to Sam Shepard, David Mamet and David Rabe portray manhood as rivalry for dominance," he is sticking as usual to American examples, but forgetting that rivalry for dominance is very often a rivalry over patriarchal status. What is being contested for is an already authorized rhetoric of domination by which one man chooses to fashion himself in competition with another. In pre-Civil War American literature, this was significantly a rhetoric which English literature had already cast into a dramaturgy of male rivalry for patriarchal eminence. It can be heard in the speeches of Satan and, dull though they are, of God in *Paradise Lost,* which induced Blake to say that Milton was of the Devil's party and Emerson to say, after Blake: "If I am the Devil's child I will live then from the Devil"; it can be heard more genially in the verbal duels of Hotspur and Glendower in *Henry IV,* Part One, in which Prince Hal defeats both of them not only in battle but, thanks to a democratic proficiency of speech which his father had failed to master, in the minds and hearts of the English people. "I can drink," Hal boasts, "with any tinker in his own language." The rivalry for possession of the language of self-fashioning goes back to Exodus and God's "I am that I am," a phrase that echoes in Shakespeare's Sonnet 121, in Emerson's "Experience," and on into several poems by Wallace Stevens.

The rhetoric of manhood is inherent in the very traditions of literary production and inspiration. It isn't simply one of literature's themes. It finds its voice in that magnification by which certain male writers come to believe in their own suzerainty. Keats, on reading Chapman's translation, wrote of the "one wide

expanse" that "Homer ruled as his demesne," and in the delirium of dying, Henry James, as I've already mentioned, thinking
most likely of the transatlantic empire he had created in his
novels, signed letters, in which he grandly discussed some refur-
bishing of the Louvre, "Napoleone." George Eliot in *Middle-
march* in her sardonic reference to those "amazing gentlemen"
who perhaps find consolation "in the sense of a stupendous self
and an insignificant world," or Gertrude Stein when she compares her acts of literary composition to the conduct of a general
in a battle, were directly contending with traditional masculine claims to imperial sway over the literary terrain. It was an
uphill struggle, and it is still going on. The sheer difficulty of
understanding Stein for long stretches is evidence, I think, that
her heroic efforts to seize the language were only sporadically
successful.

When criticism of American literature insulates itself, as
much of it does, within the quite narrow confines of American
literature and social history, it effectively short-circuits the intricate and mysterious network of connections, those echoes and
reflections by which, as John Hollander has demonstrated in
The Figure of Echo, works of literature are flexibly bound one
to another, despite national boundaries. Such Americanist criticism then hopes to reconnect the works to a social-economic
support system wherein, on new frequencies, a few of the same
echoes can be heard but without much foreign interference.
Almost always, there is a political intent behind all this cutting
and splicing: to expose the complicity of American literature
with the ideological assumptions of Western capitalism as these
show luridly forth in the conquest and settlement of a continent
and in the near-eradication of the people who already live there.
The range of inquiry is in most cases so restricted as actually
to hinder the political purpose of the whole effort. It needs
far more audaciously to show—once one has learned how to
do it—that not merely American literature but literature as an

institution has, since at least the English Renaissance, been complicit with governing economic, political, and social systems, even when it has seemed to oppose them.

Such complicity need not be either surprising or reprehensible, especially if you believe, as I do, that social systems are not imposed from without but are the product and proof of what human beings are and aspire to become. We are collectively responsible for the whole thing; we are not simply in it or out of it; we are of it. When Yeats writes, "Whatever flames upon the night/ Man's own resinous heart has fed," that first word— "whatever"—should mean as much as any of the others. Some of my dissatisfaction with the ideological bent of historicist-psychoanalytic critics like Leverenz is not that they are tough about literature but that they are not even aware of the stakes involved. They aren't nearly tough-minded enough about the institution of literature as a whole or about "whatever" is produced alongside it, including the idea of the human. They think they can clean up Western civilization by treating the literary canon as its insidious agent and not for what it really is, which is a list of works, and a continually changing list at that. As Frank Kermode argues in a brilliant chapter on the subject in *History and Value,* literary canons are indeed "complicit with power." However, since the institution of literature could conceivably exist without a canon, those who attack only the latter—the central committee, so to speak, instead of the party—incur the suspicion that, like most revolutionaries, they want only to replace some existing tyranny with a new one. "Those most hostile to the canon," as Kermode puts it, "only mean to occupy it as a reward of success in the struggle for power."

These are complicated matters, but Leverenz is in a more than necessary quandary about them. He cites one critic who asks how Hawthorne got into the canon while Susan Warner, author of *The Wide, Wide World,* didn't make it—a fair enough question—and who then attributes Hawthorne's elevation to the interventions of a cluster of male supporters. These include his old college friends Longfellow and Franklin Pierce, who became the subject of a campaign biography written by Hawthorne and who also became President of the United States. This critic then points to their influential descendants in order to explain how the canonization continues into the present century. From his demurrals in the notes, it is obvious that Leverenz finds this line of reasoning a bit embarrassing—which makes it all the more perplexing when, in the body of his argument, he sets out to emulate it. He there asks an equivalent question about Emerson and Sarah Hale, the author of "Mary had a little lamb" and the novel *Northwood,* who was also the editor of *Godey's Lady's Book.* And he comes up with an equivalent answer: "If Emerson has been canonized and Hale has not, part of the reason has to do with the constituencies they address." For Hale this was "leisured middle-class American women," and for Emerson "a new intellectual elite." Leverenz fails to mention that the "elite" included a number of these same "middle-class American women," or that writers of course always do address audiences who will listen to them. Emerson earned his audience simply by being an immeasurably better writer than Hale.

Leverenz is uneasily aware that he needs some better explanation for their different levels of accomplishment. But he mismanages the one he comes up with, and in such a way as to prove once again how sorry is any attempt to explain the American literary canon by attributing its formation to social and historical factors that do not include the determining power of literary tradition, its images and sounds. "Emerson," he says, "can presume from his privileged maleness and his privileged class to reach a much greater imaginative range, beyond any constituency in sight." While the direction of this sentence is not at all clear, it could be read as a fumbling attempt to reach the light. Leverenz might be supposed to be saying that the "much greater imaginative range" shared by Emerson and his privileged male readers was licensed by literary practices inherited from such writers as I've already mentioned, writers whose exaltations of human consciousness and aspiration were also exaltations, for the most part, of white upper-class males.

It becomes evident in his next paragraph that this is not what Leverenz has in mind, and that the phrase "greater range" is to be circumscribed by the phrase "public influence." Thus, "the male writers'" greater range of voice builds on their greater access to public influence, while the women's narration bespeaks the constraints of an audience not allowed to compete for power. "Public influence" as used here has, in fact, nothing to do specifically with a public's literary dispositions in favor of one kind of writing rather than another; it could refer as easily to partialities for political candidates or for hemlines and shirt collars. Anyone selling anything could have "access" to it. Discussions of literary access should take account, as Leverenz's kind of criticism doesn't, of the way literary traditions and modes of literary representation help to create a canonical aura for some writers more than for others.

Once the negotiating field for admission to the canon becomes bound by local circumstance, as it does in this book, there follows the inevitable question of how a writer canonical in one period ever manages to hold on to his status in a later and very different one. What happens when the writer is put "beyond any constituency in sight"? We have heard a possible answer in the case of Hawthorne—he was kept in place by the efforts of the powerful offspring of his powerful contemporaries—and while this doesn't seem even to persuade Leverenz, he manages for Emerson merely to substitute another conspiratorial party. The party came into existence, he says, with "the rise of the American university system." "Since one of Emerson's greatest virtues is to make intellectuals feel like liberating gods," he observes, "we return the favor by exercising our institutional power of syllabus-making and our professional power of canon-making to put him at or near the top of the American procession." I had always assumed that he had been helped in staying there by the recorded adulations of Friedrich Nietzsche, of William and Henry James, or by John Dewey's assessment that he is "the one citizen of the New World fit to have his name uttered in the same breath with that of Plato." Even with this kind of support, however, Emerson's status among "intellectuals," academic and other, is in no sense settled. During one decade alone, the 1980s, he was roughly treated by, among others, A. Bartlett Giamatti, in an address given while he was president of Yale, by John Updike in a very extended attack in *The New Yorker,* by Irving Howe's unflattering lectures in *The American Newness,* and by the refusal even to list him among the indispensable American writers in *To Reclaim a Legacy,* William Bennett's cultural position paper as Ronald Reagan's Secretary of Education.

Emerson has never, in fact, been sufficiently placed: he is both everywhere in American culture and nowhere, conspicuous as platitude and otherwise unrecognized. With an important exception I will get to in a moment, the philosopher Stanley Cavell seems to me right on target—as I've had to say perhaps once too often—when he argues in *In Quest of the Ordinary,*

> I take it for granted that their thinking [he is referring also to Thoreau] is unknown to the culture whose thinking they worked to found (I mean culturally unpossessed, unassumable among those who care for books, however possessed by shifting bands of individuals), in a way it would not be thinkable for Kant and Schiller to be unknown to the culture of Germany, or Descartes and Rousseau to France, or Locke and Hume and John Stuart Mill to England.

Cavell is saying that regardless of Emerson's canonical status he remains improperly or insufficiently understood. This strikes me as undeniable. It also presupposes that the situation might be corrected, in which case it will require of many other readers some of the extraordinary dedication and interpretative brilliance that have gone into Cavell's own work on Emerson. Even then, I doubt that Emerson could ever be read *into* American culture so as more significantly to shape its thinking. On occasions too frequent to be taken as exceptions, he is not the kind of writer whose thinking ever could be culturally assumed or possessed or made use of. His writing often has the effect of moving you beyond culture, in Lionel Trilling's phrase—which is a sensation to be grateful for if, more of the time, you want to understand why you prefer to be in it. He is best appreciated for his performances with words, the exemplary ways in which he asks you to be in a close, expectant, quizzical relation to the language he happens to be working with. For a reader like Leverenz, on the other hand, Emerson's language, and the language of American Renaissance writers generally, is to be read as if the range of its associations is sufficiently contained within the historical, psychological, and social coordinates established around it, as by a *cordon sanitaire* which excludes all the luxuriant mess of roots and branches.

At three different points in his book Leverenz returns to a paragraph in Emerson's essay "Self-Reliance" that is ostensibly concerned with masculine self-fashioning. He is fixated on part of a sentence at the beginning of one paragraph: "the nonchalance of boys, who are sure of a dinner . . . is the healthy attitude of human nature." That is, keep your cool. In coping with this sentence, as with the entirety of "Experience," to which he devotes a particularly unfortunate chapter, Leverenz insists that Emerson's failure to give due mention to the women in his household represents a disabling ingratitude and indifference. At one point he grumbles that to say the boys are "sure of a dinner" presumes a "faceless mothering"; at another, that the phrasing indifferently takes for granted "the supportive role of women"; and at another that "a bold male self-reliance presumes a depersonalized female support system." Presumably everything would be A-OK if only he'd mentioned mother Ruth or Aunt Mary Moody or wife Lidian. To be spared such nitpicking, would that he had. But even from the point of view of

his own limited and limiting thesis, Leverenz could have made
better use of the offending sentence.

Common sense ought to suggest that when Emerson writes
that the boys are "sure of a dinner" he is not suggesting that dinner depends solely on the women who cook it. It depends more
basically on there being a supply of food provided by men who
are competing in the marketplace for the cash needed to buy it.
What, then, is to be made of the sentence? It does sound peculiarly focused on that dinner. Why mention it at all? Emerson
himself may have wondered, since he is always alert to opportunities and detours that open up, thanks to casual uses and common phrasings. Keep in mind, too, that he is a philosopher of
profit and loss, of how, as he says elsewhere, in an echo of *King
Lear,* "nothing is got for nothing." Accordingly, further down the
page and in the next paragraph, he recalls this dinner and gets
round to the cost of it and hence the price that must be paid for
whatever assurance the dinner breeds. It is a cost the boys themselves, once grown, will also have to pay. "Society is a joint-stock
company," he writes, "in which the members agree for the better
securing of his bread to each shareholder, to surrender the liberty and culture of the eater."

While "nonchalance" may be a "healthy attitude," the health of
the body requires that we eat, and the necessary earning of bread
requires that the "attitude" be surrendered. An impasse has been
created without any notice taken of it; we—Emerson and the
reader—simply find ourselves at it, as if edged into the perplex-
ity. When he is most meaningful Emerson tends to be least
emphatic. This is his way of indicating that it is not the job of writing to resolve the irresolvable: it is only to show us how best to
get on with life, allowing for just the right degree of nonchalance.
It is no celebration of manhood to discover, over the progress of
two paragraphs, that its "healthy attitude" is reserved not to men
at all but to boys who do not need to earn a living. The only
adults so fortunately situated will appear in the novels of James,

and Emerson seems to anticipate them in a parenthetical remark which Leverenz omits from his quotations: the boys "should disdain as much as a lord to do or say aught to conciliate one."

A more adequate reader of the canonical writers Leverenz discusses must be alert to the play of voices among sentences and to the proportionate emphases due to them. Otherwise, it becomes easy to mistake self-magnifying allusiveness for gender identification. A reader who gets accustomed to *Moby-Dick* as a novel cluttered with rhetorical overreaching will not be startled when Ahab says, late in the book: "In the midst of the personified impersonal, a personality stands here . . . the queenly personality lives in me and feels her royal right."

Leverenz finds this so spectacularly convenient to his arguments about gender fixation, however, that he entitles his last and, along with the one on Emerson, least satisfactory chapter, "Ahab's Queenly Personality." But it is a mistake to suppose that Ahab is here making a cross-dressed identification of himself. He is indulging, as he so often does, in the inflationary use of allusions, as is Melville in the interests of his novel. Leverenz claims to find the lines "startling" and "strangely ambiguous"; "nothing," he says, "prepared me for this gender change."

Of course, no gender change has occurred; the allusion, which is all that it is, has been prepared for, as can be learned from notes written by Harold Beaver for the Penguin edition of *Moby-Dick*, which Leverenz himself mentions. Beaver pertinently identifies the "queenly personality" with defiance of the black goddess Kali, who figures elsewhere in the novel. Leverenz would also have been "prepared" by notes supplied to an earlier edition of *Moby-Dick* by Charles Feidelson, in which he refers us to the infidel queen of death, who puts in an appearance only three brief chapters earlier, and, more intricately, to what Ahab, closer by, calls his "unknown mother." My own contribution, if it hasn't already been made by someone else, is that the Melville who marked up *Antony and Cleopatra* more than

any other Shakespeare play might also have had in mind the
Egyptian queen who liked to buckle on the sword with which
the emperor defeated Brutus and Cassius, while she dressed
him, as he slept, in her headdresses and mantles. Also like Ahab,
and no less disastrously, she preferred to compete for empire at
sea rather than on land.

My purpose isn't to exorcise a faulty reading of the passage by
bombarding it with possible literary antecedents. It is to indicate
the characteristic feebleness of a historicism in which indifference to literary allusiveness and an incapacity to recognize it
derive from a politicized fervor for merely social referents.
Ahab's use of the word "queenly," in which Leverenz makes a
wholly inordinate investment, is not an example of "the gender
conventions flaring out of his words." It is instead an example of
a flaring-out of associations by which Ahab is extending himself
and Melville's book beyond any such limited gender identifications. While it's tiresomely all right to say that Ahab is "being
spoken by the ideology of manhood that has possessed him," it is
obtusely minimizing to propose that this ideology results only
from some social constructs of gender. Behind these constructs
is a vast literary mythology derived from the Bible and from
medieval and Renaissance literature, Spenser, Shakespeare, and
Milton especially.

Moby-Dick is a book about manhood because it is also a book
about the conventions of romance. Romance is part of the cultural accumulation turned to waste with which Melville contends. I mean "romance" less as Hawthorne defined the mode in
his prefaces than as an enactment in a work Hawthorne revered
perhaps even more than Melville did, *The Faerie Queene.*
Melville read it avidly before he read Shakespeare; it permeates
Mardi, the headnotes to some of his sketches, and *Moby-Dick.*
The Faerie Queene, like *Moby-Dick,* is about male questing,
male physical prowess and a taste for adventure and hardship,
most of it taking place in open spaces far from home and family

responsibilities. Even more closely appropriate to *Moby-Dick* is the fact that *The Faerie Queene* concerns itself with the encroachments of capitalist enterprise on the ideal forms of an older, agricultural order. By the time of Melville's America, the encroachments had become catastrophic and there was no hint that any alternative had ever existed.

When Spenser's Guyon is exposed to the appeals of filthy lucre in the Cave of Mammon, where he is also offered Mammon's daughter as a wife, he is able to resist the temptations, though he nearly faints from the exertions of doing so. He is sustained by a faith in ideals still evocable. No such possibilities are available to Melville. The *Pequod*, the ship Ahab commands, is named for an Indian tribe exterminated by Puritan settlers. Colonialism, imperialism, capital enterprise first created and now inhabit and pursue the vessel, its officers, and its crew. More than that, these same bequests of Western civilization inform the literary repertoire of the book itself—the quest romance, Shakespearean imperial dramaturgy, and allegory, which has come to depend on insane projections. *Moby-Dick* can thus be read as a horrendous meditation on its own literary and cultural derivations, to which local and immediate forms of economic competitiveness, and of the gender struggles within it, are only incidental.

What Wallace Stevens says of speech in his 1944 poem "The Creations of Sound" should be said of American and of any other literature: ". . . speech is not dirty silence/ Clarified. It is silence made still dirtier." The murkiness of these lines is perhaps proof of what they say, which is that behind speech or words is not some generative source that awaits disclosure and explanation— there are only other words. Even the first time the words were used, they were at best mediations of reality: so that when we in turn use these words, trope them to serve our needs, it only makes them "dirtier," still less transparent to any objects beyond them. More than any other kind of writing, literature exhibits and exults in this condition. A work of literature, unlike a work of journalism, makes itself responsible for the cultural inheritance amassed in the words it uses, and it does so in order to add to that inheritance. Literature does not aspire to be clear, but to be dirtier and dirtier.

Historicist-psychoanalytic criticism, especially when conducted in the FDA frame of mind, deeply resents this truth about literature, which means that often, without quite knowing it, it is deeply resentful of literature itself. The resentment is disguised even from those who harbor it by the busywork of trying to prove that the duplicity of novels and poems does not belong to the very nature of fiction but is the result instead of compromises and evasions necessitated by social and historical circumstances, or, in worst-case instances, by authorial collusion with them. It has to be granted that though any work of literature is of necessity duplicitous, it nonetheless emerges at a particular time and place, so that its duplicities will have historical implications of a local and measurable kind. No one need object, for instance, when Leverenz points to the tones of class privilege that bind narrator and reader in *Uncle Tom's Cabin* and then shows, as Gillian Brown has done, that these manage all the while subversively to glorify Chloe and women in the kitchen; or when he describes similar tactics in Frederick Douglass, where stylistic gentility is meant to indicate how high he has risen, even while in the story he intends to show how dangerous he can be in a fight.

When, however, duplicity or evasiveness in a work of literature does not ameliorate some historically verifiable problem, Leverenz can become very censorious indeed, and in a you-better-believe-it manner that is itself quite devious. It is distressingly evident that for him duplicity in literature is often only one of the many tactics by which male writers set out to seduce and then dominate him, thus perverting that heterosexual intimacy among chaps who want to share what he likes to call "real feelings." Indeed, works of literature can for him very quickly get populated with "real" instead of fictional people. He is all of a

sudden like Fielding's Partridge at a performance of *Hamlet,*
ready to rush onstage to save Ophelia. As his notes attest, Leverenz is not alone in suffering from such delusions. He approv-
ingly mentions two critics who allege that Rappaccini in
Hawthorne's story "may have raped his daughter, as his name
implies," and though he isn't quite ready to agree with three others who contend that Coverdale in *House of the Seven Gables*
killed Zenobia, he "wouldn't mind seeing him accused of a
crime. At least then he might be forced out into the open." He
can only mean forced out of the novel.

Literature, by such interpretations, is reduced to a masked
ball or to some newspaper scandal. Of Hawthorne, Melville, and
Thoreau, Leverenz writes that their "ambiguous and contradictory interpretations . . . frequently make me feel seduced into a
sneaky intellectual fraternity yet simultaneously exposed and
accused." What to a naïf might sound like the call to comradeship in *Leaves of Grass* is heard by Leverenz as a call for "possessive fusion," which "effectively denies the basis of real intimacy
in separate selves." Though he knows it makes him sound "up
tight," he "recoils" from Whitman's advances. After all, he is "a
heterosexual male" who announces that he is one. A homosexual
male might recoil, too, if, as Leverenz puts it, Whitman is
"attacking me for trying to make sense of him" while "also playing the grand seducer. Stripped of its prophetic grandiosity, his
speech promises me the moon for a one-night stand." Blue-eyed
Nathaniel, as D. H. Lawrence called Hawthorne, is almost as
threatening: "As detectives sniff and snoop through the underbrush of his tales, he lures them into the open, only to humiliate
them with their own intellectual prurience." Is this spirited? I
suppose. Is it funny? Not very. More on the order of jocular intimacy with the great, which can be dispiriting when you're being
told that they haven't been there all along.

GERTRUDE STEIN: "MANLY AGITATIONS"

Well before her death in Paris in 1946 at the age of seventy-two, Gertrude Stein had elevated herself to the ranks of the immortals: "Think of the Bible and Homer think of Shakespeare and think of me," she instructs us in *The Geographical History of America,* written in 1935. She might have thought it a bit tardy that not until 1998 was she admitted into the Library of America. But as she also once said, "history takes time," and she might want to conclude that the Library had only waited until she could occupy a sort of pinnacle, though no such thing was intended. As it happens, the Stein volumes bring the Library to a full one hundred volumes, and at a point when the century—in which it was a "woman," meaning herself, who "did the important literary thinking"—is about to pass into a new millennium.

The two volumes of Gertrude Stein total close to two thousand pages, making this the most comprehensive collection of her writings ever published. Even so, some of her work had to be omitted, such as her massive *The Making of Americans,* written between 1903 and 1911, published in 1925, a novel that has been compared in scope and achievement to *Ulysses* and *A la recherche du temps perdu.* A recent edition of it weighs in at more than nine hundred crowded pages. The Library may expect one day to publish it separately, just as it will eventually want to bring out, as a supplement to the two volumes of William James already in the series, his greatest book, and one that had a shaping influence on Stein, the huge *Principles of Psychology.*

Along with an abundance of her works, these volumes include a full and very useful chronology of Stein's life and a note on each of the various texts, along with essential information about dates of composition, important because in her case the dates of publication can be many years or decades later. And there are notes for words and phrases that would likely send readers to a dictionary but that couldn't easily be found there. No interpretative notes are allowed in Library of America volumes. It is a policy especially appropriate for a writer who tends not only to avoid allusions or big words but to insist that each of her readers be allowed the freest play of response to her arrangements of words, which are often intentionally puzzling. The final selection was left to two well-seasoned scholars of her work, Catharine R. Stimpson, renowned as an educator and as one of Stein's most acute interpreters, and Harriet Chessman, author of an instructive book on Stein called *The Public Is Invited to the Dance.* Taken from the subtitle of one of Stein's poems, Chessman's title might reassure readers otherwise shy of getting close to the writings of "one of modernism's hardest writers," as Stimpson has called her.

Any writer famous for being "hard," whether Stein, Pound, Stevens, Joyce, or Eliot, is usually thought to be so immensely self-assured as to be indifferent to the approval or disapproval of the puzzled reader. If you don't get it it's because you don't get it. An unfortunate consequence of this presumption is that the intimidated reader is likely to miss the evidence lurking in these modernist works of the often intensely conflicted feelings that can infiltrate them, no matter how aloof the writer pretends to be. The more one reads of what Stein wrote over the course of her long career, the more she seems in fact to be genuinely torn between an impulse to write for the general public and the conviction that she should be writing only for herself. It is not enough, as she once hauntingly phrased it in *The Making of Americans*, that "I write for myself and strangers"; finally it must be only "for myself." With other American writers, like Melville or Whitman or Frost, she seems in this as in many other respects to be working in a tradition of difficulty that is naggingly troubled by the fact that the writing emerges from and enters back into a democratic culture.

She was by nature a socially gregarious, immensely personable woman who could charm not only the world's great but also nearly anonymous persons like the garage mechanics who fixed her car when she and Alice Toklas drove around France making themselves useful during World War I, or the city employees in her Paris neighborhood from whom she wheedled extra rations of fuel during a coal strike, or the students who flocked to her lectures in England and in the United States, or especially the American GIs whose voices (and post-war concerns) she catches so sympathetically in *Brewsie and Willy* of 1945 and who swarmed about her when she visited them in occupied Germany after World War II. She and Toklas had spent the war hiding in the villages of Belignin and Culoz, towns in Vichy France. Meanwhile, their Paris apartment with its precious collection of modernist paintings was intruded upon only once by German soldiers, who took only a few trinkets. Two middle-aged Jewish-American women living in hostage to wartime enemies of their race and country were made safe, it seems, by the interventions of an influential friend of theirs and of Picasso's named Bernard Fay, a scholar of American history and culture and an advisor during the war to Marshal Pétain. After the war, he was sentenced to prison for life as a collaborator.

All the while, she most ardently believed that true "writing" had no resemblance whatever to social discourse, at which, however, she was manifestly successful. "When I write I write and when I talk I talk," she wrote in the very talky *Everybody's*

Autobiography of 1936, "and the two are not one." "Talking," she wrote at this same time, in "What Are Masterpieces and Why Are There So Few of Them," "has nothing to do with creating." Talking is always with or to someone; it is perforce in the language of the "outside," while writing, for her, is ideally only of and from the "inside," a foreign language to the "outside."

Stein's quite elaborate cartographies of the writing self should not be treated, as they sometimes too solemnly are, as indispensable clues to her writings or as a dependable scale on which to rank them. They are improvisations, of a kind familiar enough among novelists and poets who have immortal longing more than merely earthly ambitions. The schemes help them to explain why some of their best, most inspired work appears to them to have come from someone or somewhere else, and is therefore markedly different from other compositions which manage or are intended to be popular. It is a way to account for writing that may seem literally extraordinary. Such categories of style, and of the different parts of the self which presumably correspond to them, may shape the speech of certain characters in a work, like Ahab or like Shakespeare's Richard II, who, both a man and a king by divine right, says of himself: "Thus play I in one person many people."

Claims to multiple identity were made similarly by two American writers, particular favorites of Stein's, along with Henry James. There is Emerson, with his famous depiction of "double consciousness," wherein the "two lives, of the understanding and the soul, which we lead, really show very little relation to each other . . . one prevails now, all buzz and din; the other prevails then, all infinitude and paradise." And there is Whitman, who goes Emerson one better, imagining for himself a tripartite arrangement whereby a "real Me" keeps its distance from and is capable of being quite scornfully judgmental of "my self" and "my soul." I evoke these precedents to emphasize again that Stein likes firmly to locate herself within an American literary tradition. Her experimental writings should therefore be regarded as not so much beyond the tolerable limits of what an American experimental tradition encourages, but rather as an extreme development that significantly, importantly, reflects back upon that tradition.

Coming late to the invention of these terminological divides, Stein understandably embellishes them. Divisions already over-elaborated by Whitman are elaborated still further. The core distinction laid down in *Geographical History* (1936) goes something like this: "the human mind," which is timeless, the shared property through the ages of various writers of genius, is utterly detached from "human nature," which is historically determined and changeable and from which gender, sexual, and racial identifications emanate. This dualism is then exemplified by attendant ones having more directly to do with writing. These are anticipated in earlier works like *The Making of Americans,* and become programmatically more active thereafter. There is, for instance, "true writing" (an emanation of "mind") as against "writing" or "speech" (which are endorsed by "human nature" and by the social commonality). There is also "entity" writing (as from "mind"), opposed to "identity writing" (derived from "human nature" and content with words that have already been "identified" with things as they are). Finally, there is the distinction laid down in "What Is English Literature," one of her *Lectures in America,* between "writing to serve God" or "writing to serve Mammon," though she tends to blur it quite casually, letting the two be separated now and then not by "or" but by "and." Why not, indeed, write for both at once?

Even though the very wording of Stein's classifications might suggest that works presumably written for God are necessarily superior to works meant to serve Mammon, any critical estimates of that sort turn out to be crude or useless. There's abundant evidence, for example, that she intended *Stanzas in Meditation* to be taken as a sharp and disparaging contrast to *The Autobiography of Alice B. Toklas.* She wrote them more or less concurrently in 1932–33, the one destined to be her most popular and profitable book, the other among her most inaccessible, intended presumably as an act of penance for her efforts at selling out. But her intention in no way proves in the actual results that the hard book is superior to the easier one, though this is a familiar misconception in academic assessments not only of Stein but of most writers of the early modernist period. Even some of Stein's most assiduous readers are heard to say that the *Autobiography,* precisely because of its popularity, is actually an obstruction to any serious appreciation of her.

It oughtn't to be assumed that Stein is at her best or even her most representative in works of hers that are close to impenetrable, like the nonetheless important *Patriarchal Poetry,* written in 1927 but not published till 1953. Not only is the line between her more public and her more private writings blurred in many important instances; it is a line that gradually becomes indistinct the more closely acquainted one gets with some very difficult works, notably *Tender Buttons,* which appeared in 1914. The work is divided into three sections, "Objects," "Food," "Rooms." Except for "Rooms," these sections are then broken down into smaller pieces carrying titles like "A Piece of Coffee" or "Roast Potatoes," and followed by what purports to be descriptions. However, the descriptions are totally defamiliarizing and in words that seem only tenuously related to one another. It is left to the reader to work toward a wholly new awareness of names and of things that heretofore had been taken for granted.

A reader who wants to enter into the movements of Stein's language had best read her without caring too strictly about any of her various schematizations of private as against public writing. It is better to think of each piece, particularly when it is experimental to one degree or another, as constituting a scene in the dramatization of her degrees of estrangement from normative English. There is scarcely any work of hers, including the more conventional ones, that isn't to some extent an act of linguistic protest against traditional and agreed-upon systems of designation and against the structures of relative primacy and subordination that have been made to seem necessary, normal, and inevitable.

That her writing is often anomalous is in part, but only in part, a reflection of the fact that she is herself an anomaly, in the sense of that term that Catharine Stimpson ascribes to the anthropologist Mary Gordon. Every culture, according to Gordon, explains itself to itself through categories that are endorsed by general public acceptance and usage "that cannot easily . . . be subject to revision. Yet they cannot reject the challenge of aberrant forms. Any given system of classification must give rise to anomalies, and any given culture must confront events which seem to defy its assumptions. It cannot ignore the anomalies which its scheme produces."

Stein is an anomaly not because she is a woman writer but because, while being one, she assigns herself the role of self-designated peer of the greatest of literary geniuses, and these are, in her lists of them, always male. Similarly, while celebrating her lesbianism, she imagines, especially in her experimental writings, that her natural sexual position is the classic male position in heterosexual sex. She is, in her own words, "on top." Being thus one of the grand masters of writing, she is also a master in love, and she often readily identifies herself in either case as a man. As she puts it mischievously in her poem *Lifting Belly,* written in 1915–17:

> Lifting belly can please me because it is an occupation I enjoy.
> Rose is a rose is a rose is a rose.
> In print on top.

A declaration of literary mastery, this is also an exhibition of it. Her signature line about "Rose" as a "rose" had appeared earlier, in the 1913 *Sacred Emily,* and would be repeated in more than a dozen of her works, culminating in *The World Is Round,* her highly successful children's book of 1938, whose hero is named Rose and which in its first edition was, as one evidence of Stein's often childlike insistence, printed on rose-colored paper and illustrated by Sir Francis Rose, displaying on the cover a circle made up of the words "Rose is a rose is a rose is a rose." Toklas, it is reported in *The Autobiography,* put the line "as a device on the letter paper, on the table linen and anywhere that [Stein] would permit it that I would put it." It became a device on Stein's signet ring, used to mark the sealing wax on addressed envelopes. It was in effect her logo. Along the way, however, she quietly altered it, so that the initial "Rose," a woman's name, emerges instead in lowercase as "a rose," referring thereby not to a woman but to a flower or to the word itself. It is a word or a flower, no more than that, and by being compared only to itself it is, she thinks, thereby divested of the many significances it has acquired from its poetic appearances over many centuries. That is how she herself chose to interpret the line when she said to Thornton Wilder in 1936, as he later reported: "Now listen! I'm no fool. I know that in daily life we don't go around saying 'is a . . . is a . . . is a. . . .' Yes, I'm no fool; but I think that in that line the rose is red for the first time in English poetry for a hundred years."

But what about that line when she chose originally to print it as if "rose" were meant to describe some property of a woman named Rose? In that version of the line—and carried over into its variant regardless of Stein's intentions—the rapid repetition of "a rose" easily slips into a pun on "eros." The pun can be found also in Melville's poetry, when he plays on "rose" and "a-maroso." These erotic connotations of "a rose" are also strongly hinted at in one of Touchstone's ribald speeches in *As You Like It,* Stein's favorite Shakespeare play, which is alluded to in *The World Is Round.* Touchstone there uses "rose" to refer to the heroine's (Rosalind's) vagina, as it also does, inferentially, in Dante's *Vita Nuova.* If in one version the line is supposed to be read as an act of poetic decreation and cleansing, it is in an earlier version, which was to resurface in *The World Is Round,* invested with some of the most ancient associations acquired from the poetry of the past, associations which in fact haunt Stein's line in all her versions of it.

Thus, while the line as it appears in "Lifting Belly" and as it first appeared in "Sacred Emily" is unmistakably metaphoric, linking a person to a flower, the revised version, which was soon to follow and predominate thereafter, is meant—regardless of the impossibility of doing so—to nullify any metaphoricity. That was Stein's intention, and it cannot be realized; it can be no more than gestural. Stein was fully aware of this problem and never let it deter her freedom of movement. Any theories she might entertain about her role as the redeemer of language easily give way in practice to her larger conviction that, as a master of poetry, she is free to do whatever she wants to do with words. Not only can she disassociate a word from its acquired significances, which is sometimes all she is credited with wanting to do, but she can then, at her convenience, revive and deploy that word with all of its conventional associations.

Stein has theories about many things, but her theory of herself as a grand master in print and in bed is the mother of all her theories. As a master of language, she is "on top," just as she is "on top" when in bed with Toklas; she is a usurper who, in the very process of eradicating patriarchal structures in sex and in sentences, also reserves to herself all the privileges derived from those structures. She is a "man" in relation to other women; she is a "man" in a line of entirely male geniuses, and like her two American favorites in that line, she makes self-contradiction into an evidence of her absolute authority over words: "With consistency a great soul has absolutely nothing to do," said Emerson, then to be echoed by Whitman: "Do I contradict myself?/ Very well then I contradict myself,/ (I am large, I contain multitudes.)."

Stein's seemingly outrageous claims to preeminence and all-inclusiveness manage to charm rather than to offend, in part because they are characteristically phrased in a way that depersonalizes them. It is as if she is claiming superiority not for herself as an individual but for something much larger and more inclusive, something belonging to "the human mind," as it does in Emerson to the "oversoul." Take, for example, the exhortation that when we think of her we think only of the great, indeed the greatest: "Think of Homer and the Bible, think of Shakespeare and think of me." She is speaking less on her own behalf than on behalf of an idea that genius in writing is an expression ideally only of the human mind which is timeless, not the property of any individual who participates in it. Besides, that "mind" is indifferent to individual identity, including sexual identity, which emanates from "human nature." It turns out that Stein's sentence, appropriately and shrewdly, refers to works of literature whose authorship has in each case been in dispute for centuries. This in itself might suggest that there is a general resistance to the idea that works of genius can ever be convincingly attributed only to specific individuals. Homer, birthplace unknown and blind, has had his authorship of the *Iliad* and even more frequently of the *Odyssey* cast into doubt. Shakespeare's plays have with some frequency been attributed to the Earl of Oxford, and in the later nineteenth century, when Stein reached her twenties, the claims of Bacon to their authorship were taken seriously by, among others, Whitman. As for the Bible, who can be sure who wrote any part of it? Growing up in a Jewish family, Stein would probably have heard it said that Moses was the author of the Torah.

So that even as Stein elevates herself to this select group, the authored identity of each of them is forever a matter of dispute. She nullifies any fixed identification between the writer and the writing, which brings up a central question about the importance to her own writing, especially in its experimental phase, of gender identification and lesbian identity.

Her lesbian sexuality is important to her writing from the very outset, as evident in the first of her novels, *Q.E.D.*, written in 1903 but left untyped and unpublished until after her death. Awkwardly anxious to be conventional in form and in style, *Q.E.D.* has at its center three young women in an unhappy triangulated love affair. The three have been identified as Stein (Adele) and two of the friends she made while studying at Johns Hopkins: the lover, Helen, is May Bookstaver, who was to remain close to Stein all her life; and the other woman, in love with Helen and Adele's rival, is Mabel Haynes (Mabel Neathe in the novel).

Several good reasons can be imagined why Stein relegated the novel to her unsorted manuscripts, where Toklas and a few other of her friends happened upon it in 1932. One likely reason was Stein's apprehension that the three characters involved would be identified with living persons, embarrassing all of them, particularly the two who were soon to find husbands. But this possibility of easy recognition points to a better, more strictly literary reason for her neglect of the novel. At the time she wrote it, Stein had yet to find a way to transform the material taken from her sexual life into anything much beyond a vague recounting of it. She hadn't discovered and developed the necessary resourcefulness in language that would allow her to make connections between her unconventional practices in love and the correspondingly unconventional forms which her writing was waiting to take. She was not long in finding ways to do so. Meantime, *Q.E.D.* did little more than reveal that her clumsily conventional writing was matched by what was then her clumsy, inexperienced, and reticent sexuality, deficiencies which the outspoken Helen (Bookstaver) is quite ready to point out to her. She was illiterate in the language of the body and would remain so until Toklas came into her life in Paris in 1907. At the very end of her first portrait of Toklas, a piece called "Ada" written in 1910, Stein lyrically and movingly expresses what Toklas meant to her in those first years:

Trembling was all living, living was all loving, some one was then the other one. Certainly this one was loving this Ada then. And certainly Ada all her living then was happier in living than anyone else who ever could, who was, who is, who ever will be living.

"Living" in the Stein–Toklas household was not for a while to be "all loving" once Toklas discovered and read *Q.E.D.* in 1932. This was at a time when Stein was finishing *The Autobiography* and was hard at work on *Stanzas in Meditation.* As it turned out, Stein had neglected to mention the May Bookstaver episode when, on pledging themselves to each other, she and Toklas were supposed to have confessed to all previous love affairs. Toklas took this as a betrayal of trust, the more embarrassing because she was obliged to cooperate with Bookstaver in efforts to secure the publication of *The Making of Americans.* It was years later, while doing research on *The Making of Americans,* that the Stein scholar Leon Katz unearthed the affair between Stein and Bookstaver, and it was to him that Toklas admitted, in 1952–53, that she had gone so far as to force Stein to destroy all the letters Bookstaver had written her in the early years.

More than that, Toklas, while typing *Stanzas in Meditation,* became suspicious of the frequent appearance in it of the word "may." She was not being in the least paranoid, it seems to me, funny though the whole episode may now seem. The word "may" is in fact peculiarly recurrent, especially when concentrated, as it sometimes is, over the short space of several consecutive lines. Toklas persuaded herself that this was Stein's covert way of evoking the name of her first lover. Accordingly, she began marking these recurrences, occasionally writing "May" in the margin, and at one point typing "May B." close to Stein's "maybe." Stein got the message, and set about changing many but not all uses of "may" to alternative words. She usually substituted "can," but in a few cases "and" or "are." References to the month of May became references to April or to "month-to-day."

That these revisions often have absurd results doesn't at all prove, though it is often taken to prove, that Toklas's suspicions were themselves groundless. Most likely, she was on to something actually at work in the language of the poem. Quite conspicuously so, in my view, in passages such as one which begins with a declaration and solicitation of love, one that Toklas could normally have taken as directed only to herself. The two lines are startlingly clear, the more so in a poem of such sustained obscurity, and they are followed by a repetition of "may," in three of the next eight lines, so insistent and yet so unrelated to any other words around it, that "may" is made to seem all the more like a calling-out to a missing presence:

> Tell me darling tell me true
> Am I all the world to you
> And the world of what does it consist
> May they be a chance to may they be desist . . .
> May they come with may they in with
> For which they may need needing

But however just Toklas's complaints were, the revisions made in response to them can have no compelling textual authority. While the version of the poem as first published in its entirety in 1950, and in subsequent printings, is the version from which the offending "mays" have been banished, scholarly research, undertaken by Ulla Dydo, has persuasively demonstrated that "may" should be restored to the place Stein had originally given it. This is done in the Library of America edition, which uses as a text the corrected typescript in the Beinecke Library at Yale that does not include revisions to the word "may."

Stein's depictions of lesbian sexuality are most purposefully and playfully intended, it seems to me, when they are made nearly indistinguishable from her violations of linguistic regularity. Her personal presence is especially strong in her writing at points when she is, so to speak, in the process of discovering that her delight in the female body isn't separable from the pleasures she finds in the twisting of syntax and of individual words out of their normal or customary shapes. Either activity is for her, and she hopes for us as we are reading her, a liberation from conformity to patriarchal assumptions.

The first evidences of these ambitious purposes begin to appear in "Melanctha," written in 1905, a scant two years after the failed effort of *Q.E.D.* The principal story in *Three Lives,* "Melanctha" is also one of the most enduring works of short fiction written at the start of a century that was to witness some consummate achievements in that form. Melanctha, escaping from the brutish authority of a father who seems intent on abusing her sexually, finds temporary solace in her friendship with the more sexually knowing but untrustworthy Rose. When, in the earlier stages of their association, the two young women feel exceptionally close to each other and can manage to be alone, Stein's gradually intensifying synchronizations of their speech rhythms and their vocabulary can be brought to a pitch, as will some similar exchanges later on in the story between Melanctha and her lover Jeff, that amazingly evoke, without any direct reference to them, the accelerations of bodily movement as two people are reaching together a point of sexual climax. The story is in every respect a triumph, and yet it is not considered one of her "experimental" works to the degree that *Tender Buttons* is, written about seven years later. The reason, perhaps, is that in "Melanctha," for all its success in the rendering of lesbian sexuality, there is no recognition of the identifications Stein elsewhere makes between, on the one hand, irregular sexual practice and, on the other, the irregular deployment of words.

Tender Buttons is designed both to confirm such an identification and to induce the reader into discovering it by his own interpretative concentrations on the words. Consider a witty and audacious example, a short entry that appears in *Tender Buttons* under the heading OBJECTS:

A cutlet.
A blind agitation is manly and uttermost.

Following the title, the sentence seems wholly comfortable in its own oddity. And why should it not be? Its vocabulary is simple enough, its tone is concise and authoritative, despite the fact that the details soon begin to seem ever more peculiar in relation to one another. So that while it sounds as if Stein fully expects to be understood, we soon recognize that to arrive at any understanding of the sentence or its title will require a patient and prolonged involvement in syntactical arrangements that defamiliarize words otherwise easily grasped. The sentence is not in the least portentous and even as she is rejecting conventional syntax she invites us to enjoy with her the unfolding of alternatives to it. As she will later enjoin us in *Patriarchal Poetry:*

> Reject rejoice rejuvenate rejuvenate rejoice reject rejoice
> rejuvenate reject rejuvenate reject rejoice. Not as if it
> was tried.

Clearly, *Tender Buttons* asks us to try. To be told straight off that "a cutlet" is for some reason "a blind agitation" only confirms that it is not a slice of chicken or veal, evident enough already, since "A cutlet" is not printed under the heading reserved for FOOD. The title doesn't appear to exert any authority in determining the order of words in the sentence that follows and presumably describes or modifies it. Rather, the order given those words is wholly arbitrary, free-floating in relation not only to the title but to one another. What is or might be "a blind agitation"? By asking the question at all, the reader is assenting to Stein's right once again to do with words anything she is of a mind to do with them, and is also agreeing that she might well be making a kind of sense in her wholly unfamiliar arrangements.

To say that an "agitation" is "blind" may mean that it is not able to make visible or to identify its source. Such often proves to be the case with "agitation." Maybe it is "blind" also because the "agitation" is felt at a spot where it can be self-generated or caused by an instrument, like a hand, that blindly gropes at and stimulates the spot. All good enough possibilities, but not much to go on as we proceed, in the order given, to the word "manly." But if it is her mission to reject forms that are overdetermining, then that must include forms into which her own words have fallen. We are free, then, to skip the word "manly" for a moment and to look ahead to the word "uttermost." From the very sound the coinage seems more susceptible to interpretation than does the word "manly." "Uttermost" sounds, that is, like a word that will readily yield a number of puns, like "most utterable." There could also be an intended pun on "utter" as "outermost," a hint that this "blind agitation" may be occurring on or near the outer edge of something, perhaps some part of the body, or even that the agitation results in a projection at such an edge. Furthermore, "utter" might be a pun on "udder" (as is more obviously the case later on in *Tender Buttons,* where the word "utter" resurfaces under the title "Milk"). Let's say, then, that "a blind agitation" is "manly" because it is taking place at some "uttermost" (that is, outermost and uddermost) part of a woman's body, at the site, for example, of an erect clitoris, the female equivalent to a male phallus. Thus, "manly agitation," coming either from a man or from a woman, may produce not only an erection but a milky excretion. Most simply, then, "a cutlet" becomes a metaphor for the vaginal gap, itself a small "cut" or "cutlet."

Some readers may by now have come to feel that this metaphorical equation is so inevitable that we ought to have been aware of it from the outset. This is in itself one evidence that *Tender Buttons,* even while being a resolutely experimental and difficult work, is less radically so than are some later ones, like *Stanzas in Meditation,* where words seem deliberately estranged from one another and seem to become objects unto themselves. By contrast, Stein is committed in this earlier work to what she calls, in *Lectures in America*, the "recreation" of words. This means that she is intent on discovering meanings already lurking in them, but in such a suppressed way that they can be released only by her genius at putting some words into wholly unexpected juxtapositions to other words.

That the *Oxford English Dictionary* never attributes to the word "cutlet" the meaning Stein finds in it doesn't prove that the word had not at some point in the past carried that meaning. In fact, in Melville's story "Bartleby the Scrivener," as it first appeared in *Putnam's Monthly* in 1853, the "grub-man" at the Tombs, where Bartleby has been confined as a vagrant, is named Mr. Cutlets. Induced by a bribe to make himself "useful" to Bartleby, he accordingly approaches him with a proposal. "May Mrs. Cutlets and I have the pleasure of your company to dinner, sir, in Mrs. Cutlets' private room?" The innuendo was thought so obvious, and perhaps offensive to some readers, that either Melville or his editors deleted both the name "Cutlets" and the reference to her "private room" when the story appeared in *Piazza Tales* in 1856.

To discover by interpretation that Stein is using the word "cutlet" the way Melville had used it half a century earlier isn't, then, to discover her originality. Her originality consists in her ability to make that meaning serve her decidedly particular intentions. By her own "manly agitations" of the normative forms of English, Stein, even in so brief a piece, manages to affirm—as does her lovemaking with "Pussy," her pet name for Toklas, on which she also likes to pun—that the potentialities of vaginal power are equivalent, in both projectile and productive ways, to the male phallus, a standard sign of patriarchal dominance. That dominance, imaged in customary structures of language, as in the relation of substantives to other merely supportive units, is subverted by Stein's wordplay, but only so that she may in the process appropriate patriarchal power to herself, and in a form of her own devising.

The term "patriarchal" has become a buzz word in literary and psychoanalytic theory, most influentially in the writings of Jacques Lacan. Stein would have known of equivalents to some of these theories, picked up from her reading of two of her American precursors, Emerson and, especially, William James. Emerson's essays everywhere insist on one, absolutely essential responsibility for all serious writers: it is actively to resist in his or her language those conformities that are the price of using words to mean only what one's audience insists they should mean. At times, he is close to saying that the best, perhaps only way to do this, is to keep your mouth shut. "As soon as he has once acted or spoken with éclat," he warns in the essay "Self-Reliance," he is "a committed person." That is, he is sentenced to a jailhouse of conformity made out of his own sentences, particularly sentences designed to be understood easily. As a result, his language in the essays, notably at points in "Self-Reliance," can be nearly as difficult to negotiate as Stein's. At other times, even silence is said to be preferable to speech: "Good as discourse is, silence is better and shames it." "If I speak," he says in still another essay, "I define, I confine, and am less." And even if one manages to remain silent, it then turns out that, so far as Emerson is concerned, "Every thought is also a prison." Why should this be so? Because a "thought" is the inert, frozen product of the activity of "thinking," framed in words that cannot exclusively be one's own.

A still more evident and direct influence on her attitudes toward language came from William James. James was her favorite teacher at Harvard Annex, soon to be called Radcliffe College, when she enrolled in 1893. In 1894, James invited her to join his seminar. She was already acquainted with his writings, especially with *Principles of Psychology,* published only a few years earlier in 1891, a book widely discussed over the next few years among faculty and students at Harvard. After leaving Cambridge, she kept in touch with James while studying psychology and medicine, on his recommendation, at Johns Hopkins and,

after that, when she had settled in Paris. In 1908, two years
before his death, he visited the apartment on the rue du Fleurus
which she then shared with her brilliant but domineering
brother Leo. This was before Toklas arrived in 1910, soon to displace him. James looked at the not yet famous paintings that the
Steins had accumulated, including works by Cézanne, Matisse,
and Picasso. "I told you," he said. "I told you that you would
keep your mind open."

The clearest, most simply stated evidence of James's importance to Stein's experimental uses of language can be found in
the chapter of *Principles* called "The Stream of Thought." It is
there that he says, "Language works against our perceptions of
the truth." He has in mind two closely related features of ordinary language use. First, we tend spontaneously to name things
as their presence registers on consciousness: "so that the names
are taken as previous and explanatory." In this way we suppress
the actual experience of these things, which occurs within a
coincidental jumble of many other impressions and feelings.
Second, we come as if instinctively to build or structure the sentences we ordinarily use, having learned to accept as both natural and inevitable the privileges normally given in sentences to
substantives, to names, or to designated subjects. That is, we are
made craven before words that are "power bringing," as James
derisively referred to them in *Pragmatism,* such as "God" or
"Reality" or "Truth." In his view, these ingrained habits of naming and of structuring things have had not only undesirable but
quite brutal and brutalizing consequences on our thinking. With
considerable feeling, he observes,

> so inveterate has our habit become of recognizing the existence of
> the substantive parts alone, that language almost refuses to lend itself
> to any other use . . . All *dumb* or anonymous psychic states have,
> owing to this error, been coolly suppressed; or, if recognized at all,
> have been named after the substantive perception they led to, as
> thoughts 'about' this object or 'about' that, the stolid word *about*
> engulfing all their delicate idiosyncrasies in its monotonous sound.

Words as impassioned as these and as outraged in tone oughtn't to obscure the fact that James is not speaking out on behalf of people who have been marginalized, suppressed, made inarticulate and anonymous, by oppressive systems. What he's outraged about are the beleaguered elements in an ordinary sentence, those parts of the sentence whose presence is diminished or silenced by the dominant syntactical forms that "engulf" them, along with certain of our "psychic states." Stein is equally concerned about such matters, though in an altogether lighter tone, as in *Lectures in America* (1935–36), when she talks about "the active life of writing." She has, she says, developed on the way a fondness for verbs because "they are, so to speak, on the move and adverbs move with them." She especially likes prepositions which "can live one long life being really being nothing." And though for a while she had trouble liking or even using nouns, the equivalent of James's "substantives," she gradually found ways "to refuse them by using them," and it was then that "my real acquaintance with poetry was begun," she reports, because "Poetry is concerned with using with abusing, with losing with wanting, with avoiding with adoring with replacing the noun." This is very like a relationship between lovers trying to find their balance or between rivals testing their relative strength. Language and the writer, that is, are to be thought of as protagonists in an ongoing drama, an ever continuing and active struggle by each side against merely being "used" by the other.

"ARE THEY *MY* POOR?":
EMERSON'S STEINIAN
QUESTION

※

On earlier occasions, as far back as *A World Elsewhere* (1966) and more recently in *Poetry and Pragmatism* (1992), I have remarked on some close similarities between Ralph Waldo Emerson and his admirer Gertrude Stein. Similarities of temperament, of conviction, and in their perceptions of an inner conflict experienced acutely by American writers as grandly ambitious as they themselves admit to being. At several points in her *Lectures in America,* Stein formulates it as a conflict between "writing for God," on the one hand, or, on the other, "writing for Mammon." In the alternate phrasings she likes to allow herself, it is the difference between writing "as a writer god" or "writing [in] the way it has already been written," that is, in familiar forms assured of public understanding and approval and, thus, of marketability.

Emerson admits to feelings very similar to hers. In the opening sentences of "Self-Reliance," which is the primary focus of this essay, he enjoins the reader to speak or to write in accordance only with your own "genius," the God within you. You must, he says, articulate in public "what is in your private heart," and promises that if you do so, you will discover that "what is true for you is true for all men": "Speak your latent conviction," he reiterates, "and it shall be the universal sense." However, the thrust of the essay, as I understand it, is that if you do this too assertively you will, instead, alienate all those others who make up the "joint stock company" which is "society," an embodiment of Stein's "Mammon." You will be marginalized as an eccentric.

Emerson's sensitivity to the threat of marginalization, of being isolated within his own mind, informs all his writing and is responsible for much of the tension—and the notorious corrections of course—within his sentences or between them; responsible, too, for his rhetorical overreachings and his often abrupt and worldly-wise disclaimers of them. For Stein, the conflict between public writing and private writing is acted out less often within a single work than as a marked difference between one work of hers and another, as between, say, two works written in the same month, one as a sort of reparation for the other: the gregarious, best-selling *Autobiography of Alice B. Toklas* and the extremely private, almost wholly impenetrable *Stanzas in Meditation*.

But even Stein, popularly supposed to be the more stylistically adventurous of the two, did not imagine that these incentives for writing—for God or for Mammon—were irreconcilably in conflict, and she quite casually now and then allows the word "and" instead of "or" to separate them: "writing for God and Mammon." The desire to write for God is a condition for innovative work, but she knew that even innovative work, to make any difference, must be published. It would have no reason to exist if it were to remain unpublished, entirely unreadable and hence unread. In his essay "Intellect," Emerson declares flatly, "To genius must always go two gifts, the thought and the publication. The first is revelation. . . . To be communicable it must become a picture or a sensible object." And in the companion essay, "Art," he concedes, "No man can quite exclude the element of necessity from his labor. No man can quite emancipate himself from his age and country, or produce a model in which the education, the religion, the politics, usages, and arts of his time shall have no share."

Both Emerson and Stein were geniuses, but they were besides uncommonly intelligent and uncommonly sensible. Neither believed in the possibility of creating a new language and both admitted to the immense difficulty even of inventing new words; both were always at work *re*newing and *re*fashioning and *re*creating the words they already share with the rest of us. In her lecture "Poetry and Grammar," Stein writes, "Of course you might say why not invent new names new languages but that cannot be done. It takes a tremendous amount of inner necessity to invent even one word. . . . So everyone must stay with the language that has come to be spoken and written and which has in it all the history of its intellectual recreation." The plight Stein is alluding to here—the discovery of a "tremendous amount of inner necessity to invent even one word"—is at the dramatic center of a passage from "Self-Reliance" that we'll be exploring in a moment. It is a passage that dramatizes how Emerson himself discovers an "inner necessity" to invent a new word for the word "poor," and must instead try—quite unsuccessfully, it would appear—to endow the word "poor" with a meaning radically at odds with common usage. It is a dramatically exciting, at times self-critically comical moment that demonstrates the inconsistencies, the frustrations, the real risks of social and cultural estrangement that can result from such verbal actings-out of this "inner necessity."

The passage on the "poor" comes early on in the essay, taking up most of the seventh paragraph. This follows the paragraphs wherein Emerson has been enjoining us to "speak" or to "utter," to give vent to an inner self, an audible vocalization of "the voices which we hear in solitude, but [which] grow faint and inaudible as we enter the world." But very shortly he will be admitting that he himself fails to meet his own standards, particularly when he speaks at the level of polite social interchange. "Every decent and well-spoken individual affects and sways me more than is right," he complains. "I ought to go upright and vital, and speak the rude truth in all ways."

Why, then, doesn't he? We are already heading into troubled waters, as Emerson intends we should be, knowing all the while that his readers are apt to focus on his most hyperbolic, lofty, and memorable assertions without giving due attention to how frequently he hedges on many of them. Furthermore, the stylistic impulsiveness for which he is best known is characterized in many of his essays as a violation of the very thinking they pretend to represent. "Our thinking," he says in "Intellect," "is a pious reception"—"pious" because the "thinking" is prompted from on high, so to speak; it is actuated by our reverence for a God or genius that is lodged within us. However, the resulting thought can be contaminated by the mode of its publication, by our rhetoric: "Our truth of thought is . . . vitiated as much by too violent direction given by our will as by too great negligence."

Thus, assertions of will, though these might be supposed to exemplify "self-reliance," can as readily nullify it. This is what he means in "Self-Reliance" when, immediately after he urges us to speak out, he cautions that if we speak too forcefully, too brilliantly, we may find that we thereby become overcommitted to, imprisoned in, our own words. "As soon as he has once acted or spoken with éclat, [a man] is a committed person," he says. He is "clapped into jail by his consciousness," by his fall into language. The danger of "speaking with éclat" is that once you have done so you are henceforth monitored for consistency—this being, you recall, "the hobgoblin of little minds"—both by your fan club and by the enemies you've been making by shooting off your mouth: "watched by the sympathy and hatred of hundreds whose affections must now enter into [your] account."

How, then, does Emerson proceed in his own writing without becoming trapped in that "éclat," the eloquence which for many readers is what makes him Emerson? He manages it, quite simply, by consistently contradicting himself. Self-contradiction is for him the essential evidence that his self-reliance has remained uncompromised by his own will to signification. His writing becomes a site for repeated acts of what he calls "abandonment." Emerson's celebrations of "abandonment" in "The Poet," the shorter essay "Nature," "Circles," and "The Over-Soul" are notably impassioned. And in the magnificently eloquent last paragraph of "Circles," he directly associates "abandonment" with what he there calls "facilities of performance." For him, "performance" refers to actions taken with and within words. It is a "performance," for example, when, in the middle of the essay "Self-Reliance," he impatiently turns around on himself and on his essay and asks: "Why then do we prate of self-reliance?" For a moment at least he "abandons" his own title, and by doing so he "facilitates" his own and the reader's at least momentary release from its hold upon us, a hold that has accumulated by virtue of Emerson's own writing.

Any hope I may entertain that I can identify Emerson in his writing is generated only by a close moment-by-moment attendance on his "facilities of performance" as it creates, guides, and disrupts his sentences and paragraphs. It is necessary at all costs to avoid the temptation to conclude prematurely that any given performance has come to rest in a meaning. Commentaries on the passage we'll now turn to in "Self-Reliance" have never, so far as I've discovered, been able to resist simplistic summaries of what he is saying at the expense of what he is doing, especially when he gets round to asking his notorious question. To delineate the larger performance of which that question is only one part, I will need to quote the surrounding passage at some length:

> Good and bad are but names very readily transferable to that or this; the only right is what is after my constitution, the only wrong what is

against it. A man is to carry himself in the presence of all opposition, as if every thing were titular and ephemeral but he. I am ashamed to think how easily we capitulate to badges and names, to large societies and dead institutions. Every decent and well-spoken individual affects and sways me more than is right. I ought to go upright and vital, and speak the rude truth in all ways. If malice and vanity wear the coat of philanthropy, shall that pass? If an angry bigot assumes this bountiful cause of Abolition, and comes to me with his last news from Barbadoes, why should I not say to him, "Go love thy infant; love thy wood-chopper: be good-natured and modest: have that grace; and never varnish your hard uncharitable ambition with this incredible tenderness for black folk a thousand miles off. Thy love afar is spite at home." Rough and graceless would be such greeting, but truth is handsomer than the affectation of love. Your goodness must have some edge to it,—else it is none. The doctrine of hatred must be preached as the counteraction of the doctrine of love when that pules and whines. I shun father and mother and wife and brother, when my genius calls me. I would write on the lintels of the door-post, *Whim.* I hope it is somewhat better than whim at last, but we cannot spend the day in explanation. Expect me not to show cause why I seek or why I exclude company. Then again, do not tell me, as a good man did to-day, of my obligation to put all poor men in good situations. Are they *my* poor? I tell thee, thou foolish philanthropist, that I grudge the dollar, the dime, the cent, I give to such men as do not belong to me and to whom I do not belong. There is a class of persons to whom by all spiritual affinity I am bought and sold; for them I will go to prison, if need be; but your miscellaneous popular charities; the education at college of fools; the building of meeting-houses to the vain end to which many now stand; alms to sots; and the thousandfold Relief Societies;—though I confess with shame I sometimes succumb and give the dollar, it is a wicked dollar which by and by I shall have the manhood to withhold.

It's roughly the last third of this quotation (from "Then again, do not tell me" through "I shall have the manhood to withhold") that has excited comment both apologetic and accusatory. For example, Harold Bloom offered it (in his introduction to the Emerson volume in the Chelsea House *Modern Critical Views*) as evidence that "Emerson unfortunately believed in Necessity, including the offense of superiority in persons—and he was capable of writing passages that can help justify Reagan's large share of the Yuppie vote." Bloom then says of the passage that the concept of "Self-Reliance" translated "out of the inner life and into the marketplace is difficult to distinguish from our current religion of selfishness, as set forth so sublimely in the recent grand epiphany at Dallas." (He is referring to the 1984 Republican National Convention.) Bloom seemed content, to a degree wholly uncharacteristic of him, with an interpretation that might have come from an ephebe of the new historicism, for which he has expressed unmodified disdain. It is an analysis that pictures Emerson as complacently leaving the word "poor"—a word whose special meaning for him is clearly signaled by his italics—to wallow all the while in associations it has long since acquired from social convention and institutional use.

It seems to me quite evident that Emerson himself has already recognized and disposed of the challenge Bloom makes to the passage, as when he talks about the sorry consequences of translating "'Self-Reliance' out of the inner life and into the marketplace." Indeed, Emerson makes this problem of marketplace translation into a central linguistic drama and preoccupation of many of his essays. The tension, the defensive rhetoric of the passage, its self-lacerating changes of tone, all are meant to dramatize, through movements of style, that this problem of translation from "out of the inner life and into the marketplace" is one that Emerson took to be inevitable. It is built into the language available to him, and recognized as an obstacle to "self-reliance" which he consequently seeks out in order to test his capacities as a writer to surmount it, on the page at least. As a writer his strongest impulse is to show how it might be possible to make this translation without, at the same time, conforming to the terminologies and therefore to the ethos of the marketplace. Emerson is not, after all, making some sort of economic policy statement, and is emphatically not asking to be associated with the positions Bloom wants to assign him. Instead, as I'll be showing, he is enacting, as in a little neighborhood play, his struggles to make himself understood in the language and with the literary resources and endowments made available to him.

George Kateb's interpretation is very much at odds with Bloom's. But it creates just as many problems. Kateb has led the way in showing the importance to a political philosopher like himself of Emerson, Thoreau, and Whitman. He argues that Emerson is in no sense advising us to ignore the plight of the underprivileged. Rather, he tries to show that the complexities in the passage might guide our thinking about our obligations to others in a democratic society. In the Winter 1989 issue of *Social Research,* he writes:

> By his question in "Self-Reliance," "Are they *my* poor?" he wants to transmit the shock of Jesus' saying "The poor you have always with you"; no more than Jesus is he counseling indifference to the disadvantaged. He does not want guilt to sicken charity; rather he wants respect to inform compassion. He does not want assistance to become a mutually degrading routine. I think Emerson's attitude, because of its complexities, is a good guide to thinking about what individuals owe each other as strangers and fellow citizens in a rights-based democracy.

While these two interpretations are indeed at odds—Bloom finding evidence of a "religion of selfishness," Kateb finding evidence of scrupulous compassion—they share a number of assumptions that seem to me misplaced and inadequate to the extraordinary agitations felt by Emerson, and communicated to the reader, about the language and syntax he is using. First, each assumes that you can get at what Emerson is trying to say by quoting only a small section of the paragraph in which the passage finds itself, and it probably doesn't need to be pointed out that the predispositions of any critic do not wait to be disclosed only in analysis or evaluative comment; they make themselves known in the earlier decision as to what deserves to be quoted for analysis and what does not.

Second, and as a consequence of the first, it is assumed by both of them that the passage they quote is brought into focus by the question "Are they *my* poor?" and that this question is, furthermore, an expression, one way or another, of Emerson's feelings about people who are hurting economically. Finally, Bloom's charge that the passage reveals the alarming degree to which self-reliance is congenial to a Reaganite religion of selfishness, while being implicitly denied in Kateb's analysis, is nonetheless made creditable by it, thanks to the defensiveness of Kateb's rhetoric, and his evident feeling that he needs to protect Emerson from the charge of callousness and insensitivity by a laying-on of rhetorical pieties. As for the connections adduced by Kateb between Emerson and Jesus, my reading of the pertinent passages in Matthew, Mark, and John does not indicate that Kateb's analysis of Emerson is at all well served by his citation of the Gospels. Quite the reverse. Jesus, you may recall, has just allowed expensive oils to be poured over his head by a visiting woman. But he is then obliged to defend her act of pious generosity from those in attendance who complain of the cost. The oil could have been sold, they point out, and the money given to the poor. Jesus objects to this with a hauteur proper to a man in his condition. As the son of God, he will be on earth only a little while anyway, he points out, so he is jealous of every sign of gratitude while he's here to accept it. The poor, however, will always be with you. There'll be plenty of time, that is, to be generous to their sort.

A reader who goes back to the sentence—"are they *my* poor?"—within the large paragraph where it finds itself will notice that the sentence occurs in the last of a series of very scrappy scenes in which Emerson sounds curiously half proud of his responses and half agitated by them, or, more exactly, by the responses he *might* have made, to neighbors who call upon him to conform in his thinking, conform to the presumed legitimacy of what he calls derisively "badges" and "names." Thus the word "poor" is to be taken as only one such name or badge. And by the end of the passage he has in fact moved away from any charitable, social, or economic issues posed by the "poor," and, in a calculated tone of ranting and dismissiveness, has turned to other abuses perpetrated in the name of goodness: "the education at college of fools," "the building of meeting houses," "alms for sots." Along the way he parodies Exodus by saying "I would write on the lintels of the door-post, *Whim,*" thus encouraging people to "pass over" his house, to let him alone. And yet even as he is berating others for being cowed by "badges and names" he also disparages his own modes of speech in his supposed replies to these others. Notice that he characterizes the rejoinder he thought of making to the "Abolitionist" as "rough and graceless," and that he feels compelled to preach, or to imagine preaching, "the doctrine of hatred" only as "the counteraction to the doctrine of love when that pules and whines." Finally, he imagines himself angrily instructing "the good man," as he calls him, "do not tell me of my obligations"; and then retaliating in kind with "I tell thee, thou foolish philanthropist." What do all these confrontations have in common? First of all, we can't be sure they ever actually took place; second, they all involve one or another reference to his own speech, to writing, preaching, or telling. That is, they are largely imaginary confrontations over terminology, over badges and names—with some name-calling thrown in; they are arguments with *himself* over what to say, and how to say it, as against what already has been said so often, by "decent well-spoken individuals," as to have become socially and morally unassailable.

In this series of encounters Emerson is contending in his own mind with others for control over a terminology they share in common, since, to communicate at all, opponents must share a terminology. And in none of these encounters does he picture himself as a clear winner. The implication is that, while one can *try* to change words, it is not possible to seize them for personal use only; they always stubbornly do keep their "market" value; they always in themselves are a market of exchange. His bluster is an expression of a writer's linguistic frustrations with the fact that words are not his but communal property. So that by the time we get to his question about "*my* poor," the accumulated effect of these frustrating encounters is that the word "poor" becomes itself—for him, and in his mind—an object of contention. That is, so far as he is concerned, the word does not designate only or even principally a class of persons who need economic assistance. That common-sense meaning of the term demands from him too great a degree of linguistic and therefore of social conformity.

The word "poor" thus becomes yet another instance of verbal intimidation, a particularly insidious demand that he stop thinking of and for himself, that he simply conform to a name or a badge. He elects, therefore, to treat the word "poor" no differently from the way a self-reliant person should in his view treat any word; any word should be treated *not* as if it necessarily represents an established reality—as Jesus assumes when he says "the poor you have always with you"—but rather as "titular" and "ephemeral." The italicized word in the phrase "*my* poor" is not, then, to be taken even as a reference to some selected favorites or neighbors out of a mass of all poor men. "*My* poor" may be a reference instead to persons who might not be economically underprivileged at all. They could as easily be prosperous people who nonetheless can be called "poor" in Emerson's own radically revised sense of the term. Maybe they are linguistically impoverished or lacking in resources of imagination. Maybe they are impoverished in the way Emerson describes himself as being in "Experience": a writer whose darling infant son has been inexplicably taken from him and from life, depriving him forever of the most cherished, visible evidence of his own creative powers.

This particular moment of linguistic struggle has been prepared for by the way Emerson talks earlier in the passage about words having to do with slavery. He speaks to "the Abolitionist" in a tone as disdainful as is his tone in addressing "thou foolish philanthropist." And this little tonal precedent is meant to alert us, I think, to a more important one, which is that in this encounter with the Abolitionist, as in the later encounter with the philanthropist, Emerson is trying to change the import of the very words he perforce shares with his opponents. Noticeably, he does not say that "the Abolitionist," a bigot in disguise, should turn his attention toward "blacks" and slaves closer to home than are those he likes to talk about, a thousand miles away in Barbados. Instead, he asks the reader to approve of a question he apparently didn't dare to ask: "Why should I not say to him 'Go love thy infant, love thy wood-chopper.'" In asking for the approval of the reader, Emerson may betray his uncertainty about his imagined course of argument, but it is also a way of inviting the reader to participate in a tactic of evasion; it gives us practice in how "to carry [ourselves] in the presence of all opposition," in how, inwardly at least, to say what we often don't say aloud, or with "éclat." He is dramatizing his internal resistance to the power accumulated in certain words, like "slave" or "black" or "poor," power available even to bigots and fools, and then used by them to force him—as he admits to being forced ("I sometimes succumb and give the dollar")—into what have come to be called politically correct positions.

But merely resisting such power inwardly is obviously frustrating to Emerson. He wants also to appropriate an equivalent power to his private discourse. It is at such junctures that he seems to me to become most radical and most intricate in his writing, and where even sympathetic readers might find reason not to follow him. It isn't only that he wishes he could quite aggressively retaliate against people who use "badges," like "poor" or "slave," so as to make him conform to socially accredited attitudes. He specifically wants at these moments to invent new meanings *and* win public assent for doing so. He wants to write simultaneously for god *and* mammon, by depriving "badges," words, and "titles" of their normal representational value even while he still uses them in a vastly different, unfamiliar, and uncredited sense. He wants both to use the words and to advance alternate meanings for them, words like poor or slave, whose authority will then depend entirely on Emerson's own self-reliant, individual tropings of the terms.

A particularly vivid and moving example of this effort of his occurs in his Journal, dated August 1852:

> I waked at night, & bemoaned myself, because I had not thrown myself into this deplorable question of Slavery, which seems to want nothing so much as a few assured voices. But then, in hours of sanity, I recover myself, & say, God must govern his own world, & knows his way out of this pit, without my desertion of my post which has none to guard it but me. I have quite other slaves to free than those negroes, to wit, imprisoned spirits, imprisoned thoughts, far back in the brain of man—far retired in the heaven of invention, &, which, important to the republic of Man, have no watchman, or lover, or defender, but I.

The word "slavery," having initially referred to a "deplorable question" affecting millions of black people, is gradually troped so that it refers instead to "imprisoned thoughts." And what are these? They are the "thoughts" of a writer and very specifically so, as suggested by the direct echo in "heaven of invention" of the chorus at the outset of Shakespeare's *Henry V.* ("O! for a muse of fire, that would ascend/ The brightest heaven of invention!"). If he *could* bring about the liberation of these thoughts, could he then perhaps assure his place as America's Shakespeare?

Emerson's troping of slavery here, and in the passage from "Self-Reliance," is a clue to what he is doing with the word "poor" and to how the phrase "*my* poor" may best be understood. It is in no sense an apologetic or even an extenuating use of that phrase. It does not mean "I'm taking care of my poor, of some of the people you would also call 'poor,' but who are especially close to me." It is entirely aggressive. The question means: are those people *you* are calling "poor" really "poor" in *my* sense of the *term* "poor." Would *I* call them "poor"? By "poor" Emerson would mean, in my understanding of him, those of whatever economic class or occupation who are not receiving the support they need by way of inspiration or genius, support from the resources of language itself. It is exactly this complaint that can be heard in the opening paragraph of "Experience." There, once again appropriating the language of the market so that it refers principally—but not exclusively—to the writer's imagination, he asks: "Did our birth fall in some fit of indigence and frugality in nature, that she was so sparing in her fire and so liberal of her earth, that it appears to us that we lack the affirmative principle, and though we have health and reason, yet we have no superfluity or spirit for new creation? We have enough to live and bring the year about, but not an ounce to impart or to invest."

Who, then, to wrap this up, are those allies he has in mind when he mentions "the class of persons to whom by all spiritual affinity I am bought and sold" and for whom "I will go to prison if need be"? Once again, he brings together the market and the prison metaphors used earlier in "Self-Reliance," metaphors that describe conformity, in the one case by his referring to society as a "joint-stock company," and, in the other, by his saying that anyone who has once "spoken with éclat is a committed person." And yet this same "class of persons," with whom he here claims "spiritual affinity," manage for the very reason of that affinity to buy and sell him as in a "joint-stock company," possibly even to put him in prison.

In other words, though he may love them, they threaten him no less, and in much the same way, as do all the opponents in the essay to whom he wants to preach the doctrine of hatred. How can this be? Because, by his lights, even when he speaks in a way that reveals his spiritual affinity with others he is, nonetheless, *speaking;* he is nonetheless using words, seeking approval and support, compromising his reliance on himself. He becomes, thereby and again, a "committed person" and a conformist, in his very efforts not to be. The only escape from these cyclical losses of self-reliance is yet another determined effort to abandon even the few affinities and alliances he has acquired by his non-conformist way of talking. Only then, to recall a phrase from "Experience," might "the mind" once more and forever "[go] antagonizing on." William James may be right in thinking that "true ideas . . . lead to consistency, stability and flowing human intercourse," but for Emerson the language for discovering or expressing "true ideas" is just as likely to lead to eccentricity and isolation—to the great writer alone with and in his writing.

13

IN COLD INK:
TRUMAN CAPOTE

※

It can be said of *A Capote Reader* that to have read it once is to have read it forever. Though the best of Truman Capote's short stories are here, they are only pretty good, like "My Side of the Matter" (1945), "Master Misery" (1949), and "Among the Paths to Eden" (1960); so too with the travel sketches. But many items could easily have been omitted to make room for his first novel, *Other Voices, Other Rooms* (1948); it could honorably use the space given to *The Grass Harp* (1951), that prolonged embarrassment of a novella. We are, fortunately, given the most impressive of Capote's fictions, the novella *Breakfast at Tiffany's* (1958), which features the indomitable Holly Golightly. She is one of those smart, offbeat, warmhearted, disruptive women whom Capote tended to favor in fiction and, until cause was almost inevitably given for a break, in life. Accordingly, among the portraits are those of Marilyn Monroe and Elizabeth Taylor from *Music for Chameleons* (1980) and a vignette about Mae West from *Observations*, a book he did jointly with Richard Avedon in 1959.

Far too long to be included in the *Reader* is *In Cold Blood,* the best of Capote's works. Some excerpts would have been welcome. It was published in 1966, the year of his famous Black and White Ball for five hundred people at the Plaza Hotel in New York in honor of Katherine Graham. At the time the critic Frederick Dupee said convincingly that *In Cold Blood* "is the best documentary account of an American crime ever written." Unlike Norman Mailer in his later *The Executioner's Song,* Capote himself did every last shred of research for his book, without taking tape recordings or even taking notes during his hundreds of interviews. The book is a masterful re-creation of the brutal murder in Holcomb, Kansas, of the Clutter family— Herbert Clutter, a prosperous wheat farmer who had been an Eisenhower appointee to the Federal Farm Credit Board, his wife, and two of their children. Immediately fascinated by news reports of the incident, Capote took up the project even before the murderers, who had not known their victims, were appre- hended. He stayed with it through the investigation, the trial, the death-row incarcerations, and the executions, where he bid a last farewell at the foot of the gallows to Richard Hickock and Perry Smith, the two young wanderers who had committed the crime.

Capote never put so much of himself into anything. The fact that he studiously avoids appearing as the first-person narrator in the work means that his personal intensities are kept impressively in control. They are continually mediated and exalted by those human complications from which, as we see in the *Reader,* he usually abstracts himself by a rhetoric alternately sentimental and tart. He gave a good six years of his life to the book, much of that time spent in the small community where the crime occurred and where he gradually won the affection and cooperation of people who had never before heard of him. He spent months talking to Hickock and Smith and to other inmates at the Kansas State Penitentiary. Before he even began to write, he had accumu- lated more than eight thousand pages of research material. Such immersion, especially when it required living in areas remote from the kind of amenities and companionship he was used to, would probably (as he suggests in interviews) have exhausted the patience and energy of most of his near-contemporaries, or a particularly macho claimant like Hemingway.

The explanation for Capote's unusual dedication to this particular project isn't simply that he was tough enough to put up with the strain. While he everywhere shows a fascination with criminal behavior and with murderers (in his talk with Richard Grobel in *Conversations with Capote,* he passes on the useful tip that eighty percent of the multiple murderers he met carried some sort of tattoo on their bodies), many other writers have been similarly fascinated. Indeed, it is fashionable to describe writing itself as a transgression, a usurpation of the authority of previous writing and of the authenticity of accepted versions of an event.

It was for reasons less theoretical, and more specific to his own nature, that the crime in Kansas cast its spell over Capote. As I read it, the story of the Clutters, their neighbors, their murderers, and the apparatus of the law, including the Supreme Court, brought into glaring focus a nagging, sullen antagonism in Capote himself to any form of authority, and raised it to a level of cultural significance rare for him. Usually in his works this authority is vested in merely private household nightmares, as in the early story "My Side of the Matter," or more appealingly, for a time, in some older lady he must eventually leave behind. In his last, unfinished, posthumously published novel, *Answered Prayers,* he in effect leaves a number of them behind. A substantial part of that last book, when published earlier in *Esquire,* caused many of his lady friends to accuse him of betrayal. The sputtering-out of talent in the book suggests that it probably never would have been finished. There are nonetheless moments when its nightmare vision of social-sexual life in New York catches the vitality found throughout Mailer's *An American Dream.*

In a curious way, a certain kind of woman was for Capote a substitute for the beneficent male authority missing from his life. Capote was like Huck Finn looking for help, not from Tom

Sawyer, but from Tom Boys. He must have sensed in those news reports from Kansas, especially given Herbert Clutter's association with the Eisenhower administration, some horrendously larger, some awesome, thwarted, terrifying expression of revenge against the dereliction of the father. When, in *Other Voices, Other Rooms,* the Capote figure named Joel discovers his lost father, he is a helpless figure lying in bed, totally mute and almost totally paralyzed. Of the two murderers, Capote admitted to a special affection for Perry Smith and says of him (in an interview in *Truman Capote Conversations*) that Smith identified Clutter as "the father he loved-hated and he unleashed all his inner resentment in an act of violence."

Capote's own parents were divorced when he was four, leaving him, like Joel, to wander among the homes of relatives. At his infrequent best, he cast his own Perry Smith resentments into figures who are bitterly isolated and intransigent, like the self-insulated man in "Shut a Final Door" (1947) who, gradually bereft of all human contact, ends up a latter-day Bartleby, alone in a room where "he pushed his face into the pillow, covered his ears with his hands and thought: Think of nothing things, think of wind." The alternative as a self-image was Capote's sassy, often eccentric, sometimes wistful, but at all times rebellious women; seemingly indifferent to the opinions of others, they are nonetheless, like Capote himself, touchingly determined to be entertaining, with sometimes disastrous results. There is a ten-year-old version of Holly in *Breakfast at Tiffany's* in the earlier "Children on Their Birthdays" (1949), where little Miss Bobbit is run over by a bus on the one occasion when she moves by instinct rather than by theatrical calculation. No wonder Capote can write well about so utterly self-absorbed and legendary a figure as Jane Bowles.

Except in *In Cold Blood,* Capote was mostly a writer of romance, in the sense that the settings are designed to exert the least possible cultural influence on the speech and the action of his characters. In that sense, too, the assumption that he belonged to Southern literature is wholly mistaken. Even *Other Voices, Other Rooms* could as easily have been located, with some changes of inflection, in California or New England. Capote is not to be considered in any way equivalent to other Southern writers such as Flannery O'Connor or Eudora Welty, much less William Faulkner. And a still more powerful reason to avoid these frequently made comparisons is that Capote's characters are never, like the others', endowed with a milieu that is made culturally or theologically resonant.

For Capote, culture is represented largely as something that can be laid on—by fine writing, by something meant to sound like Literature. This is conspicuously the case in his novella *The Grass Harp* (1951). There, yet another of his boys with a free-wheeling imagination teams up with yet another endearing odd lady, this one named Dolly. To escape the tyranny of a household ruled by Dolly's sister, they move (along with three associates picked up on the way) into a tree house, while the assembled forces of law and order try to coax them down. They sit, listening to the wind, talking and (so they suppose) thinking. One of the number, a judge with what sounds like an alarmingly expanded idea of the Fourteenth Amendment, asks, for example, "How could you ever care about one girl? Have you ever cared about one leaf?"

My point is that in his more journalistic pieces, like *The Muses Are Heard* (1956), an account of the visit to the Soviet Union by an American company performing *Porgy and Bess,* or like *In Cold Blood,* Capote was forced by the independent existence of the story he was reporting to forgo such banal and egregious reminders of his own literary presence. That is, he could not as easily make a hero of himself as resident literary genius. His fiction, by contrast, abounds in a kind of lyricism that he associates, unfortunately, with liberation, even though he never adequately imagines a society from which escape is made to seem more than quixotic.

Of what, for Capote, did liberation consist? Apparently in the ability to write such sentences as this, the opening sentence of *The Grass Harp*: "When was it that first I heard of the grass harp? Long before the autumn we lived in the China tree; an early autumn, then; and of course it was Dolly who told me, no one else would have known to call it that, a grass harp." Perhaps Dolly is a reader of Coleridge, author of "The Aeolian Harp," or of Shelley, who asks the west wind to "make me thy lyre as the forest is." Obviously it was Capote who may have done the reading and who in any case had in mind the posture of the Romantic artist whose inspiration sweeps through him from forces not at all socially derived.

Such writing characterizes no one and nothing but itself. It is meant to be "beautiful" or "moving," an evidence of something in the writer that is "deeply good" and that other people ought not to tamper with. Capote was so committed to this kind of writing, and so strongly in need of it as a cover for violent feelings, that even after *In Cold Blood* he could concoct that famous piece of fruitcake, "A Christmas Memory." There the Collin and Dolly of *The Grass Harp* find their substitutes in a kite-flying duo composed of Buddy, the Capote boy figure, and his Cousin Sookie. They live, as you might guess, with relatives "who have power over us, and frequently make us cry." Capote, that is, never fully learned as much as he might have from *In Cold Blood*: that there are in American life starker versions of his own conflicted nature, and that these make his aestheticism not only outworn but irrelevant.

As his celebrated friends were to discover, vengefulness was an essential part of Capote's nature, and the best part of him as a writer. It was there from the start, however sporadically, as in the frightening little tale called "Mariam" (1945), in which a waif unaccountably turns up at the doorstep of a nice retired lady and proceeds to take over the apartment and her life to a terrifying degree, a waif who exists only as a repressed but unbanishable part of the woman herself. His sentimentability became the most public reverse side of his vengefulness, a complementary form of abstraction. The killers in Kansas were a magnified mirror image of an alienation that he knew must finally kill even a good father, or the women who are a manageable substitute for the good father. The Clutter part of American life, resting contentedly in its security, this very emanation of the Eisenhower ethos, is forced to meet elements no less American that it cannot comprehend. It collides with the fatherless, the rejected, the wandering and savage elements in America that must mark their presence in someone else's blood.

There is nothing the matter with any motive for writing—and the motive of revenge is classic—so long as the writer does not fail to make available some full and powerful measure of whatever offends him. Mailer, Bellow, O'Connor, and Roth are all contemporaries of Capote who have sufficiently done this. Too often Capote fails to do so, and instead trivializes his own deep contempt for the order of things. That includes, I suspect, an ultimate distaste for his own body and its sexual life, which by his testimony sounds as if it had been neither very active nor very pleasurable. Scarcely anywhere in Capote's writing is there a scene of any duration in which two people make physical love; one such moment, a mere vignette in *Other Voices, Other Rooms,* so disturbs the boy and girl who witness it that they then forever turn away from each other.

Nor could Capote be depended upon even in areas he did choose to write about, like social fame. His incessant gossip about the rich and famous never once extended into an inquiry into the source of their power in American society. If most of his fiction could have been set anywhere, it could as easily have occurred in any other decade or century; and this is true to a serious degree even of his journalism. It seems not to have mattered to him that he came to maturity in a period that saw World War II and the Vietnam War, the turmoil of the 1960s, and the fight the world over for racial equality. It was a period, too, when the challenge to historical authority came to manifest itself, as at last it had to do, in bitter recriminations about sexual differences and sexual hegemony. While it is not Capote, but one of his characters, who says in the story "Mojave," "Women are like flies: they settle on sugar or shit," his own views included such howlers as the statement in his conversations with Grobel that women ought to be paid less than men for the same job because "a man works harder." For all his worldly connections, he was as uninquisitive about the forces at work in contemporary culture as a writer of his ambitions possibly could be, even about the very forces that in many places still counted his own sexual practices a crime.

At the end of *Music for Chameleons*, a collection of journalistic articles that appeared in 1980, he gingerly admitted that, though not yet a saint, "I'm an alcoholic. I'm a drug addict. I'm a homosexual. I'm a genius." This is intolerably cute. Being a drug addict or an alcoholic or a homosexual is his business. When he combines these admissions with a claim to genius, however, it becomes everybody's business. To put such items in combination makes it legitimate to ask, especially in an age that has recognized the real genius of Jean Genet, why a reputed genius like Capote, so bent in this instance on self-confession, has not had something more to say about a political culture that, by its pietistic hypocritical obsessions with private conduct, manages to direct attention time and again away from the glaringly visible disasters of social and political life. After his heroic confrontation with cold blood in Kansas, Capote retreated to a tree house in Manhattan, there to play literary games for ever smaller and overpublicized stakes. He was more than amply rewarded for his games in his lifetime. But there is no need to pretend any longer that he has earned anything but a minor place in American letters.

14

MAILER'S STRANGEST BOOK

⁎

Until its final revision, *Ancient Evenings* carried the subtitle "The Egyptian Novel." It was a helpful hint that what was to follow was meant to be quite unlike the so-called American novel or the English, French, German, or Russian novel. *Ancient Evenings* is indeed the strangest of Norman Mailer's books, and its oddity does not in any important way have to do either with its Egyptian setting or with the exotic career—exotic even by ancient Egyptian standards—of Menenhetet, its protagonist-narrator, whose four lives, including three reincarnations, span 190 years (1290 to 1100 B.C.) of the nineteenth and twentieth dynasties (1320 to 1121 B.C.). What is remarkable here is the degree to which Mailer has naturalized himself as an ancient Egyptian, so that he writes as if saturated with the mentality and the governing assumptions, some of which he revises rather freely, of a culture in which the idea of the human is markedly different from what it has been in the West for the last 1,500 years or so. Mailer never before tried anything so perilous, and the prodigious demands the book makes on the reader are a clue to his ambitions. This is at once one of his most accomplished and his most problematic works.

Ancient Evenings achieves a magnitude that gives a retrospective order and enhancement to everything Mailer had written before it. It had been possible to think of him as perhaps a great writer, but one who had yet to write a great book. Many commentators have mistakenly credited him here and in his previous novel, *The Executioner's Song,* with a new degree of self-effacement. But looking back from these, one can see more clearly than before that nearly all Mailer's previous writing depended not on some prior sense of self, the famous Mailer ego, but rather on self-fragmentation and dispersal. Even when Mailer is his own subject, as is so often the case, he cannot be said to exist simply in the narrative that tells his story but is to be found instead within a larger, expressive structure of which his voice is only one part looking for other parts. Just as it radically reduces his literary, let alone his personal identity, to assume that the voice in *Armies of the Night* refers us directly to the "real" Mailer, so it is equally mistaken to assume that because that voice is absent from *Ancient Evenings* he has thereby and suddenly become invisible.

Quite the reverse. The book comes into focus only when we recognize the complicated way in which it is a particularly self-revealing work. Menenhetet, for example, carries out the implications of Mailer's more directly autobiographical writings because even as he tells stories about himself he is trying to put himself together from several different, remembered versions. This is also the case when Mailer writes about a march on the Pentagon or a championship fight: he treats the earlier Mailer who participated in those events as if he were already a soul or a spirit. The later Mailer not only records but contends with earlier versions of himself, until the work is a record of the abrasions out of which will emerge, or so he hopes, a form he can call himself or his work or his career. The form his narratives achieve is what survives of "Mailer" from the past, but the achievement is conditioned by a recognition that some of the many selves who

make up a single person have been sacrificed to the making of
form. Any form, especially for a believer in karmic roots, creates
a longing for some possibly larger and more inclusive one.
"Karma tends to make more sense than a world conceived without it," Mailer remarked in an interview, "because when you
think of the incredible elaborations that go into any one human
being, it does seem wasteful of the cosmos to send us out just
once to learn all those things, and then molder forever in the
weeds. . . . There is some sort of divine collaboration going on."

Books of sustained visionary ambition—including *Paradise
Lost* or *Moby-Dick*—are bound to have stretches of tiresome
exposition, phrasings that are ludicrous, whole scenes that
should have been not only difficult but impossible. *Ancient
Evenings* has Honey-Ball's scenes of spellbinding in "The Book
of Queens." Nearly anything can happen here, and does, and
what is remarkable is that the risks usually pay off: moments of
subliminal ecstasy, visionary descriptions of royal personages, of
pools at sunrise and gardens which bring on a kind of sexual
swooning, of floatings down the Nile. Mailer seems more at
home in the writing than in any of his books except for *Why Are
We in Vietnam?* He luxuriates, sometimes to the limits of
patience and beyond, in accounts of Egyptian low life, in the
power put into play during a royal dinner party, in details of costume and what must have been at best a truly awful cuisine.
Near the beginning Meni calmly tells us what it feels like,
moment by moment, to be eviscerated and embalmed, and
there are equally confident accounts of the practice of magic and
of the Egyptians' wholly chaotic polytheism.

Mailer has imagined a culture that gives formal and not
merely anthropological sanction to what in his other works often
seems eccentric or plaintively metaphysical, like his obsessions
with "psychic darts" and mind-reading, with immortality, with
battles of the gods (Liston and Patterson, it now seems, were later
versions of the Egyptian gods Horus and Set), with villainous

homosexuality, with magic and sorcery, and with excrement as an encoding of psychic failure or success. Having so often written as if the self had several versions, he is completely at ease with Egyptian names for the seven spirits of the self that continue to exist in different degrees of intensity after death.

Two spirit forms that figure importantly in this book are the Ka and the Khaibit. The Ka, for which the term Double is a useful but inadequate substitute, is born with a person to whom it belongs and whom it exactly resembles; even after death it is part of that person, requiring food and drink, which is left for it in the tomb. It also requires sexual gratification. Thus, the Ka of a third incarnation, say, could encounter the Ka of the first and have sexual commerce with him—which means with himself— just as could a Ka with his own Khaibit, or Memory. For example, Meni, who died mysteriously at twenty or twenty-one and thinks he may have been one of the reincarnations of Menenhetet, finds himself, soon after the novel begins, kneeling on the floor of the Pyramid of Khufu with Menenhetet's member in his mouth, and while he finds it an abhorrent experience he realizes that he may be coping with himself, as it were, and that the unpleasantness is a kind of preparation for his passage from the Land of the Dead through the horrors of the Duad to either the upper or the lower world. It is possible to assume that the two forms remain fixed in this position—the time, we can with difficulty work out, is roughly 100 B.C.—while they visualize the immensely long night of storytelling, the Night of the Pig, when any truth can be told without fear of retaliation, a millennium earlier at the palace of Rameses IX.

Whether at the palace or at the pyramid, the scene of the novel is a scene of telling, of narration, of recollection. At the palace, where the reader mostly finds himself, Menenhetet and Meni are more decorously positioned than they are in the pyramid. The older one is telling the Pharaoh the stories of his lives; the Pharaoh hopes by listening and interrogation to become

more closely identified with his great ancestor Rameses II, while
the younger, his great-grandson then aged six, nestles between
his mother, Hathfertiti (who is Menenhetet's granddaughter
and, for many years, his lover), and the Pharaoh (whom little
Meni, using his powers of clairvoyance, knows to be his real
father). His reputed father (Hathfertiti's brother as well as her
husband and Overseer of the Cosmetic Box) sulks to one side
before eventually absenting himself.

The novel does not yield to summary or to any clear sorting
out of family trees, and depends instead on the blurring of dis-
tinctions between persons or between historical events and
visionary ones. Divided into seven books, possibly in obedience
to the seven spirits or lights of the dead, it begins with the awak-
ening of a Ka: "Crude thoughts and fierce forces are my state. I
do not know who I am. Nor what I was. I cannot hear a sound.
Pain is near that will be like no pain felt before." Some central
themes are immediately announced: birth and rebirth, mystifi-
cations of identity and of genealogy, elemental dread. Once it
has slithered out of the pyramid, the Ka walks through the
avenues of the necropolis in a vague search for the tomb of a
friend named Menenhetet II. After some suitably macabre incidents, he finds the tomb in one of the cheaper neighborhoods
and gradually realizes that he is himself the Ka of Meni II and
that next to his partly exposed and deteriorating remains are
those of the renowned Menenhetet I, moved from its own much
grander resting place by the spiteful Hathfertiti.

After getting acquainted and finding their way into the great
pyramid of Khufu, they begin their recollection, which is also
their attempted recollection of themselves. Even at the outset,
and with only these two figures in question, the effort to distinguish between them takes us into a thicket. And that is where
we are meant to be. We are meant to understand that multiple
identities, identities that in their passage through time come to
blend with each other, are common among the fantastic array of

Egyptian gods and therefore among those humans for whom the gods are a paradigm of mortal existence. Any Egyptian of high birth, for example, can consider himself an Osiris, the greatest of the gods (but not always), and can find a pattern for his own past life, or anyone else's past life, in the pains and indignities that were visited upon Him. It is therefore appropriate that Meni, in his bewilderment about himself, should ask Menenhetet to tell the stories that make up the long second book, "The Book of the Gods." The story of Osiris, Isis, and the bitter, buggery-ridden battles between their son Horus and his uncle Set is a phantasmagoric version of much that happens to Menenhetet as his story unfolds in subsequent books.

Menenhetet, born the son of a whore, has an innovative skill as a charioteer which brings him to the attention of the extraordinarily beautiful and imposing Rameses II or, as he is called, Unsermare. At his side, and assisted by the Pharaoh's pet lion, Hera-Ra, Menenhetet helps turn disaster into victory against the Hittites at the battle of Kadesh. But he is then held responsible for the death of Hera-Ra, who sickened from eating too many amputated Hittite hands, and is exiled for fifteen years as a supervisor of a remote gold mine in the desert. It is there that he learns from a dying friend that a man may be born again by dying during the consummation of sexual intercourse. Bribing his way back into the court of Unsermare, he becomes the commander of troops and then Governor of the Secluded—which means that he supervises the Pharaoh's "little queens" while being forbidden their sexual favors.

He breaks this interdiction with Honey-Ball in retaliation against Unsermare for having taken him by "both mouths" before Kadesh. And when Unsermare repeats this violation, this time in the company of some of the "little queens," Menenhetet is driven to the still more dangerous revenge of embarking on an affair with the most exalted of the queens, Nefertiri, who turns out to be one of Mailer's most engaging characterizations. Even as he is stabbed to death by the Crown Prince, he manages to leave within Nefertiri the seed of his first reincarnation. He thereby becomes his own father, though his and, above all, Nefertiri's parentage must be hidden from Unsermare, who is persuaded by Honey-Ball that he has begotten the child with her. And so it goes. The urgent, exploratory stories told by Menenhetet and the others are accompanied throughout by an attendant detail so exasperatingly complete as to suggest now and then that Mailer, like Thomas Pynchon, cannot resist displays of his encyclopedic researches—said to have included a total absorption of the Egyptian funerary literature called the Book of the Dead.

Mailer has convinced himself that the book must be dense if it is also to be authentic. Thus, Meni needs to be told the intricate story of the gods, the Pharaoh needs to be told exhaustively about his ancestors, Menenhetet needs to rehearse his lives because each of them is convinced that only a person who can remember and explain his deeds when alive, or when he somehow partook of the life of another, can pass out of the Land of the Dead. And because of the endless mirroring of one life in another and in the lives of the gods, there is, for the anxious spirit, no limit to recollection, no ascertainable boundary.

While over the course of the seven books the various tales do manage to achieve some degree of narrative sequence and development—as they would have to do when all the characters are in search of some kind of teleology—each book also spirals out of and back into the scene of telling, and even that scene is set in a time when events have already become encrusted with centuries of retelling and interpretation. No American reviewer of the novel has yet noticed the crucial admission by Menenhetet to Meni in the last chapter: that what might be called the Egyptian "gospels" in "The Book of the Gods" constitute an interpretation rather than an authentication of what they report. "If you think of the story of our Gods at the beginning of our travels, I will now confess that I imparted it to you in the way that these Romans and Greeks tell it to each other. That is why my tale was familiar yet different from what you know. For our Land of the Dead now belongs to them, and the Greeks think no more of it than a picture that is seen on the wall of a cave."

Ancient Evenings to some extent resembles Faulkner's *Absalom, Absalom!* or those novels of Joseph Conrad such as *Nostromo* where, as Edward Said describes them, there is "evidence of a felt need to justify in some way the telling of a story." Faulkner and Conrad are more successful than Mailer in creating suspense and expectation within the stories, and among vividly differentiated characters; though *Ancient Evenings* is not lacking in suspense of this kind—it is there in the stunning account of the battle of Kadesh, or the intrigues between the rival Queens, Nefertiri and Rama-Nefru—the design of the book as a whole refers us finally to motives which are as vague as Mailer's or any novelist's motives for writing. Mailer offers none of the illusions, so brilliantly sustained by Conrad, that there is something we want to know and that we will eventually know it, that a center will be located in a wilderness of possibility, that the true shape of a person's life will emerge out of the mysteries that have shrouded it.

The disaffection or impatience that many readers may feel with *Ancient Evenings* likely results from the fact that telling and listening to its stories have less to do with a desire to get somewhere (unless the reader is satisfied with being told that it has something to do with the saving of souls, and is meant to help Meni and Menenhetet pass through the Duad) than with a wish to get away from something: loneliness, darkness, waste, and dissolution. Interestingly, these are conditions Mailer has worried about since the mid-1950s as peculiar to the fate of writers, especially American writers, in the last half of the twentieth century.

It is in this context that one should consider his obsession with buggery. The obsession has in the past carried Mailer into a metaphysics of human biological creativity as a compensation for meaninglessness (the forty-six chromosomes in each cell of the body are, he tells us in *The Prisoner of Sex,* "a nest of hieroglyphics") and from there to a religion of artistic creativity (he observes in *The Armies of the Night* that these hieroglyphics are "so much like primitive writing"). Like the building of Hell in the nether regions by Milton's Satan, buggery for Mailer is a perverse response to God's invitation that we join him in the creation. For some centuries—long before Rojack in *An American Dream* refers to an evil girlfriend's backside as "der Teufel"—buggery has been associated with the Devil's terrain. In nearly all his work Mailer at some point contemplates the significance of a juxtaposition, concisely described by D. H. Lawrence in "Pornography and Obscenity": "The sex functions and the excrementary functions . . . work so close together, yet they are, so to speak, so utterly different in direction. Sex is a creative flow, the excrementary flow is towards dissolution, decreation. . . ."

Though Menenhetet, like the Mailer of "The Metaphysics of the Belly" (*The Presidential Papers*), offers positive theories of scatology, the anus is mostly imagined as the site of evil. But there is also for Mailer a kind of art which is a trope for buggery. Writing about Jean Genet, he has referred to those aesthetic acts which "shift from the creation of meaning to the destruction of it," offering as further examples "the therapy of the surrealist artist, of Dada, of Beat." And he continues, speaking now of his own involvement in this dilemma: "jaded, deadened, severed from our roots, dulled in leaden rage, inhabiting the centre of illness of the age, it becomes more excruciating each year for us to perform the civilizing act of contributing to a collective meaning." *Ancient Evenings* represents such an attempt, haunted by failure, to discover "collective meaning," to create spiritual (and literary) genealogies that are as strong and mysterious as biological ones.

Questions of origin soon become, for Mailer, questions also about originality and authorship. It is impossible to claim either of these, so the book tells us, without first accepting one's incalculable obligations to a marvelous but murky antecedence. Mailer's (and our) debts to the past, it is suggested, are enormous; they are also mysteriously entangled and untraceable. It is therefore a mistake to suggest, as some reviewers have done, that because Menenhetet is given "that look of character supported by triumph which comes to powerful men when they are sixty and still strong," he is meant to represent Mailer, or Hemingway, Mailer's supposed precursor. Mailer partakes of both Meni and Menenhetet, who at the end are transformed into yet another dual figure: a triumphant Icarus–Daedalus. In the final scene Menenhetet embraces and dissolves into the young man's Ka as it tries to escape the destructive force of "the abominable onslaught of offal" and to ascend the ladder of lights, knowing it will take not goodness to get to the top but strength.

The joining has been made possible because Meni comes at last to accept all the stories he has been listening to, and, along with these, all the burdens of the past. "The tales he has told our Pharaoh, had been told for me as well. It was I whom he wanted to trust him." He cannot disown any of it because he cannot even know for sure that he did not somehow father himself or father his own father, whoever that might be, as Ra did in Egyptian mythology. At the beginning of *Ancient Evenings* we were told, "The God begets the God who will be his father. For the Gods live in the time that has passed, and time that is to come."

Genealogies confound one another to create a future that can call on the assembled strengths of Menenhetet, Meni, all the characters they have loved, the Egyptian gods, along with their latest manifestations in Christian mythology, and, not least, the now enriched figures of Mailer's earlier writings and earlier selves. The "I" in the last paragraphs is a composite of all these, but it is also the creative spirit with whom Mailer associates

himself in an apocalyptic vision that could anticipate either the
coming of, in Yeats's phrase, "the fabulous, formless darkness" of
Christianity, or the last phase of our own civilization:

> A pain is coming that will be like no pain felt before. I hear the
> scream of earth exploding. In this terror, vast as the abyss, I still know
> more than fear. Here at the centre of pain is radiance. May my hope
> of heaven now prove equal to my ignorance of where I go. Whether I
> am the Second or the First Menenhetet, or the creature of our twice
> seven separate souls and lights, I would hardly declare, and so I do
> not know if I will labor in greed forever among the demonic or serve
> some noble purpose I cannot name. By this I am told that I must
> enter into the power of the word. For the first sound to come out of
> the will had to traverse the fundament of pain. So I cry out in the
> voice of the newly born at the mystery of my first breath, and enter
> the Boat of Ra.

This is, then, Mailer's "portrait of the artist as a young man,"
but it does not allow, as Joyce's does, for much distinction
between that "artist" and the author of the book. If we are
reminded of Joyce it is certainly not for the ironic reservations
about Stephen implied in the last chapter of *A Portrait of the
Artist as a Young Man* and the first section of *Ulysses,* or even for
the moment on the seashore when Stephen imagines that "his
soul had arisen from the grave of boyhood, spurning her grave-
clothes. Yes! Yes! Yes! He would create proudly out of the freedom and power of his soul, as the great artificer whose name he
bore, a living thing, new and soaring and beautiful, impalpable,
imperishable." This is a beautiful but forever embarrassing
moment in the long history of the artist *exalté,* and Joyce meant
to bring into question the prospects of anyone in the twentieth
century who chooses to "enter into the power of the word."
Mailer has always been frighteningly naïve about this "power"
and especially—as was revealed by his involvement with writer-
murderer Jack Abbott—the privileges that should be accorded
it, and he fully endorses Meni's grandiloquence. This is his most

audacious book largely because behind it all is the desire, once and for all, to claim some ultimate spiritual and cultural status for the teller of stories, the Writer. Which is yet another ancient and perhaps pernicious story, though Mailer will always need to believe every word of it.

15

IN PRAISE OF VAGUENESS:
HENRY AND WILLIAM JAMES

From the beginning of his distinguished career, with his influential *The Reign of Wonder: Naïveté and Reality in American Literature,* on to the more recent *Adultery in the Novel* and his fluently recondite *Venice Desired,* on the literary figurations of that city since the eighteenth century, Tony Tanner has shown a rare degree of excitement and curiosity about the workings of literary style, the way words come to life in response to the performative presence within them of a novelist or a poet. This book, *Henry James and the Art of Nonfiction* (1995), is made up of three lectures at Southern Georgia University. It is a celebration of the stylistic elaborations in Henry James's travel writings, literary criticism, and autobiographical works, most of which belong to his later or, as it is often called, major phase, which includes, more famously, *The Ambassadors, The Wings of the Dove,* and *The Golden Bowl.*

Tanner takes evident delight in the task at hand and exploits it with an often brilliant mischievousness. He intends to show how readers of James will be abundantly rewarded once they forgo much of what they already have, including the conventional expectation that the reason to read great literature is to find things that are transportable, things they can carry away with them. Not a chance. At the beginning of the last lecture, he points out how precious little his interpretations have yielded by way of those facts and specifics usually to be expected, especially from non-fictional prose: "I have so far offered you a James whose travel writing deliberately disdains information, and whose literary criticism flauntingly eschews consistent method or theory. Finally, I want to celebrate James as a writer of autobiography that will have nothing to do with chronology or conventional sequence."

Tanner's enthusiasm presupposes that the style of a literary work can create a sustained interest primarily in itself. This made him something of a rarity—he died in 1998—among academic literary critics of this or any other time. Literature in English began to be accredited as a course of study in English and American universities only in the early decades of the twentieth century, and since that time readers have been enjoined to treat literary style not as something to be read for the fun of it but as something to be decoded, even if you might take a more relaxed pleasure in it outside the classroom or the literary journals. How else could English departments make "contributions to knowledge," the prerequisite for their ability to compete for prestige and funding with departments of philosophy or history or the natural sciences? What keeps a classroom hour going when all there is in front of a teacher is a poem and some students, what keeps the literary quarterlies humming, is the flat-minded, professionally opportunistic conviction that the style of a given work must be holding an encapsulated secret, and that the secret calls for a professional locksmith. Style must finally be *about* something else, and this requires us to look behind it for big meanings and big truths.

I italicize the word "about" not only for emphasis but because I want it to carry some of the implications it takes on in *Principles of Psychology*, the massive first book by Henry's brother

William, regarded by R.W.B. Lewis and others as one of the singular achievements in American writing of the nineteenth century. *Principles* never systematically or for long directly addresses the issues of language and style. When it does do so, however, it is with an urgency of feeling that links William with Henry in the conviction that, as William bluntly puts it, "language works against our perception of the truth." He means language as it is conventionally or habitually structured. It might be assumed that anyone convinced of this would admire Henry James's later style, with its evident desire to use language in unfamiliar, unpredictable arrangements. Gertrude Stein, who had a notorious determination to do so, was one of William's favored students at Harvard and he a dominant figure in its philosophy department; and she always spoke of him admiringly. All the while, William was aggressively censorious about his brother's stylistic innovations, particularly during the period when he was writing much of the prose featured by Tanner.

This standoff between the two brothers becomes even more anomalous once we take a closer look at that moment in *Principles* already alluded to. There, in the chapter called "The Stream of Thought," William complains about our tendency to focus in any sentence on words that are taken to be the most referential, be it to important topics or to familiar things. "So inveterate has our habit become," he writes, "of recognizing the existence of the substantive parts alone, that language almost refuses to lend itself to any other use." And then, in what could serve as close to a passionate justification for Henry's efforts to find alternative structures, he describes our habitual ways of using words in ways that turn out to be repressive, even murderous. "All *dumb* or anonymous psychic states have, owing to this error, been coolly suppressed; or, if recognized at all, have been named after the substantive perception they led up to, as thoughts 'about' this object or 'about' that, the stolid word *about* engulfing all their delicate idiosyncrasies in its monotonous sound."

The relation between Henry and William doesn't enter into Tanner's considerations, and neither does the likely relation between Henry's style and William's formulations of pragmatism. There are no compelling reasons why he should bother with these issues. But one of the permanently valuable achievements of his book is that Tanner's close interpretations of style encourage the speculation that to a remarkable degree Henry's writing, particularly in the later works, is an enactment in language, call it a poetic enactment, of the pragmatism somewhat later propounded in William's 1907 *Pragmatism: A New Name for Some Old Ways of Thinking.* He means "old" to philosophic thinking; he does not mean, as I do, that pragmatist thinking is as old as poetry, at least as old as Shakespeare's poetry, which evinces a desire to create realities then and there, in the words, on the spot. Nietzsche, an intense reader of Emerson, more or less proposes this connection between poetry and pragmatism, but it is left to the philosopher Richard Rorty to argue for it in a passionate and sustained manner, as he does in *Contingency, Irony, and Solidarity.*

The style of *Pragmatism* is in itself sufficiently poetic to have made many professional philosophers at the time suspicious and dismissive of it. Its arguments depend very often on mostly tonal rhetoric, and advance by means of evolving figurative patterns rather than by any rigorous self-questioning. In idealizing the pragmatist individual, for example, he prefers to evoke the kinetic energy of the body with words like "turn" or "set at work" or "actions," which sound like quite casual evocations of his outdoorsy athleticism. On inspection, they refer metaphorically to wholly sedentary activities at the desk or in the mind. When, for instance, he says that a pragmatist is one who "turns away from pretended absolutes," away from "power-bringing words" and "solving names" inherited from earlier writing, he means that if operative concepts of reality are ever to be changed, then somewhere along the line it will be necessary "to turn"—that is, in the quite ancient lingo of poetry, "to trope"—the words that have previously described those concepts. To put it in Henry's terms, one mustn't get stuck with "excess of specificity," as he calls it in *The American Scene,* a slavishness to the "scene" as it is already assumed to exist.

Tanner highlights still other passages in Henry for which equivalents can be found in William's prose. In *English Hours,* Henry exults in the evidence that so little remains of the town of Dunwich that it is "not even the ghost of its dead self." Why this fascination with ghosts? Because ghosts, it would seem, prove his contention that "there is a presence in what is missing." The existence of a ghost cannot be proved, since it would then cease to be one; it would emerge as a real presence. Ghost stories have the built-in advantage, from the point of view of a writer like James, of remaining beyond the reach of any presumably full or final interpretation, which is one reason he chose to write a number of them. One can find equivalents to all these arguments in William's *Principles.* He there focuses more directly than does Henry on the ghostly elements, as they might be called, that inhabit the structures of our sentences. He notes that some parts of speech are "impalpable to direct examination," that "large tracts of human speech are nothing but *signs of direction,*" that "they are not to be glimpsed except in flight," and warns that "if we try to hold fast the feeling of direction, the full presence comes and the feeling of direction is lost."

These compassionate-sounding observations attest to beliefs everywhere manifest in brother Henry's later style, including a belief affirmed by William that "namelessness is compatible with existence." If it is "nameless," how does language represent it? By phrasings that are calculatingly elusive and by making one's language evasive of any final interpretation or factual approximation. A remark of William's came immediately to mind ("The feeling of an absence is *toto caelo* other than the absence of feeling") when I read in the first of Tanner's lectures the estimable description of some of Henry's stylistic practices: "Absence rather than presence; shadow rather than substance; broken eloquence esteemed more than confidently replete utterance— these are central to preferences for [Henry] James."

There is, besides, a predilection shared by both brothers with earlier American writers, like Emerson and Thoreau, and later ones, like Frost and Stevens, for what each of them at some point gets to call "vagueness." So that even while admitting in an essay on Flaubert that the novelist no less than the painter is to a degree committed to a rendering of things as they are, Henry goes on to say that there is an obligation to "something else, beneath and behind, that belongs to the realms of vagueness and uncertainty." These, as Tanner points out, are "the realms with which Henry's work will unerringly concern itself," and to which, I might add, William declared an equal allegiance. Early on, in *Principles,* he announced, "It is in short the re-instatement of the vague to its proper place in our mental life which I am so anxious to press on the attention."

Once these close approximations between Henry and William are recognized—their resentment of the structures normally given to language and their intensely expressed opinion that these need to be loosened and reformed—it's all the more startling to come upon the dismissive, supercilious energies that William can bring to his criticism of Henry's writing, especially to what he calls "your third manner." He has in mind, again, the style of many of the works especially commended by Tanner, like *The American Scene,* the autobiographical writings, and James's prefaces to the New York Edition of his novels, which R. P. Blackmur in 1934 called, as I would now, "the most sustained and I think eloquent and original piece of literary criticism in existence."

What makes the strictures in William's letters to Henry even more peculiar is that in the process he can't help revealing an admiration, however suppressed, for what Henry is doing. He is quite capable of describing the "third manner" with an accuracy that is a match for Tanner's. I must again quote at length one such passage, which I discuss in the prologue to this book, since there is no good way to abridge it, and no one should want to abridge it anyway. It is in a letter written in the spring of 1907.

Dearest H. . . . I've been so overwhelmed with work, and the mountain of the *Unread* has piled up so, that only in these days . . . have I been able to settle down to your *American Scene,* which in its peculiar way seems to me *supremely great.* You know how opposed your whole 'third manner' of execution is to the literary ideals which animate my crude and Orson-like breast, mine being to say a thing in one sentence as straight and explicit as it can be made, and then to drop it forever; yours being to avoid naming it straight, but by dint of breathing and sighing all round and round it, to arouse in the reader who may have had a similar perception already (Heaven help him if he hasn't!) the illusion of a solid object, made (like the 'ghost' at the Polytechnic) wholly out of impalpable materials, air, and the prismatic interferences of light, ingeniously focused by mirrors upon empty space. But you *do* it, that's the queerness! And the complication of innuendo and associative reference on the enormous scale to which you give way to it does so *build out* the matter for the reader that the result is to solidify, by the mere bulk of the process, the like perception from which *he* has to start. As air, by dint of its volume, will weigh like a corporeal body; so his own poor little initial perception, swathed in this gigantic envelopment of suggestive atmosphere, grows like a germ into something vastly bigger and more substantial. But it's the rummest method for one to employ systematically as you do nowadays; and you employ it at your peril. In this crowded and hurried reading age, pages that require such close attention remain unread and neglected. You can't skip a word if you are to get the effect, and 19 out of 20 worthy readers grow intolerant. The method seems perverse: 'Say it *out,* for God's say,' they cry, 'and have done with it.' And so I say now, give us *one* thing in your older directer manner, just to show that, in spite of your paradoxical success in this unheard-of method, you *can* still write according to accepted canons. Give us that interlude; then continue like the 'curiosity of literature' which you have become. For gleams and innuendoes and felicitous verbal insinuations you are unapproachable, but the *core* of literature is solid. Give it to us *once* again! The bare perfume of things will not support existence, and the effect of solidity you reach is but perfume and simulacrum.

What is to be made of this? On the one hand, William concedes that in his "third manner" Henry brilliantly accomplishes with language what he sets out to do with it. And if *Principles of Psychology* along with *Pragmatism* are to be believed, that's just about what William himself wants to see happening. On the other hand, he asks Henry to desist, lest he go unread or read merely as "'the curiosity of literature' you have become." As from one of America's greatest philosophers—Tanner chooses to call him "America's greatest psychologist"—this is a way of saying that Henry somehow hasn't any right to display in his work a power of individuality that might alienate him from a popular audience, since as a novelist he can be no more than a public entertainer or a moralist. How dare this younger brother, so often patronized by the far more worldly, robust (and married) older one, come forward at this late date as if he were already one of those whom Harold Bloom calls "strong poets." Rorty adapts Bloom's idea of "the strong poet" in his revisionist definitions of pragmatism, and he does so to designate a writer who, as Bloom puts it, "will not tolerate words that intervene between him and the Word, or precursors standing between him and the Muse." This requires a style of defiant originality which may easily be taken as eccentric, a style defiantly of one's own invention. The emergence of such a style in Henry's writing seems to have proved intolerable to a brother heretofore secure in his sense of priority. To help meet this threat he summoned not only his sarcasms but the predictable opinion of those "19 out of 20 worthy readers." On their and not only on his own behalf, he pleaded that Henry grant "at least an interlude" in which "you give us *one* thing in your older directer manner"—this to a writer already sixty-four years old! Please assure us, he is saying, that, at last, you do not intend to be taken seriously.

The assumptions of superiority in this letter, apparently boisterous but on closer reading insecure, can be interpreted in the context of an 1898 lecture called "Philosophical Conceptions and Practical Results" in which William proposed that "philosophers," obviously meaning himself, "are after all like poets." Why? Because "they are pathfinders," a metaphor he immediately extended with this claim, "They are, if I may use a simile, so many spots, or blazes—blazes made by the axe of the human intellect on the trees of the otherwise trackless forest of human experience. They give you somewhere to go from." Philosophers and poets are in themselves signs, and they also make signs; they create verbal entitlement for the rest of us. Clearly he is talking only about writing, and yet he wants to make it sound, as he usually does, as if the activity of the writer is among the most physically strenuous, he-man, and even dangerous of pursuits. Axe at the ready, philosopher-poet William *is* Natty Bumpo. At least he is not at all like brother Henry, as William described him in a letter from London to his wife, Alice, in 1889:

> Henry is as nice and simple and amiable as he can be. He has covered himself, like some marine crustacean, with all sorts of material growths, rich sea-weeds and rigid barnacles and things, and lives hidden in the midst of his strange heavy alien manners and customs; but these are all but 'protective resemblances,' under which the same dear old good, innocent, and at the bottom very powerless-feeling Henry remains, caring for little but his writing, and full of dutifulness and affection for all gentle things. . . .

It can be said in extenuation that this manages to be comically outrageous, and was intended no doubt to amuse his wife, left at home. Besides, it is accepted that expressions of sibling rivalry often combine, as this does, considerable abuse with tenderness. However, it's also worth noting that William, not for the first or last time, insists on associating Henry and "his writing"—novels and novelistic prose—with inertia and powerlessness, with self-sequestration and a near paralytic curtailment of manly activity. And this, as it happens, is exactly the dreaded fate that, earlier in life, and feeling at that time close to a total nervous collapse, William had imagined as a likely end for himself.

Indeed, his assessments of Henry's "third manner" are of a piece with a long-held fear of any involvement in the arts that doesn't issue quite directly into what he insistently calls "action." With some degree of self-mockery, and self-protection, he says at one point that this "action" can be "the least thing in the world, speaking genially to one's grandmother . . . if nothing more heroic offers." But we're left again to conclude that he wants simply to avoid the admission that the only "action" that can properly be said to occur as a result of writing or of reading, which is his business in life as well as Henry's, is in the head or at the desk. William's convoluted and neurotic association of immobility with any prolonged, intensive contemplation of artistic works—surely it is this that so frequently makes him incapable of admitting to the sustained seriousness with which Henry's later writings ask to be taken.

When he does find novelists to admire, like Stevenson or Tolstoy, the admiration he expresses isn't for their actual writing, for what they can do with words, but for their representations of physical adventurousness in the world, their healthy-minded attitudes, or, as he says in commending Dante and Wordsworth, for their "tonic and consoling power." Early on, in *Principles,* he engages in a bizarre diatribe against "the habit of excessive novel-reading and theater going . . . even the habit of excessive indulgence in music," aside from composing it. And the reason? Because, he alleges, these habits inevitably produce that "contemptible type of human character . . . who spends his life in a weltering sea [Henry, one recalls, is compared to "a marine crustacean"] of sensibility and emotion, but who never does a manly

deed." It is here that he offers the one remedy I've mentioned—
speaking "genially to one's grandmother, or giving up one's seat
in a horse-car." The stubbornly held view, among those who care
to have one, is that, of the two genius brothers, Henry is singu-
larly the wimp. This has already had a decisive correction in Ross
Posnock's *The Trial of Curiosity,* the most penetrating study yet
written of Henry and William in the context of modernist social
and intellectual thought. And the idea of a "powerless-feeling
Henry" is implicitly challenged, too, by Tanner's exacting analyses, which should persuade anyone that Henry's "third manner"
constitutes in itself a "manly concrete deed," a deed, one might
say, of imperial proportions. The later style is a concerted effort
at imaginative capture. Its aim is nothing less than the liberation
of persons, places, and things from their fixed associations, so
that they may discover new accommodations within the realms
of his sentences and paragraphs, even while retaining traces of
their origins in life.

Any style pretending to such authority of appropriation inevitably meets the incomprehension if not the resistant indifference of the "19 out of 20 worthy readers" conjured up by William.
For writers of great ambition, this problem of audience didn't
begin with Henry James, nor did it end with him. There cannot be
any such thing as progress in these matters. Writers of the distant
past knew as well as he did the difficulty of finding an audience,
and, long before T. S. Eliot, they took it as a veritable sign of their
cultural and historical significance if they had proportionately
more difficulty of this sort than their contemporaries. In the 1815
"Supplement to the Preface," to go back only that far, Wordsworth
remarks that his task as a writer isn't only "to clear" but also "to
shape" his own road: "What is all this," he asks, "but an advance, or
a conquest, made by the soul of the poet?"

The authorial grandiosity of such sentences clearly asks to be
taken as charming, and this in itself is some indication that the
author knows he is communicating with a receptive if small band

of readers. No matter how heroic-sounding and solitary certain great poets and novelists pretend to be, they are all, and always, flirting with readers, even if the readers are mostly in their own heads. In the very act of writing they imagine readers who will be offended or startled and others who are willing to join in, so to speak, anxious to encourage the writing on its way, even to nudge it in certain directions. Any reader needs inducements, however, and any writer learns to provide them. Wordsworth promises that his readers will be "invigorated and inspired" by their "leader"; James is always talking about the need for "suspense" or the right proportions of "bewilderment" or the novel's "special obligation to be amusing." "All art is *expression*," he says in the Preface to *The Ambassadors*, "and is thereby vividness." To lure readers into unfamiliar territory, the writer must somehow, somewhere concede that the pleasurably familiar has an enduring claim on our sentiments. Without such authorial concessions, how could the inducements, the lures, be expected to work at all?

More acutely even than Wordsworth, James recognizes the ever increasing difficulty in modern times of at once sharing in a common language with readers while undertaking in the same breath, so to speak, radically to transform it. If, in such a situation, all a writer can count on to begin with is one out of twenty readers, how is he to sustain the interest and support, over the long haul, even of this exceptional and solitary worthy? The answer is that no writer can ever be sure just how to do it. In his own criticism James bequeaths a record unsurpassed in the history of literature of a great artist meditating on this dilemma. I have in mind two essays in which, though he is talking about other writers, he seems as surely to be talking about himself. The first is an essay on Flaubert published in 1902, when the major phase was reaching its full splendor; the second is the preface to Shakespeare's *The Tempest,* published in 1907, when his own work as a writer had been more or less completed.

Flaubert, he wrote, believed "that beauty comes with expression, that expression is creation, that it *makes* the reality, and only in the degree in which it *is,* exquisitely, expression; and that we move in literature through a world of different values and relations, a blest world in which we know nothing except by style, but in which also everything is saved by it, and in which the image is thus superior to the thing itself." He found in this aspect of Flaubert, as Tanner observes, a "magic . . . that is inestimably precious." It's as if James, in his fervor, was saying something equivalent about his own stylistic ventures. But a little further on in the same paragraph he concluded that "with all respect to Flaubert, [style] never *totally* beguiles; since even when we are so queerly constituted as to be ninety-nine parts literary, we are still a hundredth part something else." And he added, "This hundredth part may, once we possess the book—or the book possesses us—make us imperfect as readers, and yet without it should we want or get the book at all?"

Tanner greatly appreciates this passage, which gives us reason to wish that his quotation of it hadn't stopped short of that last sentence. It's a sentence in need of exactly his kind of interpretative generosity. The more one looks into it, the more puzzling it becomes. The preceding sentence poses no problem. It says that in even the most aesthetically yielding reader there is a holding back at some point. A "hundredth part" of oneself forestalls any total surrender to the beguilements of another's style and remains committed to something else, to "clumsy life," as James called it in his preface to *The Spoils of Poynton.* Only in the next sentence do confusions intrude. Here the intervention of the "hundredth part" seems to occur not before but only after we have been beguiled: "once we possess the book—or the book possesses us." Presumably it's only at this point that we become "imperfect as readers," since we'd managed earlier (hadn't we?) to let ourselves be fully possessed and possessing. But the confusion of sequence is compounded when James goes on to say that this imperfection is nonetheless responsible for our earlier desire "to want or get the book at all," meaning, I take it, in the first place, before we got into the possession game.

The objections I'm raising are inevitable, given the wording and assuming that the wording was intended to be clear and logical. The question is, then, whether or not this assumption can really be made about James's later writing. Isn't his style purposely designed to defeat clarity and logic, at least of the commonsensical kind I've been evoking? That does seem to me his intention, and he achieves it by being even more slippery, vague, and elusive than I've shown. Consider, for example, the words in the offending sentence that imply some degree of orderly development in the experience it describes but that turn out to be utterly unsuited to the task. "Once we possess" doesn't, for instance, necessarily refer to some point after we've gotten into the reading; it can refer to a time before we start, perhaps when we are only anticipating the imaginative adventure ahead of us. And the vapid phrase "at all" ("Should we want to get the book at all?"), instead of pointing to a time before we owned the book, could just as well refer to a time after we've read it and while we are cherishing the memory of how it "got" to us. When *does* reading begin? When does it end?

The analysis can go on interminably, wearing us down, opening up prospects of tiresome circularity. It's as if we are only proving how fully we've become what James wanted us to become, "imperfect readers" whose resistant "hundredth part" keeps us from giving in to his beguilements, even though, in a sense, we've already done so in our obsessions with his words. At that point it's time to admit that the passage has accomplished just what he intended it to accomplish. He wanted us to concede that the process by which the workings of style can take possession of us, or we of it, does *not* have any particular order or logic. The word "possess" suggests the kind of madness, evoked in his story of 1893, "The Middle Years," where the dying novelist

Dencombe exultantly declares: "We work in the dark—we do what we can—we give what we have. Our doubt is our passion, and our passion is our task. The rest is the madness of art."

These matters are eloquently brought into play in James's preface to *The Tempest,* unaccountably ignored by nearly all his interpreters, even by Tanner, who joins the very best of them with this book. James writes of Shakespeare as if he were proud to be an enlistee in the ranks, doing what he can to help out in an enterprise whose dimensions absolutely amaze him, reduce him, as he says, to "strained and aching wonder." Surrender and obedience are responses that in this case are more suitable, he argues, than is the "interpretive heat" or "interpretive zeal" of those who want to dig up the meaning, like so much plunder, so as to carry it elsewhere. His "merely baffled and exasperated view of one of the supreme works of all literature is," he contends, "no unworthy tribute" to it, especially when compared to the large body of commentary on the play that "abounds much rather in affirmed conclusions, complacencies of conviction, full apprehensions of the meaning and triumphant pointings of the moral."

As he continues, it becomes poignantly evident that he finds in Shakespeare's last play the very qualities he hopes, this late in his career, might one day be discovered by a critic of his own work. He speaks, meanwhile, of "the Poet's high testimony to this independent, absolute value of Style, and to its need thoroughly to project and seat itself." A bit earlier he insists that in Shakespeare "the phrase, the cluster and order of terms, *is* the object and the sense," which may be taken to mean that, whatever the realities or truths created by style, these compete with and aren't simply to be measured by any reality or truth prior to it. "It is," he goes on to say, "by his expression of it exactly as the expression stands that the particular thing is created as interesting, as beautiful, as strange, droll or terrible."

Nevertheless, as James likes to remind himself and us, any writer, even of Shakespeare's unparalled genius, who works "predominantly in the terms of expression, *all* in the terms of the artist's specific vision and genius," is in an immensely precarious position. He is forever in danger of becoming ultimately incomprehensible. Imaginative vision for a writer can only and always be an effort to arrive at one, to create it in words, and it is thanks to these words that readers may expect to share in the wonder and excitement of the effort. But the quest, the effort, the sharing assumed an implicit agreement among all participants that a good part of the pleasure depends upon keeping a delicate, forever varying balance between sense and indecipherability, each allowed to tease the other into and out of assertions of predominance.

Mostly on this score, James is willing, for a moment directly, to claim some place on the stage with Shakespeare:

> One can speak, in these matters, but from the impression determined by one's own inevitable standpoint; again and again, at any rate, such a masterpiece puts before me the very act of the momentous conjunction taking place for the poet, at a given hour, between his charged inspiration and his clarified experience: or, as I should perhaps better express it, between his human curiosity and his æsthetic passion. Then, if he happens to have been, all his career, with his equipment for it, more or less the victim and the slave of the former, he yields, by way of a change, to the impulse of allowing the latter, for a magnificent moment, the upper hand.

His glorification of Shakespeare seems to me a wholly deserved glorification of himself, and it is appropriate, too, that in this process he resorts to a descriptive terminology that William should have found irresistible: "Such a quest of imaginative experience, we can only feel, has itself constituted one of the greatest observed adventures of mankind."

16

MELVILLE'S VANITY
OF FAILURE

Melville began writing *Pierre, or The Ambiguities* in August 1851; he had just turned thirty-three and was the author of six books. The most recent, *Moby-Dick*, was set to be published, and reviews of it, largely negative in the United States and somewhat less so in England, would begin appearing while he was working on the new novel and negotiating the terms for its publication. Of the books already in print, only the first two, *Typee* and *Omoo,* had much commercial success, and even *Typee,* which made him for a time a minor celebrity, had been criticized, as nearly all his works would be, for blasphemy and untruth, prompting his publishers to ask him to revise for the second printing, adding some assertions as to the veracity of the story and cutting some unflattering references to Christian missionaries.

When he submitted the manuscript of *Pierre* to his publisher, Harper Brothers, at the very beginning of January, he was in debt to them for earlier advances. He was nonetheless surprised and disappointed when they offered a contract less generous, so he thought, than for any of his earlier books. Though he reluctantly agreed to their terms, he almost immediately began to

write sections and passages that he then added to the manuscript, and by January 21 his brother Allan was informing
Harper's that the manuscript exceeded the length originally
agreed to, possibly hoping, but in vain, that they would pay a bit
more for it. No manuscript of the novel has been found, but it
is estimated that the additions make up about thirteen percent
of the total published by Harper's in July 1852. This published
version has since been accepted as standard, and it served as
copy text for the edition published in 1971 in the authoritative
Northwestern-Newberry Edition of *The Writings of Herman
Melville,* edited by Harrison Hayford, Hershel Parker, and G.
Thomas Tanselle.

   Then, in 1996, this same Hershel Parker, a professor of English at the University of Delaware, constructed an alternative
version meant to approximate the novel Melville originally delivered to Harper's. In the absence of any manuscript copies, it is
not possible to determine exactly what or how much was added
or where such additions may have been inserted. But Parker
convinced himself that the sure mark of any supposedly added
material is that some direct reference is made in it to Pierre as a
working poet or novelist. And since, again in his view, all references of that kind begin to occur only with Book XVII ("Young
America in Literature"), he starts out by deleting that and then
goes on to cut Books XVIII ("Pierre, as a Juvenile Author,
Reconsidered") and XXII ("The Flower Curtain Lifted from
before a Tropical Author; With Some Remarks on the Transcen-
dental Flesh-Brush Philosophy"), along with bits and pieces
from other of the later Books ranging from several pages to a few
words. This means the deletion of one of the most powerful passages Melville ever wrote: Pierre's vision of the Enceladus in
Book XXV.

   In an extensive introduction, Parker tries to explain why this
new edition is worth owning, aside from the fact that it is handsomely produced by HarperCollins with pictures by Maurice

Sendak. Parker makes it clear that his reconstruction is not meant to replace the Northwestern-Newberry Edition. Nonetheless, he quite heatedly insists that his shorter version is much to be preferred. The alleged additions, he asserts, "wrecked" such precious elements as Melville's "symmetrical" time scheme and the novel's "meticulous control," though of what we're never told, and played havoc with its "hyper-coherence." By the end he is in something of a froth against any suppositious reader who might dare to disagree with him: "For readers of *Pierre* as originally published but not as originally completed, the aesthetic lesson of my evidence is that it is folly to look for ways of seeing the Pierre-as-author theme as unified with the rest of the book. To find unity in the mixed product of ecstatic confidence and reckless defiance after failure is to trivialize Melville's aspiration, his achievement, and his wrecking of that achievement—to dehumanize Melville as man and artist."

This summarizing passage cannot be called literary criticism; it is a plea of sorts, on behalf not of a novel called *Pierre* but of a man, or rather Parker's version of a man, named Herman Melville. Like the introduction as a whole, the passage fudges the critical issues it raises. Why, one wants to know, is "unity" or "hyper-coherence" so overriding a criterion, especially when in this instance it seems to involve mostly mechanical aspects of plot-making? And is the shorter version of the novel actually as "unified" as he thinks it is? *Pierre* in either version harbors a deep incoherence between its historical and its psychological dimensions, and this comes into play in the very first Book, composed well before any of the purportedly added sections. It's this evidence of incoherence that makes *Pierre,* no less than *Moby-Dick,* more interesting to think about than it otherwise might be.

The deficiencies in Parker's interpretation of *Pierre* have their source, I suspect, in his belief, perhaps inevitable in someone now completing a two-volume life of the author, that Melville's style at crucial moments is necessarily determined by his state of mind at the time of writing, or more exactly by what Parker assumes that state of mind must have been. His extravagant assertion that in making the so-called additions to *Pierre* Melville succeeded only in "wrecking his achievement" is based finally on a biographical conjecture that while writing them Melville "was bitter, overwrought, and even suicidal." Why would he not be, in Parker's view, faced as he was by emerging evidence that *Moby-Dick* would be a critical and commercial failure and, related to that, by what Parker calls Harper's "punitive contract" for the new book?

These conjectures may or may not be correct, but Melville's state of mind, whatever it was, did not necessarily dictate what he wrote at the time or his artistic decisions about where and how to insert new passages into the novel. As it happens, the longest of the Books that offend Parker, Book XVII ("Young America in Literature"), includes some of the funniest, certainly the most comically modulated writing in *Pierre.* It is a high-spirited send-up of Pierre's fame as a juvenile writer, best known for "that delightful sonnet 'The Tropical Summer'," and of literary celebrity in general.

As for the contract offered by Harper Brothers for *Pierre,* why was it "unfair," much less "punitive," given the sales and reception of most of Melville's preceding books? Melville's disappointment isn't surprising; a disappointment of that sort is common enough among writers. Any additions to *Pierre* he then proceeded to make were designed in part to increase the price of the book and thereby his own proceeds. This was not an unworthy ambition, and it is only one of the many indications of Melville's own commercial impulses and of his constantly increasing financial needs—as a writer in debt, with no private means and with responsibility for a large and growing household. If he was a martyr to commercialism, then some of the commercialism was his own. He and his publishers together were in the business of making a living, which doesn't mean that they hadn't other ambitions that worked meanwhile against financial profit-taking. He intended each of the seven books he had written by 1852 to be a popular success. At the same time he took the commercial failure of most of them as evidence of his artistic distinction and a reason for boasting of failure. Failure was a price worth paying for engaging in what he called, in "Hawthorne and His Mosses" (1850), "the great Art of Telling the Truth." In a letter of October 6, 1849, to his father-in-law, Judge Lemuel Shaw, to whom he owed a considerable amount of money, he claimed: "It is my earnest desire to write those sort of books which are said to 'fail.' Pardon this egotism." Meantime, his publishers and some other of his correspondents, were being assured that the book then in progress was also designed to sell.

Melville was genuinely confused on this issue. It is never a good idea to hold him strictly to what he said about it in any one instance, not even when he wanted to sound as if the writing enterprise was in and of itself a courageously perilous adventure. Immensely excited when he met Hawthorne in the summer of 1850, while he was working on *Moby-Dick,* and convinced, for a time, that here was another American capable, as he thought himself to be, of proving a match for Shakespeare—at once supremely great and immensely popular—he was apt to address his new friend with an exceptional degree of self-infatuated por- tentousness. He was already well into *Pierre* when he wrote to Hawthorne in November 1851, still exhilarated by Hawthorne's response to *Moby-Dick,* to whom the book was dedicated: "I have written a wicked book, and feel spotless as the lamb. . . . Lord, when shall we be done growing? As long as we have any- thing more to do, we have done nothing. So, now, let us add Moby Dick to our blessing, and step from that. Leviathan is not the biggest fish;—I have heard of Krakens," a fabulous Scandi- navian sea monster.

This is an early example of a kind of macho agonism especially pronounced among American male novelists who like to talk about landing or shooting or climbing The Big One—Mailer as Babe Ruth wanting to "hit the longest ball ever to go up into the accelerated hurricane air of our American letters," or Hemingway, who "wouldn't fight Dr. Tolstoi in a 20 round bout because I know he would knock my ears off." Obviously, what Hawthorne had dismissed as a band of "scribbling women" were not expected to produce contenders.

One of the many extravagances of Parker's edition of *Pierre* is that he chooses to call it "The Kraken Edition," presuming without clear warrant that, in his letter to Hawthorne, Melville was making "his first unmistakable reference to his new book." Melville was implying, he writes, "that *Pierre* was to be bigger, deeper in its profundity, than *Moby-Dick.*" But the reference isn't at all "unmistakably" to *Pierre.* It can refer more generally to any future work done by either of the writers. Furthermore, if applied to *Pierre,* the characterization is totally at odds with what is obviously meant to be a clear reference to the novel, not mentioned in Parker's introduction. It can be found in a letter dated January 8, 1852, by which time he had already submitted a version of the novel to his publisher which Parker now claims to have reconstructed, and when he had, besides, begun to write the material he intended, according to Parker, to add to it. The letter this time is not to Hawthorne but to Hawthorne's wife, Sophia, thanking her for what he terms her amazing insights into *Moby-Dick.* He then remarks: "My dear Lady, I shall not again send you a bowl of salt water. The next chalice I commend will be a rural bowl of milk." Clearly, "a rural bowl of milk" is expected to suit the tastes of the general public, though it may be significant that in the novel Pierre's appetite for bowls of milk provokes from his mother the mock warning that he is becoming a milksop. In any case, "a rural bowl of milk" is a most unlikely habitat for a kraken.

If the two images are put together, however, then a kraken in a rural bowl of milk, an upsurging, destructive turbulence that finds itself trapped within a pacifying and confining domesticity, is quite appropriate to *Pierre.* It is, besides, an apt enough description of a writer whose lifelong financial needs and intense desire for fame compelled him to hope for commercial popular success, even as the hope simultaneously provoked in him a revulsion against the concessions he would be required to make to stylistic and formal conventions. Thus, in the opening sections of *Pierre* as in the opening sections of *Moby-Dick,* Melville initially commits himself to familiar modes of romantic and domestic fiction, only then progressively to disown these in both instances.

One reason why many people admit to confusion while reading this novel is that Melville indulges himself in literary conventions about which he holds an instinctive suspicion—as indeed he does of all uses of language. At crucial points it is impossible to determine whether or not or by how much he intends parody. He seems particularly given to exaggerated versions of styles that are themselves inherently exaggerated, like the pastoral-heroic idyll or the Gothic, antecedents for which include Byron's *Manfred* and, I would guess, Richardson's *Clarissa,* where a coffin is used as a writing desk. Melville had read Spenser before he took up a close study of Shakespeare in early 1849. ("If another Messiah ever comes," he then wrote a correspondent, "twill be in Shakespeare's person.") He found in the plays precedents for the rhetorical overreachings of Ahab and of Pierre, along with the use of minor characters for commentary in the manner of the porter's scene in *Macbeth.* Some of this is quite clumsily managed, and the echoings of Lear and Hamlet in the speeches of Ahab and Pierre can be taken either as a heroic questing of mind or as mere folly. There's often no way of knowing how to take them. Uncertainties and puzzles of this kind, which abound in Melville's work, can be assessed as disablements or as relatively inconsequential in the context of his enormous imaginative ambition and attainment.

Great literary and intellectual ambition can assume a variety of forms when it comes up against the mediating counterforce of formal conventions. In Melville, as in other writers given to works of encyclopedic dimensions, from Spenser to the Romantic poets to Joyce and his successors, it often manifests itself as a celebration of the heroics of authorship, of the effort to cope with the cultural accumulations that over the centuries have been building up within literary practice. The reader is then invited to attend not only to the actions of the characters but to the activity of the writer, a designation that may include the fictional hero as well as the author himself, as it does in *Pierre.* One result is an often quite direct foregrounding of literary technique. Attention is called to the manipulative prowess required of a writer who even as he makes use of inherited modes also tries to show that they have, at best, only a temporary utility. Particularly in the last century and a half a tendency has developed, comic or plaintive as the case may be, to highlight the inadequacy of available techniques to the organizational tasks they are expected to perform. And the evidence of this inadequacy includes the nurtured incoherence and asymmetry of the work at hand. Failure of a sort thus becomes a sign of the lonely bravery of authorial effort in the modern dispensation, of the writer's willing self-sacrifice in the service of some necessary but unspecifiable cultural change.

Melville in *Moby-Dick* wrote a version of *Ulysses* before he wrote, in *Pierre,* his version of a portrait of the artist as a very confused young man. As his career developed, he was overwhelmed by his sophisticated doubts about literary composition, including at last his own compositional efforts. It is as if he increasingly measured his achievements by the degree of critical corrosion he could bring to bear on the cultural and literary origins of his own writing, along with its contemporary viability, and this became more important to him than any similar scrutiny of the cultural or literary or historical origins to which his characters might lay claim. Origin and originality are the issues that matter most to him in *Pierre.*

The plot of the novel can only superficially be derived from the chronology of its events or the murky psychological developments in its characters. Any coherence or "hyper-coherence" inferable from these factors proves to be illusory. Rather, the plot evolves from obsessively repeated discoveries of likenesses where none were expected, of topographical namings and renamings, of reflections, of multiple, slightly varying portraits of the same person, of mirrorings and echoes, including echoes of other literary works. All these increasingly call into doubt the familial and historical lineages that give Pierre an initial sense of his identity. His peculiar avidity in seeking out possible likenesses, as between what he already knows and what he chances upon, gradually erodes whatever trust he might have had in the distinctness of his inheritance or origins. And with that comes a confusion, too, as to the standards in terms of which he might confidently affirm some degree of individual variation or originality.

The prose of the first Book is cluttered with literary allusions and mimicked styles, as if to suggest that, initially at least, Pierre is contented to be "heaped," as Ahab complained of being, by the accumulated weight of inherited forms and models. There are hints, however, that he will in due time feel compelled to release himself from these by inventing, like a Melvillian novelist, alternative forms and models. As the novel opens, much is made of the fact that Pierre is heir to every possible advantage. These advantages are described in the language of the fairy tale, however, an early suggestion that his heritage will in some degree prove to be fraudulent. Physically beautiful and athletic, the only child of a startlingly youthful-looking widowed mother, he is at eighteen destined to own a vast, idyllically situated estate in upper New York State. All round him are visible evidences in the family properties of the heroic military feats by which his near-ancestors took violent possession of the land during the Indian and Revolutionary Wars. He is engaged to a seventeen-year-old neighboring beauty, also of a distinguished and wealthy family, named Lucy Tartan. When we first meet them, they are speaking to each other in the language of *Romeo and Juliet* or, rather, in the Petrarchan mode of the first scene, more appropriate to Romeo's discredited mooning over Rosalind. Their dialogue—"'Smell I the flowers, or thee,' cried Pierre. 'See I lakes, or eyes,' cried Lucy, her own gazing down into his soul, as two stars gaze down into a tarn"—finds its equivalent in Melville's commentary: "Love sees ten million fathoms down, till dazzled by the floor of pearls."

Such writing has to be called intolerably bad or taken as parody. Melville wants no decisive choice to be made on that score, however. If he allowed his own writing at such moments to become clearly parodistic, then obviously the equivalent language used by Pierre and Lucy would be an object of ridicule, and he is determined not to expose his hero to that possibility. At several points in the opening Book, entitled "Pierre Just Emerging from His Teens," Melville intrudes directly to caution the reader—much in the manner of Henry James in *Portrait of a Lady,* on behalf of his own romantically youthful Isabel Archer—not to judge precipitously someone destined to suffer unduly. Paragraphs in which his characters are allowed to exult in their situations tend to conclude with dropped hints of bad things to come, and when these same characters use idealizing literary allusions, they often do so with a kind of distortion that only confirms the unreality of their expectations. When, for example, Pierre's mother says to her son, "You are a Romeo," she then has to add that she trusts he will be married "not to a Capulet, but to one of our own Montagues; and so Romeo's evil fortune will hardly be yours. You will be happy." She cannot know, though he may already have a premonition (he interjects at this point "The more miserable Romeo!"), that by grotesquely fulfilling her wish that he marry within the family he will destroy everyone, including himself. He will soon tell her a lie calculated, he likes to suppose, to protect her and his late father from disgrace. He is already married, he will say, to a strange, beautiful girl named Isabel, about whom no one, including Isabel herself, knows much of anything. He wants desperately to disguise what he impulsively believes to be true, that Isabel is his illegitimate and long-forsaken half sister, a ruse by which he hopes to bring her under his intimate protection and at the same time redeem, without revealing to anyone, the sins of his father.

Pierre is even more given to literary allusions than is his mother, who "looked the daughter of a General, which she was." And though of Pierre we are told that "on both sides he sprung from heroes," Melville gives greater emphasis to his literary interests and inclinations: "not in vain had he spent long summer afternoons in the deep recesses of his father's fastidiously picked and decorous library; where the Spenserian nymphs had early led him into many a maze of all-bewildering beauty." His heroic lineage, his literariness, and his surroundings all suggest a figure in heroic-pastoral romance, which is consistent with the style of the first Book. It isn't enough that he has "a delicate and poetic mind"; he is credited also with having "the complete polished steel of the gentleman," an allusion, possibly, to another sixteenth-century writer, George Gascoigne, in whose satire "The Steele Glas" the hero can see not only his own faults but those of kings, lords, and knights. Pierre will similarly come to see the faults of his father mirrored in the little portrait he has cherished of him as a debonair young man, a portrait that, once he is persuaded by the story of Isabel, he will throw into the fire.

Being more exactingly literary than his mother, Pierre is haunted early on less by *Romeo and Juliet* than by Dante's *Inferno,* and even as he anticipates an evening with Lucy when they plan to look through a book of Flemish prints and of Flaxman's illustrations of Homer—yet further references to copies and reflections—he emphatically rules out in his mind any inspection of Flaxman's Dante. He has a fearful premonition that he would find there too close an approximation of the face of the mysterious girl that has haunted him for weeks, though he has seen her only once and doesn't yet know that her name is Isabel:

> No, we will not open Dante. Methinks now the face—the face—minds me a little of pensive, sweet Francesca's face—or, rather, as it had been Francesca's daughter's face—wafted on the sad dark wind, toward observant Virgil and the blistered Florentine. No, we will not open Flaxman's Dante. Francesca's mournful face is now ideal to me. Flaxman might evoke it wholly,—make it present in lines of misery—bewitching power. No, I will not open Flaxman's Dante! Damned be the hour I read in Dante! More than that wherein Paolo and Francesca read in fatal Lancelot!

A novel whose hero is as obsessed as this one with finding possible relations, reflections, and origins for himself is necessarily crowded with figures drawn from history, painting, poetry, and mythology. Many of these, just as necessarily, are distorted by his compulsion to shape life so that it fits his illusions. Pierre's agitations about Dante are an example of how, especially in the opening Books, Melville characterizes his hero as someone who has immersed himself in literature so as to probe the mystery of his psychological states and at the same time lend them a grand historical or mythological dimension. He is here alluding to one of the most celebrated passages in the *Inferno,* where, in Canto V, Dante and Virgil meet the shades of Francesca and Paolo. These two thirteenth-century contemporaries of Dante were the central players in a famous scandal: discovered in the illicit act, they are murdered by Francesca's husband, who happens to be Paolo the Handsome's hunchbacked older brother. They have been consigned to the circle reserved for carnal sinners, and all the lovers found there have been made known to later times mostly through ancient epics or medieval romances or will be immortalized, like Paolo and Francesca, through Dante's poem.

The importance to their story of Lancelot and Guinevere is wholly invented by Dante, and it is significant that Melville makes a point of mentioning it. These two earlier lovers betray King Arthur doubly, as both husband and ruler. So do Francesca and Paolo betray Giovanni Malatesta, since he is husband to the one and elder brother to the other. It is their exposure to an actual text of the Lancelot–Guinevere story that, according to them, induces the sinful act that leads to their deaths. Melville thus creates a hall of mirrors. He has contrived to have a character in his novel look forward to an evening over the books with a young lady he loves, in which, during a scene of reading, they will look into a text wherein they will discover another romantic couple also involved in a scene of reading, and that couple, nearly a half century before, were in their turn also finding in their text the same illicit and initial moment of intimacy between a still earlier couple, the legendary Lancelot and Guinevere. Paolo and Francesca can claim literally to have been mutually seduced by the book they are reading, as were Lancelot and Guinevere by the pander Galleoto. Indeed, in her speech to Dante and Virgil, Francesca, speaking of the book they read, says, "A Galleoto, that book."

Though Melville makes no mention of this remark, readers are free to think of it as one of the many indications that much of Pierre's trouble comes from his desire to imagine life for himself as if it were part of one or another of the more conventionalized literary masterpieces. This is hinted at in the early paragraphs of the novel when it is said that Pierre looks upon the perfection of his life at Saddle Meadows as an "illuminated scroll" and that there is "only one hiatus discoverable by him in that sweetly-writ manuscript. A sister had been omitted from the text." That is, even before he catches sight of Isabel, he has invented a place and a specific role for her in his "text." His life is likened to an evolving work of art which, for the very reason that it is so conventional, artificial, or scroll-like, is ready to accommodate any romantic revisions he wants to make in it.

While Parker may complain, as did some of *Pierre*'s first reviewers, that Melville didn't directly identify Pierre as a writer until Book XVII, and didn't go back to insert earlier mentions of this, a pattern of metaphors nonetheless abundantly exists in the opening sections, starting with the first passages of Book I, suggesting that Pierre treats his life, disastrously, as if it were already a literary work in progress and he its composer. To discover such compositional patterns doesn't thereby make a novel any better than its many adverse critics have said it is. Nor does it suggest that without the added material on Pierre-as-writer the book would have been, in Parker's phrase, "a masterpiece," or that with the additions it is nonetheless, as Sacvan Bercovitch claims in his massively detailed interpretation in *Rites of Ascent,* "a work of sustained brilliance," "a major text not only in but about American literary history." Simply because close analysis may reveal some potentially complex meaningfulness in *Pierre,* or some scaffoldings of a coherence among certain of its metaphors or submerged strands of allusiveness, does not thereby recommend the book the more. At most, it merely offers clues about some of the author's powerfully registered intentions. It is not proof that he ever fully or adequately realized or executed those intentions. What ought to concern us are not adducible meanings but the manner in which these are made available and whether or not they allow themselves to be experienced at the pace of civilized, educated reading. This is a pace rather different from systematic decoding only of certain passages.

Why, since its first publication, have many intelligent readers who admire a book as erratically put together as *Moby-Dick* confessed that they find *Pierre* more or less unreadable? They don't mean that it is indecipherable. Henry James put it best, I think, in his 1884 lecture "The Art of Fiction":

I can think of no obligation to which the "romancer" would not be held equally with the novelist; the standard of execution is equally high for each. Of course it is of execution that we are talking—that being the only point of a novel that is open to contention. This is perhaps too often lost sight of, only to produce interminable confusions and cross-purposes. We must grant the artist his subject, his idea, his *donnée*: our criticism is applied only to what he makes of it. . . . We may believe that of a certain idea even the most sincere novelist can make nothing at all, and the event may perfectly justify our belief; but the failure will have been a failure to execute, and it is in the execution that the fatal weakness is recorded.

By intellectual conviction Melville was deeply wary of the pleasures afforded by any of the fictional modes familiar to him. He was persuaded in his own mind that a book could indeed be "a Galleoto." But he wanted and needed to believe that he could freely indulge in these conventions while also engaged in "the great Art of Telling the Truth." In April 1852, months after Parker claims he had finished his additions to *Pierre,* he wrote to his English publisher (who in the end refused to publish it) that the novel "possessed unquestionable novelty, as regards my former ones," but was at the same time "very much more calculated for popularity than anything you have yet published of mine." He is doubtless saying that he has tried to cater to the popular taste for pastoral romance combined, as it is in *Pierre,* with urban and Gothic sensationalism. At the same time, however, he is also choosing to forget his own complicated mockings of these same qualities and, especially, the sometimes formidable density of his prose. One probable attraction for him of Canto V of the *Inferno* is that it masterfully bridges any such difficulties. It is among the most popular parts of the poem while also being especially complex of purpose, in its implicit critique of the romantic clichés it is successfully making use of.

The passage about Dante in *Pierre* is notable not simply or even primarily because of Pierre's allusion to the lovers. More significantly, it alludes to Dante's mythic method and Melville's variation on it. This is a method of juxtaposition that scarcely waited to be invented by Joyce, as Eliot once claimed it had been, and in which an ongoing experience finds an explanatory version of itself in some apparently similar experience already represented in the literature and mythologies of the past. The implication, in Melville and in Dante, is that while the mythic method may prove expedient in literary composition, it is to be avoided by people who, like Francesca or Pierre, might use it to create excuses for conduct in life that has been marked in the past by tragic consequences. Deployed in this manner, the method becomes not only a great convenience to the literary magnification of experience but a moral instrument, warning against the naïve appropriations of the power at work in literary texts.

I suspect Melville especially appreciated the way Dante indulges Francesca in her bold assertion that it was her reading the story of Lancelot and Guinevere with Paolo that caused, even as it forever glamorizes and immortalizes, their fateful and, as she would have it, unpremeditated act of sexual love. Melville goes a step further in indulging his hero: he lets him revise Canto V so that he may conjure up a figure carefully left unmentioned by Dante, namely, Francesca's daughter. At the time of the murder, Paolo was a married man with two children and Francesca, married for ten years, was the mother of a nine-year-old daughter. To have brought this daughter onstage would have compromised Dante's poignant if critical characterization of the mother. Even though condemned for eternity, Francesca remains touchingly devoted to the romantic cliché of her reputation and the projection of her romantic image. Mention of a daughter, particularly a daughter whose age in those days would have qualified her to be engaged to be married, would have crippled her effort to appear as a historical exemplification of young love and of the fatal consequences of a first surrender to an unthinking romantic impulse. Pierre's abrupt introduction of this daughter's face as a suitable image of the haunting face of Isabel is another example of the extent to which Melville indulges his hero's compulsive illusion that he is free to blind himself not only to reality but even to reality as represented in literary inheritances and, with that, to family and historical inheritances.

Along with these early and repeated characterizations of Pierre as a literary illusionist in his responses both to life and to the texts that purport to represent it, there is a concurrent development in the novel, strictly relegated to authorial commentary, in which Melville reveals his intense disdain for the perpetuated illusions, scarcely restricted to his hero, about patriotic, military forebears and the nobility of their contribution to the founding of America. In the first dozen pages, before Isabel is introduced and long before any of the material to which Parker takes exception appears, Melville remarks on his hero's view that there was "only one hiatus" in the "illuminated scroll of his life." And we have already been alerted to "deeds of his ancestors" far more reprehensible than the siring and desertion of the illegitimate child who might one day fill the "hiatus." Just a few paragraphs before the passage about the omission of a sister from the "text," Melville refers to a more damning cover-up—of how "vindictive" was the war by which the "sires" had come into possession of Saddle Meadows (named, in fact, after one of the battles over the property): "The Glendinning deeds by which their estate had so long been held, bore the cyphers of three Indian kings, the aboriginal and only conveyancers of those noble woods and plains."

The derision in this wording could easily be missed and may have been intended to be missed. The quasi-parodistic style of the opening Books does not invite the attentiveness required of the pun here on "cyphers," which can mean both hierogylphs and also non- or obliterated identities, or the pun on "deeds,"

referring both to legal title and to these acts of brutal appropriation that first secured that title. It is as if Melville wants to
disguise or even hide from his general audience a good part of
his historical-political intentions. Equally troubling, Pierre himself is completely insulated from this ongoing critique of his historical inheritance. Melville intervenes directly to protect him
("I beg you to consider again that this Pierre was but a youngster
as yet") from any reader who, if he has managed to catch what
Melville has been insinuating, might then choose to question the
"proud, elated sort of way" in which the hero has been brought
up to think of his ancestors. A case in point is the grandfather.
Famous for his exploits in the Revolution and, before that, in
the Indian Wars, this "mildest hearted and most blue eyed gentleman," measuring six feet four in height, "had annihilated two
Indian savages by making two reciprocal bludgeons of their
heads." There is an ironic, quasi-Swiftian pitch to Melville's
prose at such moments, as when he compares English to American pedigrees, "pedigrees I mean in which there is no flaw," and
then quietly moves on to the innocently delivered conclusion
that Americans have as much inherited right as the English to
take credit for imperialist excesses.

Not just as a "youngster," but even in his later rhetorically
grandiose expressions of general despair, Pierre never participates in or even indicates an awareness of the author's ongoing
acts of historical deconstruction. As I've suggested, this gap or
failing in the novel, as I take it to be, is perhaps best understood
as a consequence of Melville's desire to keep his critique of
America from becoming a more public, more audible factor in a
book that he imagined would be open to the usual complaint that
he was irreligious, blasphemous, and indecent, especially with a
hero clearly intent on some sort of incestuous career. Of course,
incestuous compulsions by themselves might constitute a desire
to discredit and then destroy "the great genealogical and real-
estate dignity" of a family line. It is a time-honored device for

bringing great families to ruin, a classic literary sign of degeneracy, often following on the discovery of some great earlier family sin. By itself, however, it carries no specifically targeted historical content, and it isn't given any here either by Melville or by his hero. In fact, it is made evident from the outset that Pierre has incest on his mind even before he finds someone to incite the erotic feelings that go with it. Among the first things we're told about him is that he and his mother address each other as "brother" and "sister" and that Pierre nonetheless feels cheated of a real sister. In Melville's account there is a perplexing blend of prissy elegance, prurience, and superciliousness:

> He mourned that so delicious a feeling as fraternal love had been denied him. Nor could the fictitious title, which he had so often lavished on his mother, at all supply the absent reality. The emotion was most natural; and the full cause and reason of it even Pierre did not at that time entirely appreciate. For surely a gentle sister is the second best gift to a man; and it is the first in point of occurrence; for the wife comes after. He who is sisterless, is a bachelor before his time. For much that makes up the deliciousness of a wife, already lies in the sister.

I focus on this passage because it encapsulates some of the complications that make this a fascinating novel, one that fails partly because it is overloaded with possibilities of meaning—something Melville was prone to do—without bringing them into a sufficiently reciprocal or productive relationship. What is most interesting here are the hints that while striving to be a proto-Faulknerian novel about a young man's need to discover the true nature of a historical and landed inheritance (assuming such a discovery is ever possible), the book is even more, but quite separately, a very confused psychological novel about the hero's profoundly destructive erotic needs. These needs find an object in the "face" or vision of Isabel, the very tenuousness of whose claims to sisterhood allow her also to be called his wife, and, we can confidently assume, to engage with him physically in that capacity. She represents the precise confusion in a single flesh-and-blood woman that he desperately seeks, in part to displace the frighteningly virginal Lucy. He contrives that Isabel shall give him both the "delicious feelings of fraternal love" and the "deliciousness of a wife," two satisfactions customarily kept separate but joined in the passage by Melville's rather leering repetition.

In a passage so gushingly benign in its phrasing, this repetition would likely seem devoid of ulterior motive if it was noticed at all. And in what sounds like a still further effort to muffle, even while acknowledging, the remarkable perversity of Pierre's project, the sentence which begins by stating that his "emotion was most natural" immediately admits that the emotion is murky: "the full cause and reason of it even Pierre did not at that time entirely appreciate." The time will never come when he will, and it's evident that Melville isn't sure what he himself means to be communicating here. Perhaps he is saying only that Pierre hasn't yet become aware of the existence of his half sister Isabel. But her existence has nothing to do with any "cause" or "reason" for the "emotion"; the "emotion" has always made him feel the want of someone like her. It's this prior emotion that wishes or dreams her into existence, and once she has appeared on the scene he will thereafter remain perplexed by his ready acceptance of her claims.

This compulsion to create a sister-wife for himself seems impelled by motives more mysterious and destructive than any understood by him; and whatever they might be, they are never effectively woven into the novel. Pierre's incestuous impulses are evidence, apparently, of an unconscious and for that reason all the more desperate determination to bring his line to an end, to disown his inheritance, and to terminate everyone closely associated with him, including himself, his mother, Lucy, his cousin and counter-image Glen, whom he murders outright, and of course Isabel, who is there to assist him in these efforts. And yet the motive brought forth by Melville is phrased in such a way as to suggest, grotesquely, that his incestuous desires are linked to literary aspirations. That is, he wants to correct that "hiatus"— a word with interesting anatomical suggestions, under the circumstances—in the "sweetly written text of his life." In doing so, he will transform that text into a family nightmare, a Gothic novel of incest.

Faulkner, who learned something from Melville and more from Conrad, makes far better use of an incestuous situation similar to Pierre's in *Absalom, Absalom!* He successfully develops its connections, as Melville never does, to specific and psychologically energizing historical circumstances. Faulkner's would-be agent of incestuous retribution is a young man, part Negro but easily passing for white, named Charles Bon. Close to the beginning of the Civil War, Bon discovers that, by his partly Negro mother in Haiti, he is the never acknowledged, even if financially assisted, son of the now remarried, immensely propertied Mississippi planter Thomas Sutpen. This also means that he is the half brother of Sutpen's daughter Judith. She falls in love with him, attracted by his physical resemblances to her adored brother Henry, who must, in the end, kill Bon to prevent the marriage, though he, too, loves him. Meantime, Bon has all along been prepared to release Judith, or so it is conjectured by some of the narrators of the story, if only the father will offer even a private gesture of recognition. The novel ends, as *Pierre* does, with a pile-up of bodies and with Sutpen's Hundred—on property, like Saddle Meadows, taken from its original Indian owners and with a house built by slave labor—in ruins.

Pierre's incestuous venture is given no such resonance, and it remains from beginning to end dissociated from the social-historical components that surround it. Whether one is reading the standard version or Parker's revised version, the novel proves to be incoherent in its conception. Of course, incest in life need not be joined to any social or historical motivating cause, but we are not reading life. We are reading a novel, and one that requires us, besides, to think at every point about novels as a genre. When, for example, Pierre is persuaded after the first of two chapter-long interviews with Isabel, that she is the sister who has been denied him, Melville gives prominence less to the hero's disenchantments with his father than, of all things, to the novel form! That's the culprit. It's the novel, the English novel it would seem, that has deceived and lied to our hero.

Once again, the structures of his feeling are revealed to us through metaphors having to do with literary structures:

> In [Isabel's] life there was an unraveled plot; and he felt that unraveled it would eternally remain to him. No slightest hope or dream had he, that what was dark and mournful in her would ever be cleared up into some coming atmosphere of light and mirth. Like all youths, Pierre had conned his novel-lessons; had read more novels than most persons of his years; but their false, inverted attempts at systematizing eternally unsystematizable elements; their audacious, intermeddling impotency, in trying to unravel, and spread out, and classify, the more thin than gossamer threads which make up the complex web of life; these things over Pierre had no power now . . . while the countless tribes of common novels laboriously spin vails of mystery, only to complacently clear them up at last; and while the countless tribe of common dramas do but repeat the same; yet the profounder emanations of the human mind, intended to illustrate all that can be humanly known of human life; these never unravel their own intricacies, and have no proper endings; but in imperfect, unanticipated, and disappointing sequels (as mutilated stumps), hurry to abrupt intermergings with the eternal tides of time and fate. So Pierre renounced all thought of ever having Isabel's dark-lantern illuminated to him.

This confession of Melville's own artistic despair comes in Book VII, not even halfway toward Book XVII, presumably inserted later, where we learn that Pierre is himself an unsuccessful practicing novelist. Examples like this make it evident-

that Parker has failed to read attentively enough his own preferred version, much less the standard one, even though he has
been an editor of both. Against the shared opinion of just about
every other commentator, he asserts, "Melville conceived and
wrote the original *Pierre* in a mood of intense exaltation"—as if
Melville's realization that he could not write a popularly successful novel and, if he could, would have scorned the results, came
to him only when his publisher refused to pay what he wanted
for this one or when some reviewers attacked the one before it,
Moby-Dick. Already implicit in this passage from Book VII is the
confession made by Pierre in one of the supposedly added chapters: that his own, alternative and Melvillian novelistic experiments cheat him of the truth as much as have any conventional
practices. He complains of "the universal lurking insincerity of
even the greatest and purest written thoughts. Like knavish
cards, the leaves of all great books were covertly packed," and he
adds, "He was but packing one set the more; and that a very poor
jaded set and pack indeed."

From beginning to end, in every crevice, and in whatever version, *Pierre* is an allegory of Melville's thwarted career as a novelist. It is a totally self-absorbed performance in which failure is
attributed to the nature of literature itself and to language as a
necessary betrayer. The claims in all this to a lonely cultural
heroism on the part of the writer was to become familiar to readers of twentieth-century modernist literature. It is a claim, fortunately, that seems by now nearly to have worn out its welcome.

WHITMAN: THE END GAME

⁜

With the publication of volumes 8 and 9, some ninety years after the appearance in 1906 of the first volume, all two and one half million words of Horace Traubel's *With Walt Whitman in Camden* are now in print. Altogether the volumes cover the last four years of Whitman's life, from 1888 to 1892, and consist of nearly day-by-day renditions of Whitman's conversations, correspondence, and such activities as he was still up to, along with reports of his last illnesses and lingering death. Traubel constructed this record from notes sometimes taken in the half-light of Whitman's sick room in the little house Whitman owned on Mickle Street in Camden, New Jersey, or jotted down later from memory, when he returned home to his wife and family or to his desk at the bank that employed him.

Whitman very seldom acknowledged that his conversations were being recorded. But he made it clear that as a form of biography he preferred this method to anything more studied, more given to summaries, interpretations, and speculative conclusions. In an August 1890 exchange with Traubel, he remarked on the unique value "in the matter you are piling together . . . personal memorabilia, traits of character, incidents, habits—the pulse and throb of the critter himself. Oh, how I have looked for just that matter in connection with great men, some of whom I have met, some not, yet it is the thing we get least of—is really a desideratum." And he enthusiastically agreed when Traubel interjected: "The real life of a man can often be written in the scraps the formal biographer refuses" (IV, 44).

A sprawling accumulation of "scraps" like *With Walt Whitman in Camden* is understandably congenial to the poet's lifelong habits of evasion and concealment, punctuated as these were with hints that at some point a "secret" is to be revealed, perhaps, as he teasingly remarked to Traubel, about "a period in my life of which my friends know nothing" (II, 316). His way of soliciting interest—even as he refused to take questions about his history, his daily habits, his studied variations of tone and mood—required of him a kind of unrelenting and stylized composure. Whitman's composure finds its equal among American writers only in Henry James. With majestic aloofness, he liked, as he wrote early in *Song of Myself,* to be "both in and out of the game, and watching and wondering at it."

And like the games James plays in *The Turn of the Screw,* Whitman's are intended to create mysteries, to hint at exposures, to turn mystification itself into the subject of inexhaustible interest. For Whitman as much as for James it is a serious game indeed, the place where aesthetic and ethical practice come together, and where the hoped-for consequence is that the reader will learn a reverence for the unknowable, along with a kind of amused wonder at the way human inquisitiveness persists in the face of its defeats. Such reverence and wonder is the antithesis of the "brilliancy, smartness" (II, 187) for which Whitman repeatedly expressed disdain. "The disease of our time," Traubel reported him as saying in June 1891, "is its smartness, cleverness—that hellish New England hunger to know something" (VII, 272).

Perhaps he was forgetting, for he surely knew, that it was the New Englander Emerson who put the matter even more powerfully in the essay "Experience." In a paragraph in which Emerson proclaimed that "the value of life lay in its inscrutable possibilities," he launched an attack on the "theoretic kidnappers" of our minds: "The grossest ignorance does not disgust like this impudent knowingness." That last is a particularly resonant phrase in its association with Whitman. The word "pudency" derives from *pudenda,* the bodily site of human creation, a derivation we're reminded of later in the essay: "The art of life has a pudency, and will not be exposed. Every man is an impossibility until he is born." Emerson, like Whitman, was in effect arguing that the source of creation is itself unknowable, thereby suggesting, as Whitman extravagantly liked to do, a mysterious link between poetic creativity and the most elementary forms of sexual production, including the production of sperm itself. Whitman intended that he and his ever emerging *Leaves of Grass* should, by his own obfuscations, be made immune to "impudent knowingness."

In an obviously deeply pondered remark to Traubel in September 1888, he maintained, "If there is anything whatever in *Leaves of Grass*—anything that sets it apart as a fact of any importance—that thing must be its totality—its massings," the accumulations, it might be said, of the marvelous mess that resulted from the poem's nine editions between 1855 and 1892, a textual maze of additions, deletions, revisions, and rearrangements. It could, he insisted, be "comprehended at no time by its parts, at all time by its unity" (II, 373), even as it forestalled any imposition of unity upon itself. The assertions of identity, notorious in some parts of *Leaves,* are meant to exist in a taut relation to his questionings of identity in another. The most poignant expression of despair for himself and his work, his doubts of the authenticity of both, is to be found fairly early, in 1860, in one of the greatest of his poems, "As I Ebb'd with the Ocean of Life," notably the second section, which I have discussed in greater detail in chapter 2:

As I wend to the shores I know not,
As I list to the dirge, the voices of men and women wreck'd,
As I inhale the impalpable breezes that set in upon me,
As the ocean so mysterious rolls toward me closer and closer,
I too but signify at the utmost a little wash'd-up drift,
A few strands and dead leaves to gather,
Gather, and merge myself as part of the sands and drift.

O baffled, balk'd, bent to the very earth,
Oppress'd with myself that I have dared to open my mouth,
Aware now that amid all that blab whose echoes recoil upon me I have
   not once had the least idea who or what I am,
But that before all my arrogant poems the real Me stands yet
   untouch'd, untold, altogether unreach'd,
Withdrawn far, mocking me with mock-congratulatory signs and bows,
With peals of distant ironical laughter at every word I have written,
Pointing in silence to these songs, and then to the sand beneath.

I perceive I have not really understood any thing, not a single object,
   and that no man ever can,
Nature here in sight of the sea taking advantage of me to dart upon me
   and sting me,
Because I have dared to open my mouth to sing at all.

None of this self-doubting despondency about his poetic creations is to be found in the millions of words Traubel credited to
Whitman in his final years. By then he was intent only on monu-
mentalizing himself, even while the conversations turned, time
and again, to his corresponding efforts to prepare, with Traubel's
help, the final, so-called deathbed edition of 1892 of *Leaves of
Grass,* and to the ongoing construction of a massive and expensive tomb, intended to house himself, flanked by a parent on
either side.

Whitman meant these volumes to be his last invocation, which
is the title of one of his most exquisitely turned poems, first published in 1868, long before he was readying himself for death. It
is in fact a poem not about death so much as about the mystery
of immortality, including literary immortality:

> At the last, tenderly,
> From the walls of the powerful fortress'd house,
> From the clasp of the knitted locks, from the keep of the
>   well-closed doors,
> Let me be wafted.
>
> Let me glide noiselessly forth;
> With the key of softness unlock the locks—with a whisper,
> Set ope the doors O soul.
>
> Tenderly—be not impatient,
> (Strong is your hold O mortal flesh,
> Strong is your hold O love.)

The poem asks that this "me" be released from the flesh, which it is somewhat sad about leaving, since flesh is the instrument of human, bodily love. But the nature and identity of this "me" is puzzling; it cannot be defined as readily as the "body" it is leaving or the "soul" which is asked to make the act of separation as "tender" as possible for this "me." We are left to conjecture that this "me," like "the real Me" that in "As I Ebb'd" is said to "stand yet untouch'd, untold, altogether unreach'd," exists not only prior to the body but also before and independently of the soul. In "As I Ebb'd" it stands aloof also from his poetry, so that it cannot be identified, either, with any descendent muse. It is some part of Whitman that always has been immortal and always will be. Perhaps this "Me" is the "genius" that he exhibits in his poetry and that might insure the immortality of that poetry. Whitman, the living man, aspires to be, like this immortal "me," beyond and contemptuous of questions and explanations. So, by implication, is the immortal *Leaves.*

Repeatedly in his conversations with Traubel, Whitman asked that his great book be accorded the same reverence, the same deference that he wanted shown to this immortal "Me." Discussing a study of 1883 by his devoted friend Richard Bucke entitled *Walt Whitman,* he insisted to Traubel that his endorsement of the book was never meant to extend to its interpretations:

as to his *explication*—no, no, no—that I do not accept—for *Leaves of Grass* baffles me, its author, at all points of its meaning—so that things perhaps plain to Doctor are not so plain to me. . . . Leaves of Grass never started out to do anything—has no purpose—has no definite beginning, middle, end. It is reflection, it is statement, it is to see and tell, it is to keep clear of judgements, lessons, school ways—to be a world with all the mystery of that, all its movements, all its life. From this standpoint I, myself, often stand in astonishment before the book—am defeated by it—lost in its curious revolutions, its whimsies, its overpowering momentum—lost as if a stranger, even as I am a stranger on this earth—driving about with it, knowing nothing or why or result. (VIII, 320–321)

In other words, this is a man who is content to leave what he has done in life in some natural state of "mess," as represented by the random assortment of papers on the floor of his sickroom. The mess is a visible rejection of any proprietary claims that may be put upon his life or his work by housekeepers or critics,versions, he would suppose, of the same thing. As Traubel described Whitman's room early on in the first volume: "There is all sorts of debris scattered about—bits of manuscript, letters, newspapers, books. Near by his elbow towards the window a washbasket full of such stuff" (I, 155). For Whitman, however, it wasn't a mess at all, but, rather, a way of assembling things so that only he could then exert maximum control over them, much as he asserted his authority over *Leaves,* by claiming that he was mystified, while explicators, who ordered it and sorted it out, were not.

In defense of the explicators, it's obvious that Whitman's poetry and prose do at times yield quite readily to flat translation and to *parti pris* interpretations. Traubel, an ardent democratic socialist to whose writings the Soviet newspaper *Izvestia* would one day devote an entire issue, was persuaded that he had discovered an ally in Whitman, even as did Whitman's many early admirers in England, like Edward Carpenter and John Addington Symonds, men of great cultivation, who seemed taken with his poetry primarily because it spoke for and to gay men like themselves. He is at his frequent best, however, when his poetry is least negotiable in the hands of people who read it on the look-out for what they hope to find there. He knew himself to be a great poet, a man privileged to receive the awesome and often close-to-terrifying visitations of genius. It is about the gestations of that poetry that he frequently wrote, as if in self-wonderment at his own figurations, especially when they evoke, in relation to the making of poetry, certain sexual acts and positionings the exact nature of which are puzzling. A most interesting example occurs in the 1855 *Song of Myself*:

> . . . myself waiting my time to be one of the supremes,
> The day getting ready for me when I shall do as much good as the best,
>   and be as prodigious
> Guessing when I am it will not tickle me much to receive
>   puffs out of pulpit or print;
> By my life-lumps! becoming already a creator!
> Putting myself here and now to the ambushed womb of the shadows!
> (1045–1049)

Poets who have achieved immortality take the same risk as poets who haven't: some of the words they once confidently used will be so overtaken by time as to become comical; Whitman's ambition to "be one of the supremes," for instance, might now remind the modern ear of Diana Ross and her partners. But the passage gives plenty of evidence that he'd have been more "tick-led" than distressed by so unintended a suggestion. Because while the grand ambitions expressed in the passage are very seriously meant, so are the associated sounds of high-spirited irreverence, as in the blustering oath "By my lumps!" What can be meant by this exclamation? I take "my life-lumps" to be a ref-erence to his own just-ejaculated sperm. The passage joins many others in the early editions of *Leaves* where masturbation is described far more frequently and graphically than any other inferable sexual act. Not, as some have alleged, because masturbation was necessarily Whitman's sexual activity of choice, but because in his imagination it figured as an analogy for equally solitary acts of poetic creation, of works destined to create future generations of readers. "This day," he announced at one point, "I am jetting the stuff of far more arrogant republics" (line 1003). His "seed," as he sometimes refers to his poems, would one day produce those comrades and lovers addressed in "Whoever You Are Now Holding Me in Hand." They would hold him by holding his book and "thrusting beneath your clothing/ Where I may feel the throbs of your heart and rest on your hip." "By my life-lumps" is an oath taken on his own "jettings" and begettings, making him "already a creator." The intentional obscurity of the trope is calculated to offend polite literati, to announce that his entrance into the line of great poets will be an intrusion of unprecedented rudeness. More, he wants it understood that his semen is not itself destined for conventional use. It does not jet forth into an engendering womb or even into someone else's hand. It is far more mysteriously destined: for the dark, for an eventual and threatened entrance into the womb of the future. And that womb is already "ambushed" by his perennial enemies—critics, other poets, academics, even friendly ones—who threaten to extinguish his chances for a future life among the "supreme" poets.

Such witty intricacies are a match for anything in Emily Dickinson, who knew all about what might happen to a great and as yet unrecognized poet as he or she approached "the ambushed womb of the shadows." But when they occur in Whitman, intricacies of this sort are apt to be missed even by very alert readers, for the obvious reason that they call forth a kind of compacted language not normally to be expected from a voice as fast-paced, declarative, and democratically intended as his. Nor are the sexual figurations here, or elsewhere in his poem, meant to represent Whitman's own habits, however often they are taken to do so. This is not a call for all masturbators of the world to throw off their chains and join him. The sexual images are designed with extraordinary precision to serve the highly particular significances he wants to communicate about his conceptions of poetry and of his poetic career.

A poet capable of such audacious multiplicity of sexually compromising suggestiveness put at the service of another purpose entirely cannot be expected to like or even tolerate direct, simplistic questions about his life. On one occasion, Traubel mentions an inquiry about the poet coming from a mutual friend, which Whitman agreed should be answered: "'but answer for yourself, don't answer for me. Do I ever answer questions?' He laughed quietly. 'Horace I made a puzzle; it's not my business to solve it'" (II, 228).

The production of mess, of puzzle, might be called his method if not his métier. Mess, like America itself, is infinitely expansive, and, because of that, it can endlessly postpone the finality of any answer as to what and where it is or will be. The mess on the floor at Mickle Street was not at all the result of his feeling too ill to straighten it out. It represented the consciously exercised preference of a lifetime. One of his young favorites, Harry Stafford, who was eighteen when he and Whitman began to share a close attachment and, whenever opportunity offered, the same bed, reported to Traubel years later that when Whitman stayed at the Stafford home, "he would make a great mess of his papers and mother would fix them up after her own notions, and he would say when he got back and saw it—'Susan you have set things right—that is, have mixed them all up for me'" (IX, 493).

According to Traubel, Whitman had much the same reaction to any efforts to bring order to his accumulations in the Mickle Street quarters: "People often criticise Mrs. Davis because of the confusion in the parlor and W's bedroom. The fact is W. does not encourage any interference even by her with his papers. She has been cleaning some this week, W. being rather disposed to joke about it. "'I hate to see things after they are 'fixed.' You get everything out of place and call it order'" (I, 280). Whitman was greatly amused by the effectiveness with which the mere sight of the mess in his room frustrated an inquiring preacher who visited him one evening. "I believe," he laughingly tells Traubel, that "the old man came to me with a set purpose to deliver a speech—to question me about the 'Leaves,' about my philosophy, politics, what I thought of Lord Byron, Percy Shelley, Burns. But when he got into the room, the debricity . . . of things—the confusion, the air of don't care, the unusual look and atmosphere—must have struck him, abashed him, staggered him. For he hardly said a word beyond greetings!" (IX, 59).

The mess over which he ruled disarmed questioners; it thwarted efforts at classification meant to reduce the mystery that invested his poetry and his life; it became a device whereby he hoped to nullify, by the confusions of intermixture, the alleged importance of others, especially Emerson, in shaping his career. More instrumentally, it allowed him to manipulate, in this case with Traubel's help, the disposition, recovery, and subsequent reading of important documents, a process that created suspense and unpredictability in an account of the final years that might, over so long a work, have degenerated into a record of mere illness and decline.

The mess functioned as an archive for both of them. In an entry for October 17, 1891, in the last of the volumes, Traubel reported: "Kicking about the floor as often, I turned over a couple of yellowed letters fastened by a gum band and, picking them up, found my heart stand still at the inscription that met my eye. The Emerson 1855 letter at last! And by the strangest accident, which no one could have foreseen. Often he had promised me this letter . . . Now to have its thousand eyes look at me from this heap of debris! . . . 'I have made a great find

Walt.' 'What is that Horace?'" (IX, 44). If Horace has a right to be thrilled, Whitman has a long-held motive for staying cool: "I will keep it for a day or so—look it over. Don't forget to remind me of it when you come tomorrow!"

The 1855 letter represented an extraordinary act of generosity and prescience from the greatest man of letters America had yet produced to a man who, unbidden, had sent a copy of his first book, a man whom Emerson had never heard of and whose previous work was mostly hack journalism. With exalting magnanimity, the letter begins: "I am not blind to the wonderful gift of *Leaves of Grass.* I find it the most extraordinary piece of wit and wisdom that America has contributed. It makes me very happy in reading it, as great power makes us happy . . . I greet you at the beginning of a great career, which yet must have had a long foreground somewhere, for such a start."

From conversations scattered throughout the preceding volumes, it has already become evident that Whitman is bent on establishing his independence from Emerson. This final "discovery" of the original letter, which Traubel disingenuously (or superciliously) says "no one could have foreseen," has all the trappings of a staged event. With ever increasing anxiety Whitman had for some years been trying to squelch any suggestion that he was, early or late, Emerson's ephebe. A year before Traubel began recording their conversations, for example, Whitman wrote to William Sloan Kennedy, an admirer who once worked on the editorial board of the widely circulated *Saturday Evening Post,* that "it is of no importance whether I read Emerson before starting L of G. It just happens to be that I had *not.* If I were to unbosom to you in the matter, I should say that I never cared so very much for E's writing." He is quite shamelessly lying. In 1847, writing in the *Aurora,* he praised a lecture on poetry he had heard Emerson deliver, and the next year, in another newspaper, he praised Emerson's "Spiritual Laws." Reminiscing to Townsend Trowbridge in 1860, he admitted that it was Emerson who had "brought him to a boil."

Efforts later on to affirm a lonely independence were among his efforts to depict himself as having always been insufficiently appreciated by his own countrymen. There were, of course, some justifications for the complaint. When are there not? Longfellow, whom he characterized as "essentially a borrower— adapter and adopter" (III, 159), consistently sold more copies than he could hope ever to see in print. *Hiawatha* sold as many as ten thousand copies a month in 1855–56, while *Leaves,* despite some good reviews, including three unsigned ones written by Whitman himself, sold so few that in his 1883 biography, Bucke reports that the first edition had "no sales" and the second edition, a year later, "little or no sales"). But that in no way alters the fact that Emerson did his very best to call attention to *Leaves of Grass,* not only in America but in England.

Traubel knew all this, and on several occasions tried to remind Whitman of his earlier testimonies to Emerson's help and references to Emerson as "Master." "Now you repudiate the word," Traubel complained at one point. "What did you mean by it then?" Whitman responded with defensive irritability, ending with the advice that since he made it abundantly clear that "questions are my bête noire" and that in fact "even you at times, damn you, try me" (II, 20), Traubel had better look for an answer elsewhere. In the "mess" perhaps? "Maybe if you look long enough you'll find what you're looking for" (IV, 132).

Traubel's interventions on behalf of Emerson, along with repeated reminders that he'd been promised the original of the 1855 letter, culminated in a surprising, most revealing episode in which Whitman tried to put the matter to rest. In January 1891, he actually gathered together some documents, rolled them up, and, with Traubel's name written on the outside, presented the documents to him:

> "This may have an especial value—on several accounts. That slip in there of the Emerson letter is an original, printed at the time, when it

was first used; it has an interest, even to me. And the list of English names—that I have never written before that I remember." Afterwards, reflectively, "I meant to make plain there, as never before, the sense of the debt I feel for my English rescuers in the dark years of my Camden sojourn. No one can know as I know the depth of the need, the nobility of the response. It was veritably a plucking from the fire as I describe it. No one, not my best friends—know what it means to me. It was life or ruin—to this side continuance, to that wreck—and these men saved me—and with true sacrificing zeal, espousal. I know that London is full of cads, flunkeys, fools, evil-doers—all that—but here, too, were several hundred as generous, devoted souls as men could know. I have no mind to forget them—even though Gilder and some of the fellows here declare there's nothing to it." I referred to the Emerson letter. "The original is here still," he said. "I think I can lay my hand on it. Why do you want it? You shall have it without a question from me: if you want it, it is yours." But when I touched upon its spiritual value in connection with what must be the future of "Leaves of Grass," W. replied, "It is well not to be quick on that point: who can know the certainty among all these uncertainties? It is a hard word to say—the sure word. Who can say it?" (VII, 419)

By the "dark years of my Camden sojourn" he was referring to a period beginning in 1873 when, after suffering the first of two paralytic strokes, he had moved from Washington to live with and be cared for in the Camden home of his brother George and George's wife, Louisa. These years also marked the death of his favorite sister-in-law, Jeffe's wife, Mattie, and the devastating blow of his mother's death. "The only staggering, staying blow & trouble I have had—but *unspeakable*—my physical sickness, bad as it is, is nothing to it," he wrote to one of his mother's woman friends. He was at the same time separated from the young men he liked to hang out with, particularly Peter Doyle, to whom he wrote in 1875, "I get desperate at staying in—not a human soul for cheer, or sociability or fun, and this continues week after week and month after month." Emerson, alas, further increased his feelings of neglect and isolation by inexplicably failing to print even one of his poems in *Parnassus,* his 1872 anthology of American poets. It took an English journalist, Robert Buchanan, in the London *Daily News,* to publicize the complaints already made by William Michael Rossetti (brother of Dante Gabriel and Christina) and other English literati: that America was barbarously disdaining its greatest poet. But a rescue operation in the London press only made matters worse at home; the backlash in the American press predictably included personal attacks on Whitman himself.

During this same period, and starting in the late 1860s, Whitman found comfort in some effusive expressions of regard that he began to hear from a growing number of English admirers, many of them distinguished men of letters or on their way to becoming so. Whitman was not the first and would scarcely be the last great American writer to cultivate an English audience as compensation for the lack of an assured one at home. There are obvious instances in Henry James, Eliot, and Frost, all of whom effectively launched their careers while living in England. This was perceived as the most effective way both to impress and to outflank the timid, genteel Anglophilia of the American literary establishment.

In his effort to establish an English clientele, he was ready to take risks that, as he confessed to Traubel, he later wished he hadn't taken. Most conspicuously, there was his agreement to a proposal from William Rossetti for the publication in England of what Whitman himself considered an expurgated edition of *Leaves of Grass.* Much earlier, he had flatly rejected Emerson's suggestion that by making some changes of wording here and there he could more readily appeal to a considerably wider audience in America. In fact, what Rossetti proposed and then published in 1868 did not, properly speaking, involve expurgation. Rossetti did not change or omit any words in the poems he printed. He simply left out any poems whose sexual vividness he believed might offend squeamish readers: "Song of Myself" and most of the poems that had appeared under the headings "Children of Adam" and "Calamus."

Nevertheless, it was easy enough to infer from the poems he did print that Whitman's calls for democratic camaraderie are at least inferentially an encouragement of the expression of sexual love between men. Already admired by such luminaries as Swinburne and Tennyson, and now reviewed quite favorably, Whitman's poetry was thus given a substantial lift in England by Rossetti's edition. But perhaps most rewarding, it excited interest among young university men who were thrilled to find the poet celebrating the kind of love that dared not speak its name. In their enthusiasm, they sought out the poems Rossetti had omitted, especially the Calamus poems, and then expressed their gratitude in letters to Whitman that are close in some cases to love letters. He was for them a prophet of what has come to be called gay liberation, though of course the word "gay" did not yet carry the meaning it has since been given and even the term "homosexual" wouldn't be much used till the early 1890s. They didn't know just what to call themselves; neither did Whitman. But his poems were taken as poetic evidence that, whatever they were called, they existed in great numbers and might one day expect to be united as "camaradoes." A letter sent in 1874 to Whitman by Edward Carpenter, a young English poet, is a representative example, introduced by Whitman in a conversation with Traubel fourteen years later, in 1888. "I seem to be very close to his heart and he to mine in that letter," Whitman remarked. "It has a place in our personal history—an important place":

> Because you have, as it were, given me ground for the love of men, I thank you continually in my heart. (And others thank you though they do not say so.) For you have made men to be not ashamed of the noblest instinct of their nature. Women are beautiful; but to some, there is something that passes the love of women. It is enough to live wherever the divine beauty of love may flash on men; but indeed its

real and enduring light seems infinitely far from us in this our day. Between the splendid dawn of Greek civilization and the high universal moon of Democracy there is a strange horror of darkness upon us. (I, 160)

Quite a few of the others referred to in Carpenter's letter did in fact come forward, including John Addington Symonds, author of *History of the Renaissance in Italy,* married and the father of three; Edmund Gosse, biographer, Scandinavian scholar, and friend of Henry James; Charles Warren Stoddard, a literary scholar who wrote ecstatically to Whitman describing his lovemaking with boys in the South Pacific; Bram Stoker, author of *Dracula,* who visited Whitman in Camden; and, later on, Oscar Wilde, who visited twice in 1882. Wilde remarked: "There is no one in this wide great world of America whom I love and honor so much."

Whitman, if one may judge by his scattered discussions of these figures with Traubel, was not in the least bothered by the evidence that they had read *Leaves of Grass* quite narrowly for its favorable views of physical love between men. In his reply to Stoddard, for example, he approved of "his emotional, adhesive nature," suggesting only that he could better put it to the test in America, where the "hard gritty . . . qualities in American practical life also serve," while preventing the "extravagant sentimentalism" of Stoddard's experiences in the South Seas. The only time he took offense was with Symonds, though he everywhere spoke of him with fulsome admiration and fellow-feeling. In a letter of 1872, which Whitman didn't answer for more than twenty years, and in subsequent letters, Symonds pleaded for just the sort of response to inquiries that Whitman most resisted. Addressing Whitman as "My Master," he wrote, "I desire to learn from your own lips—or from your pen some story of athletic friendship from which to learn the truth." When Whitman entered this letter into the record with an unusual degree of exasperation, Traubel openly wondered what made him so agitated and advised him simply to answer it. In doing so, however, Whitman exaggerated a claim made before, though few had believed it: that in his travels across America he had fathered and left behind a child or two (in the letter to Symonds this became six, four of whom, he carefully stipulated, survived). Compassionately, Symonds simply dropped the matter.

To return now to the problem Whitman created for himself when, having literally wrapped together a copy of the Emerson letter of 1855 (which Whitman had used in the launching of his career) with a list of English admirers (whose letters, he says, rescued him from depression some fifteen years later), he presented the package to his Boswell. The unintended and unfortunate effect of putting these two documents in direct competition was that Whitman's laudable expression of gratitude for support from some English readers was transformed into a challengeable effort to relegate Emerson's letter to a subordinate position. As a result, both Traubel and the reader are forced to object that, compared to Emerson's response to *Leaves,* this particular English response is rather selectively based on only a few parts of the huge and still expanding poem, mostly the Calamus pieces. Theirs was a reading altogether inadequate to what Whitman liked to call the "totality" of *Leaves of Grass,* a totality, he continually insists, his readers should attend to.

From the time of the first edition, and with the sole exception of Rossetti's volume, he adamantly rejected any rearrangement of parts of the poem by editorial hands or through interpretative selectivity of emphasis. At one point he said that if Lowell is "a palace," then *Leaves of Grass* is "a seashore, a mountain, floating cloud, sweeping river, storm, lightning, passion, freedom—and all the tremendous, vital, throbbing, resistless overwhelming, stupendous forces . . . included in, implied by these" (VIII, 179). Isn't it exactly this "initial force" that Emerson singled out for praise, when he referred to Whitman's "free and brave thought," to his "courage of treatment which large perception can only inspire"? "I am happy in reading it," he wrote, "as great power makes us happy."

"No man has the right to possess me," Whitman remarked at one point (VII, 238), and Traubel never tried. There seems to me no evidence that he was possessive of Whitman or of his poetry in a lifetime of tireless devotion up to his own death, aged sixty-one, in 1919. After Whitman's death he oversaw the publication of three volumes of *With Walt Whitman in Camden* and left the finished manuscript of the six additional volumes that have been published since. In 1894 he founded the nationwide Whitman Fellowship and guided it for the next twenty-five years. And this was scarcely all. As we learn from the concise account of Traubel's life by Ed Folsom, which serves as the foreword to volume 9, by the time Traubel began his daily visits to the sickroom in 1888, he had already held a number of jobs, as a typesetter, paymaster in a factory, employee in his father's lithography shop, and correspondent for the *Boston Commonwealth.* During the years of his vigil and for many years thereafter he worked as a bank clerk, supporting a wife, whom he married in Whitman's house in 1891, and two children.

He chose to believe that Whitman's work was sympathetic to his own radical socialism, though politically the poet was far more conservative than he. By the late 1880s he had already acquired a reputation for his radical writings. These were frequently published in the journal he founded in 1890 called *The Conservator,* which almost always included reviews of Whitman and of books about him. Over time he corresponded in a mutually admiring fashion with Emma Goldman, Jack London, Upton Sinclair, and Hamlin Garland, and he was read and admired, so it is said in the three books written about him between 1913 and 1919, by Lenin. From what Folsom reports, it seems likely that in his middle years, from about 1899 to 1905, he had a passionate love affair with the leader of the Boston chapter of the Whitman Fellowship, a dentist named Gustav Percival Wiksell.

Traubel's relationship with Whitman began when he was fourteen, and in the course of their conversations there are some tender and joyous recollections of their early walks together, their discussions of Byron and Emerson, their excursions on a ferryboat. During one such conversation, Traubel asked Whitman to recall a day when a well-dressed man, leaning against the rail of the ferry and "watching us intently . . . called me by crooking his forefinger. I got up and went over to where he stood. 'Say,' he said—'say, bubby, is that Walt Whitman the man who writes the dirty novels?'" To which the boy replied yes, and was then, as he told the quietly amused Whitman about it, convulsed with laughter. One of their happy days together.

ACKNOWLEDGMENTS

I'm grateful to my dear friend Edward Said, who encouraged me to write many of these essays, and to Elisabeth Sifton for proposing that they be brought together as a book and for her always considerate help in bringing this about. G. Thomas Tanselle suggested a number of essential changes, as did my associate at *Raritan Quarterly,* Suzanne Hyman. Karl Miller and, later, Mary-Kay Wilmers of the *London Review of Books,* and Leon Wieseltier, literary editor of *The New Republic,* were exceptionally generous in the space they provided in their journals for the publication of earlier versions of a number of these pieces.

INDEX